CHEERING FOR THE CHILDREN

Creating Pathways to HOPE for Children Exposed to Trauma

CASEY GWINN

Cheering for the Children: Creating Pathways to HOPE for Children Exposed to Trauma

Published by Wheatmark®
1760 East River Road, Suite 145, Tucson, Arizona 85718 USA
www.wheatmark.com

ISBN: 978-1-62787-243-0 (paperback)
ISBN: 978-1-62787-244-7 (ebook)
LCCN: 2014922864

rev201501

To Kayden Brooke Orender
and countless other children …
who deserve futures without trauma—
filled with safety, hope, and joy.

Contents

Foreword by Dr. Vincent J. Felitti vii

Introduction 1

1. Life without a Cheerleader 9

2. Going Deeper into the Impacts of Childhood Trauma 40

3. Saving the Children of America... 62

4. The Camp HOPE Story... 90

5. HOPE Heals 122

6. Be a Mentor to Other Children... 131

7. The Power of Affirmation in the Life of a Child 157

8. Praising Children for Who They Are 172

9. Learning How to Be a Child's Cheerleader 182

10. Practical Steps to Success (Work the Plan) 203

11. Dealing with Trauma in Children of Faith............................ 231

12. What Works in Dealing with Childhood Trauma 249

13. Leaving a Legacy 272

About the Author.. 285

Acknowledgments... 287

Endnotes 289

Foreword

In my beginning is my end.[1]

— T. S. Eliot

I HAVE BEEN HONORED to spend the last thirty years of my medical career helping to understand the connection between emotional trauma in childhood and the pathways to adult pathology. The journey to uncovering some of these profound connections began while operating a major weight-loss program for Kaiser Permanente in San Diego, California. Multiple counterintuitive observations there involved seeing patients losing large amounts of weight and then inexplicably fleeing their own success and dropping out of the program. We soon began to recognize that weight loss is often physically or sexually threatening and that some of our most intractable public health problems, such as obesity, are unconscious, or occasionally conscious, compensatory behaviors put in place as solutions to problems dating back to the earliest years but hidden by shame, by secrecy, and by social taboos against exploring certain areas of life experience.

It became evident in this early work that traumatic life experiences during childhood and adolescence were far more common than generally recognized, were complexly interrelated, and were associated decades later in a strong and proportionate manner with outcomes important to medical practice, public health, and the social fabric of a nation. Our findings in our weight-loss program led to the now nationally and internationally known Adverse Childhood Experiences (ACE) Study.

The ACE Study was carried out in Kaiser Permanente's Department of Preventive Medicine in San Diego, in collaboration with Dr. Robert Anda of the US Centers for Disease Control and Prevention (CDC). The ACE Study cohort had more than 17,000 participants —half men and half women. It was a solidly middle-class group with an average age of 57. We studied eight categories of adverse childhood experiences in the first phase and then added two neglect categories in the second phase. The ACE Study, including our findings, is described in more detail later in this book. The findings have been profound and widely accepted, attracting international attention.

Cheering for the Children is one of the first books focused on educating the general public about the ACE Study. Former San Diego City Attorney Casey Gwinn has had a distinguished career in his work addressing domestic violence and the related physical and sexual abuse of survivors and their children. In *Cheering for the Children*, he connects the ACE Study to the needs of at-risk and high-risk children and teens. *Cheering for the Children* seeks to point the way forward to necessary paradigm shifts in the criminal justice, juvenile justice, and social service arenas based on the social implications of the ACE Study.

Casey Gwinn's visionary creation of Camp HOPE exemplifies the many promising practices we must develop as we seek to understand how to mitigate the potential consequences of high ACE scores. The earlier we identify children with high levels of trauma, the sooner we can begin to mitigate and ameliorate their potential for adverse consequences. *Cheering for the Children* will help community-based domestic violence programs, rape crisis centers, family justice centers, and child advocacy centers look for ways to collaborate around their shared interests in meeting the needs of high-ACE-Score children and teens. Even as the medical and mental health communities continue to look to implement the findings of the ACE Study in practice and policy, we need people across this country to better understand the implications of the ACE Study and the deep significance of childhood trauma in our most intractable social and public health problems.

The findings of the ACE study provide a credible basis for a new paradigm of medical, public health, and social service practice. Such a practice would start with the biopsychosocial evaluation of all patients, clients, and victims of violence and abuse. Such a practice would include similar evaluations of criminal offenders facing incarceration and treatment. We have demonstrated in our work that this approach is individually acceptable to patients and is affordable and beneficial in multiple ways. The potential gain is huge. So too appears to be the likelihood of clinician, institutional, and public resistance to this change. Actualizing the benefits of this paradigm shift will depend on first identifying and resolving various bases for resistance to it. In reality, this will require far more planning and public discourse than would be needed to introduce a purely intellectual or technical advance. But it can be done. It is our calling if we truly want to meet the currently unrecognized needs of multitudes of trauma-exposed children and adults.

It is my earnest hope that elected officials, legislators, medical and social service professionals, business leaders, police officers, prosecutors, and practitioners from all disciplines will one day understand the true implications of the ACE Study.

Vincent J. Felitti, MD

No one has ever cheered for me before.

—Jasmine, 10
2007 Camp HOPE camper

Introduction

ALL CHILDREN NEED at least one person to passionately love, cheer for, affirm, encourage, and believe in them. We all hope that person will be a parent, and hopefully children will have two parents who passionately love them, cheer for them, and believe in them. But there are millions of children growing up in this country every year who are profoundly impacted by childhood trauma and don't have anyone cheering for them.

Cheering for the Children is a challenge to every caring young person and adult to become one of those cheerleaders in the life of at least one child. We don't need government programs for all of it. We don't require legislation for all of it. We need caring people and organizations to apply the practical challenges of this book. We need a social movement around childhood trauma and its impacts. We need more incentives for those who can and should invest themselves in the lives of children. We must ask adults who have achieved healthy adulthood to reach back and help a struggling child. We should expect more from the health, faith, education, and business communities. We should expect more of ourselves.

It has been said that it takes a village to raise a child, but I believe it takes a village of cheerleaders—caring young people and older, wiser adults—to raise a child. It is not just a village. It matters who is in the village. It matters what the village does for and says to the children. And the reason the old African proverb says a village is needed is because more positive, healthy people are better than fewer people. If there were truly a whole village of people cheering for every child, we would be stunned at the results in the lives of those children. But perhaps before we aspire to find a village for every child, we can just dream of having one cheerleader in the life of every child.

Right now, most parents and adults don't view it as their job to invest in other people's children or grandchildren. Most adults who are not impacted by trauma don't think it is their job to help the children who are deeply impacted and traumatized by abuse. We want social service agencies to handle that. "Community organizations and churches should take care of those children who don't have the support they need at home." "The government should probably work on that." "I think they have a program at the YMCA for that, right?" And all those things are happening. Many organizations are doing good work mentoring and investing in at-risk children. The Obama administration has done tremendous work in this regard. President Barack Obama and Attorney General Eric Holder created the Defending Childhood Initiative to focus on helping children exposed to violence and abuse and children without healthy parenting in their lives.

Great organizations and initiatives focused on supporting at-risk children exist across the country. Hundreds of social services, faith-based groups, and mentoring organizations are trying to help children, but most of these efforts are a small drop in a very large bucket. Each year millions of children experience significant trauma and abuse in their lives. If you counted up every mentoring program in America, you'd probably find that they aren't personally connecting with more than two hundred thousand children per year across the country. The need is hundreds—no, thousands—of times greater than the number of available mentors and caring adults currently involved with trauma-exposed children. We will look at the costs of this failure in America as the book unfolds. The costs are immense, almost immeasurable.

Today, we have more children growing up mired in the impacts of trauma—more children living without a positive self-image, without an understanding of what they have to offer others, and without a sense of their God-given gifts and abilities—than perhaps at any other time in American history. A friend and mentor, Dr. Robert Ross of the California Endowment, has called childhood trauma the greatest public health issue in America that is "hidden in plain sight." Some children impacted by toxic stress and major traumas need professional help. Many children and their families need to be wrapped in comprehensive community responses and support systems. But every child needs one thing at the top of the list. They need one person to passionately believe in them, love them, and support them. After years of working with abused and neglected children and raising my own children, I can say without equivocation that for kids to grow into healthy, caring, kind, responsible adults, *they need someone to cheer for them!*

The title of this book was inspired by one of those children. A number of years ago, we were running one of our Camp HOPE weeks for children exposed to domestic violence. I remember praising a little girl named Jasmine for being so kind and gentle with the frogs she loved to hold on the shore of the lake where Camp HOPE operated at the time. She smiled such a big smile when I praised her, so that night at the campfire, I decided to publicly praise her in front of all the kids and adults at camp. After I did, everyone clapped and cheered for her for being so kind and loving with those little frogs. After the campfire, she came up to me and said something that shocked me: "No one has ever cheered for me before." I could not say anything at first, as I absorbed what she had said. Then I looked at her, hugged her, and told her she deserved to be cheered for every day.

I never forgot Jasmine's words: "No one has ever cheered for me before." And I wondered how many children grow up saying that. If you are in team or individual sports, you get cheered for sooner or later. If you are a high achiever in school or have unique skills that get cultivated as a child, sooner or later a group probably cheers for you—at least for what you have accomplished. But if you are not one of those kids, who cheers for you? Who claps for you? *And if they are clapping for you, is it about who you are or who you are becoming, or is it simply about what you did or how you performed?* From my time working with children growing up in violent and abusive homes, I have come to realize that most children don't get cheered for at all.

When trauma-exposed children don't have cheerleaders, bad things happen to them in life and many end up in the criminal justice system. In America, we raise our criminals at home. The vast majority of all adults we incarcerate for all crimes grew up in homes with some mix of domestic violence, child abuse, and/or drug and alcohol abuse. I made a living putting them in jail for many years.

After growing up in a small community in the Santa Cruz Mountains of Northern California, I went to Stanford University and then on to UCLA School of Law. After law school, I became a prosecutor in San Diego, California, focused on the prosecution of domestic violence, child abuse, and sexual assault offenders.

For many years, I focused on locking up those adult survivors of childhood trauma for their crimes—I just didn't know it. In 1996, I became the elected city attorney of San Diego with a developing passion for finding better ways to help victims and perpetrators of family violence and their children. In 2002, we opened the San Diego Family Justice Center, the first center of its kind in America, which brought together police officers, prosecutors, advocates, counselors, doctors, nurses, chaplains, and other professionals—more than 120 people—under one roof in order to help victims and their children. In 2003, Oprah Winfrey profiled the family-justice-center model on her show. In 2004, President George W. Bush created the President's Family Justice Center Initiative (PFJCI) and called for the creation of family justice centers across America. I was honored to help lead the PFJCI. Soon after the PFJCI started, centers began to develop across the country and around the world—all established with the simple idea that victims should be able to come to *one place* for everything they need.

After opening the San Diego Family Justice Center, my wife, Beth, and I, along with many other friends and supporters, created Camp HOPE, the first dedicated camping program in America focused on children exposed to domestic violence and related physical and sexual abuse. Camp HOPE was just a local program in San Diego for nearly a decade and then an inspired family justice center (One Safe Place Shasta) in Redding, California started the second Camp HOPE in America. We soon realized that all family justice centers should have a Camp HOPE. All children dealing with major childhood trauma in California and across America should get to go to camp each summer. I share the story of Camp HOPE in this book and all the proceeds of this book will benefit Camp HOPE.

After we started Camp HOPE California and brought children to camp from across the state, we knew we needed to prove that camping actually made a difference. Our goal was to give children hope. But could we measure hope? Could we prove that greater hope in children changes their lives and reduces the impacts of childhood trauma?

We discovered there is actual research on the power of hope. We partnered with Dr. Chan Hellman, one of the leading researchers on what is called Hope Theory, at the University of Oklahoma. After two years of using the validated Children's Hope Scale (which produces a Hope Score) with the hundreds of children coming to Camp HOPE, we can prove that Camp HOPE changes the way abused children view themselves and their futures. The results have been amazing.

As Camp HOPE began to flourish in California, Idaho, Oregon, Oklahoma, Georgia, Texas, and other states I had the opportunity to reconnect with Dr. Vincent Felitti. We had met many years earlier during my career as a prosecutor. Dr. Felitti is one of the leading researchers in America on childhood trauma, the author of the famous Adverse Childhood Experiences (ACE) Study at Kaiser Permanente, and a passionate advocate for helping children exposed to major childhood trauma and helping adults deal with many of the long-term consequences of growing up with trauma and abuse. Dr. Felitti is one of my personal mentors, and his visionary work will have a profound impact on those working with trauma-exposed children for generations. Dr. Felitti challenged us to use the ACE question-naire (ten questions on childhood trauma) at Camp HOPE and to start comparing Hope scores with ACE scores in order to figure out how to help and cheer for children otherwise destined for a lifetime of profound consequences from childhood trauma.

This book focuses on that need in the life of every child (and indeed every adult). We all need affirmation, encouragement, and praise. Resiliency grows from it. Competency is grounded in it. We thrive with it. We slowly die inside without it. It is not just true of children, though that is the focus of *Cheering for the Children*. Marriages get sick and die without two cheerleaders. Employees end up demoralized without cheerleaders. We all long for praise, affirmation, and encouragement from others in many areas of our lives. But long before they become adults, children need someone cheering for them.

I have written this book from a personal place. My own life story is woven into the pages of this book. Like most of us, I grew up in a home with both good and bad. I grew up with praise and affirmation *and* verbal, emotional, and physical child abuse. I know the power of praise and affirmation, and I know the dark, long-lasting pain of abuse. The genesis of the abuse goes back generations in my family. My father was severely abused by his father including being whipped often and punched in the head every day as his father woke him up for school. My father used some of the same techniques on me. But there was good too. The cheering, particularly from my dad, helped me find my way in life. I did not however, grow up fully understanding what it means to praise someone for *who they are, not what they do.* Much of the praise I received from my father was performance-based praise. Praising others for what they do is not all bad, but for me it left me much more focused on doing things than being someone. It inspired me to strive and achieve academically, athletically, and professionally, but it also caused me to raise my children with too much focus on what they did, rather than who they were.

After the death of my dad in 2009, I struggled deeply with my own identity, what I believed, and how I had raised my children. I have realized that my view of myself is deeply connected to my own ability to cheer for others. It is true for all of us. As I wrote this book, I decided to sit down and interview each of my children about how some of my struggles impacted them during their growing-up years. Interviewing your children to see how you did as a parent is not for the faint of heart. The lessons learned from my children are shared throughout the book. I found I needed to learn to love myself far more in order to be able to love others well.

How many others need to take this journey as adults? How many others need to learn, as Jesus said, how to love themselves before they can truly love and cheer for others? So this book is part personal story, part individual challenge, and part clarion call. It is written for all caring adults who want to make a difference in the experience and journey of children in their lives. It is strongly focused on helping children who have witnessed domestic violence, lived through an ugly divorce between their parents, experienced physical or sexual abuse, or were raised by an alcoholic, drug-addicted, or abusive parent. But I hope all parents will read it. You can use the principles in this book to become a better parent, grandparent, or mentor to children other than your own. You can learn things in this book that may help you become a better advocate for social and public policy change geared toward helping at-risk children in this country.

What should all parents know and focus on as they raise their own children? What should all grandparents know? What do adoptive parents need to know? What should parents, gay or straight, single or married, use as a road map in helping children navigate the dark waters of trauma and insecurity? What should all coaches, teachers, pastors, youth leaders, priests, rabbis, neighbors, and caring adults know about cheering for the children? The good news is that *it is not too late,* even if you have made mistakes, even if you have ended up missing out on the healing power of affirmation and encouragement in the lives of children—your own or others. You can learn to cheer for your children and your grandchildren. You can learn to connect more effectively with and encourage more powerfully the children you come in contact with in all chapters of your life. We can all practice the techniques and ideas shared in this book. We can all support the national and local policies and strategies mapped out here. And we can impact many more children in a positive and lasting way than we ever have before if we take seriously the call of this book to become more effective cheerleaders for children.

It is my hope that many more people, by the choices they make with the children in their lives, will leave a legacy of *Cheering for the Children*.

Casey Gwinn
Husband, Father, Grandfather
Founder, Camp HOPE America
April 2015

One

Life without a Cheerleader

I was one of those kids, and I never went to camp. In the course of my life, I ended up devaluing myself and letting others abuse me for so very long, until I finally came to understand who I was, what I was worth, what I deserved, and what I had to give others.

— Laura
Camp HOPE Adult Volunteer

EARLY IN MY life, I noticed cheerleaders. Yes, the real ones with pom-poms and catchy cheers. They stood on the side of sporting events and cheered. In those years, almost all the cheerleaders were girls and most all the athletes were boys. Over the years, that has changed. Now we have thousands of female athletes, and cheerleaders include both males and females. But from my earliest memories, they were all girls, and even as a young child, I liked to cheer along with them. They inspired me to cheer for and inspire others.

As I grew older and became an athlete, I loved cheerleaders even more. They were full of life, bubbly, and made me feel better about myself. They always seemed positive. They would get the crowd going at a sporting event, and then many more people were cheering for me as an athlete. And it worked. I tended to play better at home games than away games. In fact, a great deal of research has documented home-field advantage in high school, college, and professionals sports. Why? Why do teams play better at home? Why do individual athletes perform better for the home crowd? The answer is

9

cheerleaders. The adulation of the crowd inspires them. Brain chemistry and physiology are impacted by the power of affirmation and encouragement and the bond formed through the adulation of the crowd.[1] A hometown crowd increases the energy levels and performance of the athletes.[2] This advantage exists in high school, college, and professional sports and has been identified in certain Olympic events as well.[3]

Without the home crowd, sports teams don't win as often. Without "cheerleaders" and a "home crowd," children and adults don't do as well in life either. Life without a cheerleader is a tough journey. Life in an ugly, negative, and abusive home is traumatic. It is much easier to get discouraged, much harder to bounce back from setbacks, and immensely more difficult to overcome trauma without a cheerleader.

As we begin, let's define "trauma." Trauma results from an event, series of events, or set of circumstances that is experienced by an individual as physically and emotionally harmful or threatening. It can have lasting adverse effects on the individual's physical, social, emotional, and spiritual well-being. Trauma can be acute—caused by one incident, or it can be chronic—caused by repeated traumas. Most children (66 percent) grow up with some level of trauma in their lives. We will come to understand trauma in the lives of children much more specifically, but this is a good starting point. We will also talk about "trauma-informed" practices and programs. For now, let's define "trauma-informed" as simply understanding better how trauma impacts children and adults. We can then learn how our personal interactions can better help trauma survivors in dealing with the stress they are experiencing from abnormal events in their lives.[4] I have learned it is always better to ask, "What happened to you?" rather than focusing on inappropriate behavior and asking, "What is wrong with you?" It is always more productive to better understand what a child or adult has been through than to focus on his or her weaknesses, struggles, or poor choices in the aftermath of the trauma. I look forward to the day when we can all share openly with each other about childhood trauma and what we struggled with as children—without shame, embarrassment, or rationalization. Honesty without shame and rejection is the beginning of hope and healing.

Many children growing up with trauma are able to overcome it and go on to become functioning, healthy adults. Those who do overcome the impact of that trauma always have a cheerleader or multiple cheerleaders of some kind in their lives. Some also need professional, trauma-informed counseling and support. We will spend most of the book examining ways we can help children and even adults overcome the impact of childhood trauma, but before we do that, we must devote time to being honest about the odds against trauma-exposed children and the profound life-changing, long-term impact of such trauma when there are no mitigating factors or intervening cheerleaders.

There is strong evidence today that traumatic stress in childhood is closely related to the leading causes of morbidity, mortality, and disability in the United States: cardiovascular disease, chronic lung disease, chronic liver disease, depression and other forms of mental illness, obesity, smoking, and alcohol and drug abuse.[5] There is equally strong evidence that exposure to violence and abuse profoundly impacts learning and damages brain development.[6] Children with severe exposure to violence and abuse are at much greater risk for post-traumatic stress disorder (PTSD), additional victimization, unhealthy and early sexual behaviors, delinquency, and rage-based violence and abuse against others.[7] Perhaps one of the most significant works in the past thirty years to help us understand the life-changing impacts of trauma in childhood is the Adverse Childhood Experiences (ACE) Study.[8] Dr. Vincent Felitti and Dr. Robert Anda led the way in this work, and it is an important starting point for this book.

The Adverse Childhood Experiences Study

Dr. Vincent Felitti and a team from Kaiser Permanente began fascinating research in the 1980s while working with morbidly obese adults in San Diego. Dr. Felitti was one of the leading preventive medicine experts in California at the time and was focused on developing successful weight-loss programs for extremely overweight patients. The weight-loss program's use of "supplemented absolute fasting" allowed patients to lose up to three hundred pounds in a year without surgery. The program was extremely successful in helping adult men and women lose large amounts of weight but had a high dropout rate after patients were successful. Dr. Felitti began exploring the reasons for the high dropout rate. He initially found a strong correlation between child sexual abuse and morbid obesity. Extreme obesity was a protective measure for survivors of child sexual trauma—physically and emotionally—and when women lost the weight, they felt vulnerable again to sexual abuse.[9]

Dr. Felitti later wrote:

> "It became evident that traumatic life experiences during childhood and adolescence were far more common than generally recognized, were complexly interrelated and were associated decades later in a strong and proportionate manner with outcomes important to medical practice, public health, and the social fabric of a nation. In the context of everyday medical practice, we came to recognize that the earliest years of infancy and childhood are not lost, but like a child's footprints in wet cement, are often lifelong."[10]

Dr. Felitti's groundbreaking work related to obesity and childhood trauma eventually led to the famous Adverse Childhood Experiences (ACE) Study. The ACE Study was conducted with 17,421 Kaiser Permanente patients in cooperation with the US Centers for Disease Control and Prevention (CDC) and eventually published by Dr. Felitti and Dr. Robert Anda from the CDC.[11] Participants were from the general membership and not from the Obesity Program. They were comprehensively evaluated between 1995 and 1997 and then followed for nineteen years. "Everything we've published comes from that baseline survey of 17,421 people," notes Anda, "as well as from what was learned by following those people for so long."[12]

The ACE Study has become famous over the years and the ACE Questionnaire has become a validated instrument used in child-welfare programs and many other settings across the country.[13] The ACE Study, which is nearing its twentieth year, has clearly found that children facing adversity from abuse or other forms of trauma do not fare well through childhood or later in life.

The short- and long-term outcomes of these adverse child experiences (ACEs) include a multitude of health and social problems. The evidence is overwhelming and indisputable. It is changing the way we think about childhood trauma.

The ACE Study uses the ACE score, which is the sum of the total number of categories (not incidents) that respondents report on a questionnaire. The ACE score is then used to represent the total amount of traumatic stress during childhood and has demonstrated that as the number of categories of ACEs increases, the risk for the following health problems increases in a strong and proportionate fashion:

- Alcoholism and alcohol abuse
- Chronic obstructive pulmonary disease (COPD)
- Depression
- Fetal death (miscarriage during pregnancy)
- Health-related quality of life
- Illicit drug use
- Ischemic heart disease (IHD)
- Liver disease
- Risk for intimate partner violence
- Multiple sexual partners
- Sexually transmitted diseases (STDs)
- Autoimmune disease
- Smoking
- Suicide attempts

- Unintended pregnancies
- Early initiation of smoking
- Early initiation of sexual activity
- Adolescent pregnancy[14]

The adverse childhood experiences that participants identified in the original ACE Study at Kaiser Permanente were categorized as Abuse, Neglect, and Household Dysfunction. The following subcategories were then assigned to each category:

Abuse
Emotional Abuse—Often or very often a parent or other adult in the household swore at you, insulted you, or put you down and sometimes, often, or very often acted in a way that made you think that you might be physically hurt.

Physical Abuse—You were sometimes, often, or very often pushed, grabbed, slapped, or had something thrown at you or were hit so hard that you had marks or were injured.

Sexual Abuse—An adult or person at least five years older ever touched or fondled you in a sexual way, had you touch their body in a sexual way, attempted oral, anal, or vaginal intercourse with you, or actually had oral, anal, or vaginal intercourse with you.

Neglect
Emotional Neglect—You often or very often felt that no one in your family loved you or thought you were important or special or your family didn't look out for each other, feel close to each other, or support each other.

Household Dysfunction
Mother Treated Violently—Your mother or stepmother was sometimes, often, or very often pushed, grabbed, slapped, or had some-

thing thrown at her and/or sometimes, often, or very often kicked, bitten, hit with a fist, or hit with something hard, or ever repeatedly hit over a period of at least a few minutes or threatened or hurt by a knife or gun.

Household Substance Abuse—You lived with anyone who was a problem drinker or alcoholic or lived with anyone who used street drugs.

Household Mental Illness—A household member was depressed or mentally ill or a household member attempted suicide.

Parental Separation or Divorce—Your parents were ever separated or divorced.

Incarcerated Household Member—A household member went to prison.[15]

Higher ACE scores have now been correlated with destructive choices later in life, drug and alcohol addiction, illness, disease, and reduced life expectancy. An ACE score of six, for example, on average reduces life expectancy by nineteen years! Child trauma and adverse childhood experiences, without mitigating interventions and therapeutic help, are literally a premature death sentence for many children exposed to violence, abuse, and trauma.

Not everyone in the ACE study had high scores. Approximately one-third of the population in the study had an ACE score of zero. Two-thirds of the study participants had an ACE score of one or higher. Very few had a score of only one, however. If participants had one trauma marker, the vast majority had at least a score of two. This showed that people who had an alcoholic father, for example, were likely to have also experienced an additional category, say physical abuse or verbal abuse. In other words, ACEs usually didn't happen in isolation. One in six individuals had an ACE score of four or more.

One in nine individuals had an ACE score of five or more. Typically, the doctors and nurses found that the higher the ACE score, the more difficult the patient was to deal with in a medical setting. Interestingly, women were 50 percent more likely than men to have an ACE score of five or more. Fifty-four percent of depression cases and 58 percent of suicide attempts in women were attributable to adverse childhood experiences.[16] High ACE scores were also connected to other major health consequences in the lives of trauma victims.

We will not take the time to look at ACE Study replication studies in 25 states and the District of Columbia since the original study, but virtually every time the ACE questionnaire has been administered the results are stunningly similar to the original findings. The sample in the original study at Kaiser Permanente in San Diego, CA with primarily white, middle class patients did not skew results or in any way produce results different than many other populations studied in recent years.

The six graphs below from the original ACE Study visually show the correlation between high ACE scores and increased rates of smoking, alcoholism, attempted suicide, sexual assault later in life, prescription drug use for depression, and unexplained medical symptoms.[17]

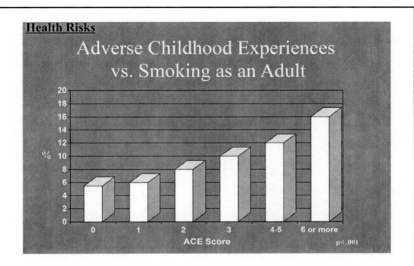

(Chart A) While some become addicted to nicotine without trauma, higher ACE scores increase the likelihood the child will become a smoker as a teen or adult and later produces a 300 percent increase in the likelihood of lung cancer.

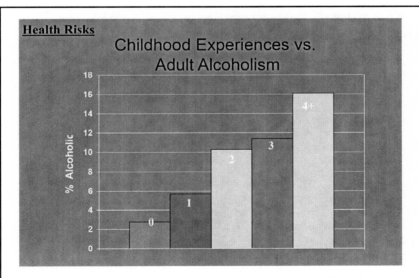

(Chart B) Higher ACE scores correlate to higher rates of alcoholism in adulthood and the increased health risks associated with alcohol abuse. Alcoholism increases by 800 percent with an ACE score of four or more.

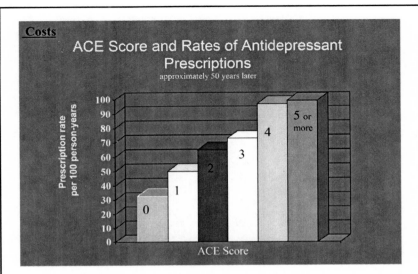

(Chart C) Drs. Felitti and Anda correlated the hundreds of millions spent to treat depression with higher ACE scores. Depression is 450 percent more likely in those with ACE scores above four.

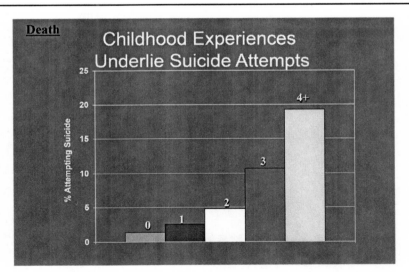

(Chart D) Higher ACE scores are connected to subsequent suicide attempts in adulthood and likely connected to teen suicide attempts as well.

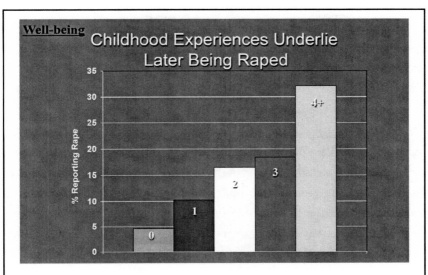

(Chart E) Research connects childhood trauma with being a rapist later in life and connects childhood trauma with an increased likelihood of being a victim of sexual assault later in life.

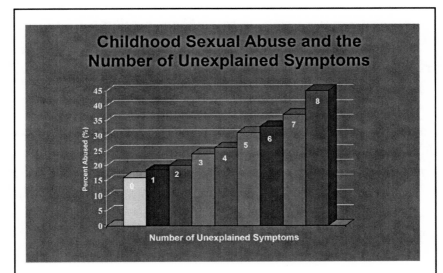

(Chart F) High ACE scores strongly correlate with high numbers of unexplained health symptoms. Physical symptoms are not irrational or imaginary. They are the body's normal reaction to abnormal trauma.

The implications of these findings are significant and will resurface regularly throughout the rest of this book in stories and strategies to help survivors deal with the impacts of trauma. In drug- and alcohol-treatment programs, there is little doubt that facilitators and therapists should be delving into the underlying trauma that may have produced the alcoholism or drug addiction (Charts A and B). In a related finding in the ACE research, a male with an ACE score of six has a 4,600 percent greater likelihood of becoming an injection drug user than a male with an ACE score of zero.[18] As to prescription medication use (Chart C), it makes total sense that childhood trauma would cause greater depression later in life, which in turn would lead to greater use of antidepressant medications. The possibility of childhood trauma should be evaluated much more closely in suicide or suicide attempts (Chart D). Suicidality is 1200 percent more likely if your ACE score is four or greater than if your ACE score is zero. Suicide is the loss of all hope. It is getting to the end of all options and seeing no way out of the pain and darkness of a life impacted by severe trauma. So much of the pain and loss finds its foundations in childhood trauma and then manifests itself in adult life as the cumulative impact of trauma—whether from childhood abuse, involvement in war and violent conflict, head trauma, natural disasters, or other loss and pain.

The correlation between childhood trauma and later sexual assault (Chart E) is not a topic many want to focus on today, even amid the current national focus on the epidemic of sexual assault on college campuses. We don't want to "blame the victim." We don't want to excuse the rapist. But we cannot ignore the research that connects childhood trauma with both becoming a sexual predator and with later becoming a victim of sexual assault.[19]

I want to point out the correlation between higher ACE scores and unexplained health symptoms (Chart F). Doctors seem to take a special class in medical school to call things "psychosomatic" if they cannot come up with a medical explanation for a symptom in a patient. I always understood "psychosomatic" to mean, "It's all in your head." So I found this element of the ACE Study fascinating. While the causality does lie in memories "all in your head," the end results of those brain changes express themselves "all in your body." Your brain and your body remember trauma from childhood. If you were sexually abused as a child, the number of medical symptoms you might describe to a doctor—symptoms for which the doctor cannot find a medical reason—will go up significantly. They are your body's normal reaction to the abnormal trauma you suffered long ago.

The charts above are only a few of the illustrative correlations that the ACE Study has profiled. The ACE Study has made clear that childhood adversity and trauma affects the pleasure and reward center of the brain (nucleus accumbens). It inhibits the development of the prefrontal cortex that is necessary for impulse control. Dr. Bruce Perry and others have shown through MRI scans that there are measurable differences in the amygdala, the brain's fear response center, in children exposed to trauma and children without trauma and adversity. These impacts often cause children to engage in far riskier behavior in life than children with an ACE score of zero. But even if children don't engage in risky behaviors, they are still in trouble because of the impact of trauma on the so-called HPA axis— the brain's response system that governs fight-flight-freeze.

How does it work? I am not a medical doctor, but the concept of the HPA axis is best understood in thinking about walking in a forest and seeing a bear. Immediately, your hypothalamus sends a message to your pituitary gland that sends a message to your adrenal gland that says, "release the stress hormones." The stress hormones are adrenalin and cortisol. They cause your pupils to dilate, your airways to open and get you ready to fight, run, or freeze. This is a normal reaction to an abnormal situation and it may save your life! The problem comes when you are not in a forest, there is no bear, and the threat is your father or stepfather or mom's boyfriend. And he comes home from work every night and your HPA axis is activated over and over, day after day, year after year. Your response, as a child, goes from being healthy, adaptive, and lifesaving to being unhealthy, maladaptive, and damaging. Children are especially vulnerable to this repeated (chronic) stress activation because their brains and bodies are just developing. These high doses of adversity and trauma caused by abuse dramatically affect the developing immune system and hormonal system. Later in life, adults face the consequences of these effects in the absence of being able to heal from this highly unhealthy and chronic state of arousal and stress.

This is why we all need to find our ACE score and figure out how to release the childhood trauma that may have been impacting us for years or even decades. Later in the book we will look at successful interventions that help children and adults release the childhood trauma and allow many to live healthy and productive lives even after severe trauma and abuse.

What Is Your ACE Score?

I would recommend that every reader of the book take the ACE test.[20] Whether you aspire to be a mentor to other children or you are reading this book to process your own journey with trauma and abuse, it might be helpful to know your score. It may help explain some of your demons and some of the challenges you still face as an adult and even a parent. The ACE Study is one of those powerful modern evidence-based research studies that confirm the old Biblical adage that "the sins of the parents are visited on the children to the third and fourth generations."[21]

Any individual or group can use the ACE score sheet, but consideration should be given to providing emotional support for those completing the questionnaire. It can trigger significant discomfort in participants. It will help you understand and process some of your own struggles if you have an ACE score higher than one. It will also help you understand the needs of trauma-exposed children and adults, even if your score is zero.

Finding Your Own ACE score

While you were growing up, during your first eighteen years of life:

1. Did a parent or other adult in the household often or very often ...
   Swear at you, insult you, put you down, or humiliate you?

   Or

   Act in a way that made you afraid that you might be physically hurt?

   Yes   No   If yes, enter 1_____

2. Did a parent or other adult in the household often or very often ...
   Push, grab, slap, or throw something at you?

   Or

   Ever hit you so hard that you had marks or were injured?

   Yes   No   If yes, enter 1_____

3. Did an adult or person at least five years older than you ever ...
   Touch or fondle you or have you touch their body in a sexual way?

   Or

   Attempt or actually have oral, anal, or vaginal intercourse with you?

   Yes   No   If yes, enter 1_____

4. Did you often or very often feel that ...
   No one in your family loved you or thought you were important or special?

   Or

   Your family didn't look out for each other, feel close to each other, or support each other?

Yes　　　No　　　　　　If yes, enter 1_____

5. Did you often or very often feel that …
   You didn't have enough to eat, had to wear dirty clothes, and
   had no one to protect you?

   Or

   Your parents were too drunk or high to take care of you or take
   you to the doctor if you needed it?
   Yes　　　No　　　　　　If yes, enter 1_____

6. Were your parents ever separated or divorced?
   Yes　　　No　　　　　　If yes, enter 1_____

7. Was your mother or stepmother:
   Often or very often pushed, grabbed, slapped, or had something thrown at her?

   Or

   Sometimes, often, or very often kicked, bitten, hit with a fist,
   or hit with something hard?

   Or

   Ever repeatedly hit for at least a few minutes or threatened
   with a gun or knife?
   Yes　　　No　　　　　　If yes, enter 1_____

8. Did you live with anyone who was a problem drinker or alcoholic or who used street drugs?
   Yes　　　No　　　　　　If yes, enter 1_____

9. Was a household member depressed or mentally ill, or did a
   household member attempt suicide?
   Yes　　　No　　　　　　If yes, enter 1_____

10. Did a household member go to prison?

Yes   No   If yes, enter 1_____

Now, add up your "Yes" answers. This is your ACE score.

I recommend that you talk to a close friend or a trusted person after taking your ACE score. If you scored a one or more, go back through this chapter and look at the charts and other data about higher ACE scores. If you scored a zero, it does not mean that you are perfect or don't have challenges as a partner, parent, or adult caregiver in life! But it does mean you have much to be thankful for when it comes to the home you grew up in.

Dear Doctor

During the writing of this book, Dr. Vincent Felitti shared with me a letter written a number of years ago by an adult survivor of childhood sexual abuse. It encapsulates all that the ACE Study and other research has found about the impact of such abuse. Her ACE score may have been as low as one, but the impact on her life is evident in this letter. With permission from *The Permanente Journal*, I want to share the actual letter.

Dear Doctor,

I am your patient. We have known one another for a long time, and I want to thank you for healing me so many times. At present, you know me only from annual checkups as a healthy 58-year-old, divorced, Caucasian female; 120 lbs., 5'6"; two adult children; parents and all four siblings living; family history of diabetes, epilepsy, alcoholism, bowel cancer, and heart disease; no medications.

You met me first ... in Pennsylvania. I was a normal 5 lb. 6 oz. infant, born under general anesthesia. My mother nursed me for eight months, and I grew normally. You were surprised and concerned when I returned in six weeks for a well-baby check and immunizations. I had developed an extremely loud heart murmur, but you assured my worried mother no surgery was needed. After I turned three, you saw me often in New Jersey, Virginia, Alabama, and Massachusetts. I had frequent, severe ENT problems, ear infections, strep throat, double pneumonia, scarlet fever, mumps, measles, chicken pox, "grippe" viruses, and a host of other pediatric problems. It is fair to say that sulfa and penicillin saved my life.

You may have noted in your chart that I was thin, compliant, and quite withdrawn. When I turned seven, you bandaged a deep cut on my thigh. You surgically removed my tonsils and adenoids. Later that year, you irradiated a regrowth of my adenoids. You also irradiated my enlarged thymus in a hopeful, experimental procedure. The hypothesis was that removal of the thymus gland would increase my immune system. Unfortunately, it had the reverse effect.

You probably made a note that I missed many months of school each year due to illness and that my lips and fingernails frequently turned blue. You x-rayed my teeth frequently and filled my numerous cavities every year for decades. You met me at a medical convention when I was a shy, embarrassed 12-year-old. As a group, you examined my heart, amazed at the murmur that could be heard without a stethoscope. You noted my thinness and suggested an enriched diet. You extracted four teeth for my braces. When I was a pretty, studious, 14-year-old in Louisiana, you bound my fractured left arm to my body for six weeks after I was thrown from a horse. Later that year, you carefully put 167 stitches in my face after I was thrown face first through the passenger side of a non-safety-plate windshield during an automobile collision. Safety belts had not yet been developed. You told me it was a miracle my eyes were not damaged, because the glass cut through both eyelids. The following year in Texas, you removed the keloid scars, but I was no longer pretty. In fact, a priest who came to visit me in the hospital fainted when he saw me.

You treated me for acne. You catheterized my heart before I went to college and found a persistent superior right vena cava, extra brachial arteries, and a valve defect. You told me not to climb mountains or go deep-sea diving. You extracted my wisdom teeth. You put me in a steam tent for a week in my Ivy League college infirmary for treatment of bronchitis. You treated me for severe dysentery (shigella) when I returned from my junior year in Europe. I had diarrhea all my life, so I did not call you until I was very ill. You told me how fortunate I was to be alive.

I was prevented from joining the Peace Corps due to the heart murmur. Instead, I went to work in Central America after college graduation. While there, after I made a conscious decision to have my first love affair, you hospitalized me for a month. You explained I had a 50-50 chance of living and surgically lanced a severe pelvic inflammatory infection. Both fallopian tubes were closed due to scarring. You explained gently that I probably could not have children but that I was fortunate to be alive. In my later 20s, in California, you treated me for a fractured bone in my foot, yeast infections, and more dental cavities. After I biked up a mountain and had heart pains that radiated down my left arm, you reiterated the restriction not to climb mountains. You told me I was fortunate to be alive.

You listened to me for a year as I wept for my younger sisters (I took the 14-year-old for an abortion and brought the 15-year-old to live with me due to severe anorexia). I am grateful you never prescribed medication for my grief. Through my employment, you taught me about biofeedback, which served to reduce my anxiety. When I finally got the courage to fall in love again, you prescribed birth control pills, in case we were wrong about the infertility. You gave me a hysterosalpingogram that showed a tiny opening in one fallopian tube. You gave me immunizations before I went to live overseas, then treated me for head wounds in Thailand when I was beaten up by a stranger. After I went deep-sea diving and had heart pains that radiated down my left arm at 50 feet below the surface, you reiterated the restriction that I avoid deep-sea diving. You told me I was fortunate to be alive.

When I was 27, I received a letter from you about the radiation treatment 20 years before. You said I was at high risk for thyroid cancer due to the heavy dose to my throat area. You gave me a procedure that showed no cancer. It also showed I had only half a thyroid. I felt fortunate to be alive. You gave me a Wasserman test [for syphilis] before my marriage at age 33.

To our mutual surprise, you determined I was pregnant at age 37 and probably carrying twins. I stopped drinking alcohol the day you told me I was pregnant. I didn't tell you and you didn't ask:

I didn't tell you I drank too much and had blackouts.

I didn't tell you every relative I had was probably alcoholic.

I didn't tell you my husband drank every night and used nonprescription drugs with increasing frequency.

I didn't tell you about his scathing comments and humiliating treatment of me, and how I couldn't seem to leave him.

I didn't tell you I had joined Al-Anon, a support group for spouses, families, and friends of alcoholics.

I didn't tell you I had smoked a pack of cigarettes per day for ten years until I was 36 years old.

I didn't tell you about the daily headaches that stopped, along with the cravings for cigarettes, after ten biofeedback sessions.

I didn't tell you that I worked part-time for many years because of fatigue, distress, and inability to concentrate.

I didn't tell you I had left my faith practice for over two decades and felt lost and alone.

I didn't tell you that as a child, I was moved to a new house every other year.

I didn't tell you that as an adult, I moved nearly every year in a vain effort to run away from my feelings.

I didn't tell you about the fear, loss, and depression I felt, even when times were good.

I didn't tell you about my suicidal ideation.

I didn't tell you about my phobias of elevators, enclosures, injections, electricity, public speaking, and groups.

I didn't tell you about the rage I felt when someone was maltreated.

I didn't tell you that as a child I compulsively read everything I could find about the Holocaust.

I didn't tell you how in adulthood, books on incest made me nauseous.

I didn't tell you about the "covert" sex abuse by a family member who told me dirty jokes and gave me "funny" back rubs.

I didn't tell you I had joined an incest survivors support group.

I didn't tell you how spacey and jumpy I felt at times, especially when surprised.

I didn't tell you about my frequent nosebleeds in childhood.

I didn't tell you I kept a baseball bat by my bedroom door as a child.

I didn't tell you about my terrible nightmares in childhood.

I didn't tell you that I could not remember much of my childhood.

You didn't ask me, and I didn't think to tell you.

After several months, you determined through amniocentesis and fetal monitoring that there was only one healthy male fetus. You kept careful track of my potential for diabetes and my loud heart murmur.

The pregnancy was unremarkable until seven months of gestation, when I developed high blood pressure and edema (which you diagnosed as preeclampsia), despite my good diet and high socioeconomic status. You put me on complete bed rest, but the water broke six weeks before my due date. After I labored for 12 hours, you did a Cesarean section with full anesthesia and delivered a healthy male child with an Apgar score of 9. I remained in the hospital for five days, although my son remained in an incubator for another five days. He had severe colic but was otherwise healthy. I nursed him for a year.

Twenty months later, again due to preeclampsia, you put me on complete bed rest at seven months gestation during my second pregnancy. You scheduled me for a second Cesarean, and I delivered a healthy 6 lb. 7 oz. full-term female child. We met frequently thereafter. My physical health deteriorated from stress as I turned 40 years old with a nursing infant and a toddler. You treated me for bronchitis, "flu" viruses, and a severe breast infection that brought an end to breast-feeding my one-year-old daughter.

I met you again because I could not swallow due to canker sores. You suggested prednisone, which I declined due to side effects. You biopsied tissue on my cervix, breast, ear, and back.

You used the term "precancerous cells" but explained that surgery was not needed yet.

I met your colleague, a PhD nutritionist, through the yellow pages and began an intensive vitamin regime that reversed all my symptoms after six months. I knew I was fortunate to be alive.

You immunized my children and treated them for frequent ear infections and sore throats. You treated my son at age four for a strange rectangular patch on his foot, which you diagnosed as cellulitis. You treated my daughter at age four for a kidney infection. After catheterizing her, you found a valve defect between her bladder and kidney.

You examined me when I had a ten-minute episode of intense pain in my vaginal area. You found nothing physically wrong. You listened patiently as I wept about my failing marriage and alcoholic father and encouraged me to move on. After my divorce, you treated me for pneumonia.

You removed my uterus and ovaries after I bled for two years. You told me I had fibroid tumors. You gave me light general anesthesia for this surgery because I finally told you I was a recovering alcoholic and my body was very sensitive. You listened to my grief at the end of my miracle of childbearing. You prescribed estrogen and ten years later stopped the prescription because of the potential side effects.

You gave me annual general medical checkups, mammograms, colonoscopies, Pap smears, and blood tests. You continued to monitor my heart murmur with annual specialty examinations, electrocardiograms, and echocardiograms.

During my occasional bouts of angina, you would conduct a stress test but could find no reason for the pain. I was not able to buy life insurance because I was a high-risk patient. You were as mystified as I by the occasional sharp pains I felt in different parts of my body and odd brief periods of malaise.

In 1988, after another automobile accident, you flushed my eyes to remove the glass that flew from an exploded mirror. A car had crossed the highway median and hit mine with such momentum that the other car flipped twice and landed upside-down. You patched my left eye and later found a corneal scar. You commented that I was fortunate to be alive and still sighted and prescribed glasses so I could see more clearly.

Then, in 1989, my life turned upside-down. My post-divorce life finally settled down, and my children began elementary school. I decided to look for the reason for the extensive childhood amnesia and why I felt so miserable despite my comfortable lifestyle. For the first time, I told you about the amnesia and asked you for hypnosis. I then began having frequent nightmares of dying animals and killing fields. Fortunately, you did not prescribe sleep medication.

For therapy, I found a nonphysician who specialized in treating sexually abused women. He did not believe in medicating emotional symptoms but rather, finding the source of the pain. This remarkable therapist, a former police investigator, understood that amnesia occurs for a very good reason. He spoke gently, compassionately, and simply. He had good boundaries, strong ethics, and a spiritual understanding. He knew that his clients may feel fragile but are actually very strong. He had a program of simple education about amnesia, dissociation, and the chemical changes that take place in the body during trauma, coupled with worksheets for his clients to complete. I told him about the experience I had at age seven, of being spanked with my pants pulled down. I explained I had talked about this event many times but never felt relief from the pain. I described a nightmare that plagued me, consisting of the sounds of the clink of a belt buckle and the zip of a zipper.

One pretty April morning in 1989, I went to the therapist's office. He led me through a relaxation exercise, instructing me to tense, and then relax, each major muscle group. He then asked me to go to a well and find the child I used to be, nurture her, and ask her what happened. I did that and found myself as a distraught seven-year-old. I began talking about that day when I was spanked on my bare buttocks.

Suddenly, I began reliving the event. I refelt the sharp slaps. I saw the pants legs as my head hung down across the adult's knees. I refelt the humiliation and pain. Then, just as suddenly, I stopped reliving the event. It felt as if I had pressed the "pause" button on an emotional and mental video of my life. I hung there, suspended in the midst of acute pain.

The therapist asked quietly, "Then what happened?" It felt as if I pushed the "play" button. I refelt being pulled up by my left arm and heard the clink of a belt buckle and zip of a zipper. I refelt the terror as I was pushed to my knees, and the adult sat back down on the edge of the bed. I refelt his hand on the back of my head as he pushed his penis into my mouth and moved my head back and forth. I retasted the ejaculate. I refelt being pushed to the floor, and left, like a used condom, as he went out of the room. I gagged and wept uncontrollably. And finally, I felt relief from that event.

It has not troubled me since that day. A hidden psychological abscess had finally been lanced, and my mind quickly healed itself. This began a five-year therapy period, during which I was able to fill in many of those blank places in my childhood. Each week I would remember just a little more, no more than I could bear. Some days, I could only relive a few minutes of the past. The pain at times felt unendurable, but the therapist assured me that I would feel better. I would scream with rage and fear on the drive home from his office. That's how I healed from each remembered betrayal. What I remembered was about my grandfather, who was a physician. He went to war when I was an infant and returned in 1946, when I was three years old. He then began to harm me in every way imaginable. Some of you will not want to believe this. However, children exposed to this kind of abuse are someone's daughters and sons, and they will someday be some-

one's spouse, parent, and patient. Will you recognize them in your practice, or will you look away?

My therapist once wondered aloud why I was not committed to the back ward of a state psychiatric hospital. I answered, "I dissociate well." He and I agreed I was fortunate to be alive. I don't need to go into detail about the crimes and brutalities I endured. I'm sure you've seen patients who experienced similar events, although you may not have recognized them. My purpose is not to shock but to teach that children can display few psychological symptoms; that the body takes the brunt of the psychosomatic effects in those of us who dissociate well.

The purpose of my letter is to tell you what happened a year after I began trauma recovery. I went to see you for my annual cardiology examination. You listened to my heart, as you had for the past four and a half decades in different countries, different states, different hospitals, and different offices. You listened again, not looking at me. Then you did a quick electrocardiogram and glanced at my thick file. And listened again, with a puzzled look on your kind face.

Finally, you looked directly at me and said, "There is no more heart murmur. I can't explain why. But you no longer need to see me for annual examinations."

I applied for a life insurance policy the very next day, which I continue to have as a talisman of healing. My physical health has been excellent, despite other life stresses, ever since I began unearthing the buried events from my childhood that broke my heart. The angina and sharp pains resolved as soon as I remembered the origin of those pains. My emotional health and sense of well-being improve daily.

A physician colleague of yours in the Southern California Permanente Medical Group found that the long-term medical consequences of incest, rape, and molestation are

- *Chronic depression*

- *Morbid obesity*
- *Marital instability*
- *High utilization of medical care*
- *Gastrointestinal distress*
- *Recurrent headaches.*

He also found that the more adverse childhood experiences a person has endured, the higher the rate of

- *Alcoholism*
- *Drug abuse*
- *Depression*
- *Suicide attempts*
- *Smoking*
- *Poor health*
- *Sexual partners*
- *Sexually transmitted disease*
- *Ischemic heart disease*
- *Cancer*
- *Chronic lung disease*
- *Skeletal fractures, and*
- *Liver disease*

[Dr. Vincent Felitti's] research is extraordinarily validating to me, since I have a majority of the after-effects he describes. I believe that by storing the traumatic memories well out of consciousness, my immune system collapsed, resulting in illness and structural damage. The stress of repeated trauma may indeed have blown a hole in my heart valve. By remembering, talking about, and grieving these events, I found that the intense psychological pressure was relieved and my body simply healed itself. Nature prefers homeostasis. Even broken hearts can heal.

At a child abuse conference in Sacramento ... a psychologist, Dr. John Briere, remarked that if child abuse and neglect were to disappear today, the diagnostic and statistical manual would shrink to the size of a pamphlet in two generations, and the prisons would empty. I agree. As physicians and particularly as pediatricians, you are in a position to help end this epidemic of child abuse. You must do so with great care, because perpetrators have gained inroads in the systems that are supposed to protect children. But you are in a unique position, and I encourage you to work together in this serious matter.

I am writing to thank the hundreds of you who treated me throughout my life, particularly when I was young. I am forever grateful for your concern for my health and well-being and for your gifts of antibiotics. I am even more grateful that you gave me biofeedback and relaxation as an adult rather than medication to blunt symptoms of my childhood trauma, so that the encapsulated, abscessed memories could surface and heal. I am, indeed, fortunate to be alive.[22]

Anonymous

Her ACE score may only have been a one. Her trauma? Child sexual abuse. It nearly destroyed her entire life. Remembering her story, telling it, and being believed opened the door to hope and healing.

The Backstory

We will focus in this book on how to change the endings for high ACE score children and adults, but first you need to hear a little known backstory. The ACE Study was not the first time childhood sexual abuse had been identified as deeply connected to psychological trauma and its physiological consequences. The genesis of the ACE Study was Dr. Felitti's identification of child sexual abuse in morbidly obese Kaiser Permanente weight clinic patients. But one hundred years earlier, doctors in Paris and Vienna found the same connection;

then they buried it, a stunning cover-up, until Dr. Felitti rediscovered it and so much more in 1995.

In the late 19th century, a French neurologist named Jean-Martin Charcot first identified the relationship between childhood sexual abuse and profound symptoms later in adulthood during his study of "hysteria" in women.[23] "Hysteria" was the diagnosis for women with major mental health issues that ended up in a hospital (asylum) outside of Paris. It was considered to be a female disorder and was grounded in profound cultural bias against women and girls. Charcot was a well-known French doctor that began studying the phenomenon of "hysteria" first. He soon discovered that the deeply troubled women in the asylum, once interviewed or hypnotized and then interviewed, disclosed consistent stories of victimization during childhood by rape, incest, and other forms of sexual abuse. The disclosure of their stories was a collaborative effort between the doctors and the patients.[24] And early on it became clear that if patients could tell their stories, they would begin to heal.

It attracted the attention of Sigmund Freud, today known as the father of modern psychology. Sigmund Freud traveled to Paris to study Charcot's work and then began focusing on documenting the stories of women diagnosed with hysteria in Vienna as well. Freud called the process of helping them remember and telling their stories of abuse "catharsis" and later "pscyho-analysis." One patient of Joseph Breuer (a colleague of Sigmund Freud), known as "Anna O.", dubbed the investigative process of figuring out what happened to the women as little girls and then being able to talk about it, as "the talking cure." The more they talked about what had happened to them the faster their recovery seemed to take place.

Sigmund Freud became deeply focused on the relationship between "hysteria" and childhood sexual abuse and authored a major piece on the topic in 1896. He wrote in part: "… at the bottom of every case of hysteria there are one or more premature sexual experiences, occurrences which belong to the earliest years of childhood…"

Dr. Judith Herman tells the story best of what happened after Freud issued his *Aetiology of Hysteria*: "Hysteria was so common among women that if his patients' stories were true, and if his theory was correct, he would be forced to conclude that what he called 'perverted acts against children' were endemic, not only among the proletariat of Paris, where he had first studied hysteria, but also among the respectable bourgeois families of Vienna, where he had established his practice. This idea was simply unacceptable. It was beyond credibility."[24] What did Freud do? He recanted his findings, covered up his research, and never again spoke publicly about his earlier findings. He depended on the wealthy families of Vienna for his living. Surely, he could not accuse them of participating in endemic child sexual abuse.

Dr. Herman continues and her analysis is important to our willingness to reject Freud's cowardice and tell the truth about trauma and abuse and its consequences in the lives of children and adults:

> Freud stopped listening to his female patients…Out of the ruins of the traumatic theory of hysteria, Freud created psychoanalysis. The dominant psychological theory of the next century was founded in the denial of women's reality. Sexuality remained the central focus of inquiry. But the exploitive social context in which sexual relations actually occur became utterly invisible. Psychoanalysis became a study of the internal vicissitudes of fantasy and desire, dissociated from the reality of experience. By the first decade of the twentieth century, without ever offering any clinical documentation of false complaints, Freud concluded that his hysterical patients' accounts of childhood sexual abuse were untrue."[25]

Not until Dr. Vincent Felitti and the ACE Study did the truth re-emerge along with clinical documentation of the short and long-term impacts of childhood sexual abuse and all other forms of life-altering trauma to children and adults. We must never ignore victims again. We must never sacrifice truth on the altar of expediency. Freud sacrificed the truth to save his career, protect his livelihood, and avoid the reality of a culture that subjugated, demeaned, abused, and minimized women and girls. We still fight those battles today but we must win them. We must become advocates of the "talking cure" and stand by the truth of the trauma still being experienced by so many children.

We must be advocates for justice. What does that mean? Let me paraphrase a definition of justice from Bishop Desmond Tutu: "Justice is three things: Telling the truth about injustice; Repairing the harm of injustice as much as humanly possible; and then changing the conditions that caused the injustice in the first place." We have no higher calling. The ACE Study has given us our marching orders in what should be a lifetime calling for each of us.

Reflections

If you didn't calculate your ACE score, go back and do it. Don't be afraid of knowing if you have a score higher than zero. Most of us do. We need to know so we can begin the journey toward healing and hope. My dad would have scored a six on the ACE Index based only on what I know about his story. He lived most of his life with unmitigated and unresolved childhood trauma. I scored a three. My adult children, during the writing of this book, scored a zero. My wife scored a zero—for which I am extremely grateful. She has her own struggles in life, but I am thankful that many times she has been able to be my advocate and supporter in my journey of dealing with my own ACEs. We can break the generational cycle identified in the ACE Study. My family is breaking the cycle. All our families can.

Two

Going Deeper into the Impacts
of Childhood Trauma

Behind every person who's committed an unimaginable crime is
an adult who committed unimaginable violence against them as a
child. Violence begets violence, and that violence begets even more
violence.

— Ji-young Gong

ONE DEAR FRIEND told me during the editing of this book
that he needed a shower after reading chapter 1 and could not bear to
read any more about the impacts. If you need a shower, go to chapter
3 now. For those working in the field professionally, studying these
topics in school, or simply wanting to know even more about the
research on the impacts of childhood trauma, read on. Beyond the
findings of the ACE Study, research has found dramatically increased
rates of drug and alcohol abuse, gang membership, generational
abuse of children, violence against women, sexual victimization, and
low levels of academic achievement in children growing up in homes
with child abuse and domestic violence.[1]

Gang Violence and Childhood Trauma

In 1999, I had the opportunity to meet with a small group of
former gang members working with the nationally recognized Tarik
Khamisa Foundation (TKF) in San Diego. I had been invited by their

executive director to talk to them about their life journeys. These former gang members were now working with TKF and focusing on helping other children to stay out of gangs. During our hour together, I told them some of my family history with violence and abuse. Though I had never joined a gang, I wanted to know if any of them had family histories of domestic violence or child abuse. I always find that sharing my story enables others to more easily share their own stories. The TKF men were no different. In fact, all twelve of the participants that day described coming from homes with some mix of child abuse and/or domestic violence.[2] There was no exception.

Other research has confirmed my own findings with former gang members.[3] First-generation gang membership is almost always about dysfunctional family dynamics. Children go looking for a supportive family. They go looking for respect. They go looking for control. It is why every gang prevention and intervention program should include a focus on domestic violence and healthy parenting skills. The solution to gangs and violence is intimately connected to families and to children receiving the love and support they need at home. Gangs often become organized crime syndicates in the second and third generations and are more difficult to unravel or understand. But first-generation gang membership is almost always made up of children and teens coming from violent and abusive homes in neighborhoods with high levels of community violence.

In Richmond, British Columbia, a few years ago, I was speaking at a community domestic violence awareness event. During the first session, I noted very little law-enforcement presence in the room. I asked the organizers about it, and they said that area law-enforcement officials were preparing for a major press conference on gang violence and their plan to address it. I was stunned that any well-educated law-enforcement professional would think the gang issue could be addressed without a discussion about family violence. I encouraged the organizers to send out their own press advisory and link the two issues that very afternoon. The law enforcement leaders held their

press conference across town, and late in the afternoon I was interviewed about domestic violence and gangs. I have little doubt that
my sound bites that night angered the local law-enforcement leaders,
but I was speaking the truth in a community that needed to hear the
truth. I'll never be invited back to do law-enforcement training there,
but at least the truth was spoken! Gangs, at their core, are always
about domestic violence.

Marie De Santis, executive director of the Women's Justice
Center in Santa Rosa, California, recently challenged law-enforcement leaders in her community attempting to deal with gang issues
to recognize the connection between gang membership and domestic
violence. "If local officials truly want to prevent gang violence, they
can't keep dodging an examination of their own role in creating it.
When police refuse to bridge the language barrier for Latina victims
of domestic violence, they condemn both the Latina mothers and
children to stew interminably in the pressure cooker of violence at
home. There's no more potent recipe for promoting gang violence.
The mother's control of her children is extinguished. And the child
is steeped in a cauldron of terror and fear. Can there be any surprise
when that child becomes the adolescent who seeks refuge and expression of rage in a gang?"[4] De Santis has rightly found the connection
between gangs and domestic violence. There is a reason children join
gangs. They are looking for a family. They are looking for refuge and
a safe place to express their rage. The gang becomes the cheerleader.

Epigenetics and Trauma

The study of genetics and epigenetics has established that childhood trauma can actually impact gene structure, resulting in health
issues later in life.[5] One recent research initiative actually found that
trauma impacts change the telomeres, the small caps on chromo-
somes in our DNA.[6] And interestingly, there was a gender disparity
found. The study, conducted with children five to fifteen years old
in the greater New Orleans area who had witnessed family violence,
found that the DNA alteration impact was profoundly greater in girls

witnessing violence than in boys! The notion of genetic engineering in laboratories that has become so controversial in America has gotten far more attention, but we have not been paying attention to the more important issue. While further studies are now underway, there is no doubt we will find impacts on both girls and boys. Genetic engineering has been going on for generations via the child abuse, domestic violence, and related trauma that children experience. Their DNA is changed because of violence and abuse, and then the genetically altered DNA is passed on to subsequent generations.

Robin Karr-Morse began to identify this issue many years ago in *Ghosts from the Nursery* when she wrote: "If the caregiving relationship is inadequate or traumatic, especially in the first thousand days of life, when the brain is chemically and structurally forming, the part of the brain that allows the baby to feel connected with another person can be lost or greatly impaired. A child may mature lacking the ability to attach or to relate in any profound way to others. Absent adequate nurturing by an emotionally competent caregiver, the baby faces an unpredictable tide of unregulated emotions … We have yet to recognize that if a child's experiences are pathological and are steeped in chronic fear, the very capacities that mitigate against violent behavior—including empathy and the capacity for self-regulation of strong emotions—can be lost."[7]

Incarceration and Family Violence and Abuse

Let's examine the financial impacts of the cycle of family violence and abuse by simply looking at whom we lock up in California and across America every year. In California, the "all-in" costs for incarceration in the state Department of Corrections are approximately $47,000 per year per inmate (not including health care costs), for a total of nearly $8 billion per year![8] Most research has found that the large majority of all inmates in the prison system in California and across the United States grew up in homes with some mix of child abuse, domestic violence, and/or drugs and alcohol.[9] We are raising our criminals, the children of trauma and abuse, at home in

America, and the taxpayers are funding the bill—billions of dollars in incarceration costs and billions of dollars to operate a criminal justice system that keeps incarcerating the next generation of criminals and the generation after that.

Recently, I was speaking in El Centro, California, with a large group of criminal and civil justice system professionals, and I said, "The vast majority of all criminals we lock up in this state for all crimes grew up in homes with some mix of child abuse, domestic violence, and/or drug and alcohol abuse." At the next break, a man came up to me quite aggressively, red in the face, and said, "You are wrong." Not sure what he meant but assuming he thought I was overstating my case, I apologized that I had offended him but told him that was my personal opinion. He got a funny look on his face and said, "I oversee four prisons in Imperial and Riverside Counties in California for the state Department of Corrections. I have been in this position for twelve years. You're wrong because you said 'vast majority.' I have *never* met a man in prison in the last twelve years who did not come from a home with some mix of child abuse, domestic violence, and drug or alcohol abuse."

Indeed, today in the United States we are locking up more people per capita than any country on planet Earth, but we are not solving the issues of crime and delinquency. We are only creating a conveyor belt of children and young adults moving from abusive homes into poverty, prison, and pain. And no one comes out of prison more functional, more effective as a partner, or more equipped as a parent.

The connection to capital murderers is equally clear. Mike Green, the former district attorney of Monroe County, New York, said in an interview a number of years ago: "In all my years as a district attorney, I never prosecuted a capital-murder case where the defendant did not have a serious history of child abuse."[10]

Life without a cheerleader is a life without the tools and the ability to overcome abuse, trauma, and adverse childhood experiences. We as a society are doing a very poor job of addressing this issue in the lives of most children growing up with trauma. We expect someone else to do it, someone else to solve it, and someone else to care. Most people don't see it as their job. Some organization will take care of them. Somebody else is keeping track of all those children, right? And so the pattern continues. As the nuclear family declines and more children grow up with only one parent or with warring parents, the issues only get worse.

If you were one of those children, don't get discouraged. Keep reading. We all need to understand how we were impacted by those difficult experiences in childhood and adolescence. If you grew up in a healthy, two-parent family without abuse or major trauma, you can be thankful, but you should keep reading. We must all learn how we can be the cheerleaders our children need and how to find cheerleaders in our own lives in order to weather the storms ahead.

So, let's break it down a little more. What are the impacts of particular types of trauma and abuse? What do these adverse childhood experiences do to a child's brain development? What kind of short- and long-term consequences have been found? And as we look at each area of abuse, let's remember the nature of polyvictims (victims of more than one type of abuse) and the clear research on the cumulative impact of these traumas.

Physical Abuse as a Child

A great deal of research has documented what happens to a child who suffers significant and even chronic physical abuse at the hands of a parent. Abuse has been linked to childhood and adult obesity.[11] While discipline can be healthy and appropriate, when discipline crosses the line to abuse or parents simply take out their rage and anger on their children, bad things happen in the brain, body, and psyche of a child. Physical child abuse is highly correlated to mental disorders in children, suicide, eating disorders, substance abuse (drug and alcohol), and risky and premature sexual behavior.[12] In my own family, during the writing of this book, my sister disclosed to me her own struggle with an eating disorder in college due to my father's verbal and emotional abuse, which began in childhood. It was the first time she had ever shared it and the first time I had looked closely at the strong linkage to eating disorders in the literature.

Physically abused children learn to believe the behavior is normative and appropriate.[13] Former Minnesota Viking running back Adrian Peterson recently reacted with some shock after being indicted for child abuse of one of his children. He issued a press release saying in part, "I am not a child abuser."[14] He went on to say that he disciplined his son the way he was disciplined. But saying you are not a child abuser does not relieve you of the moral and legal responsibility for your abuse. Adrian Peterson believed it was right and normal behavior until he was indicted and the story and pictures of a four-year-old beaten by a powerful, muscular NFL football player became public. Adrian Peterson needed help as a child to stop the abuse of his father. He needed help as a teen to deal with his trauma. He never got that help. As an adult, he needed to work through it to ensure he did not repeat the cycle into the next generation with his own children. Instead of getting the help he needed, he has had to face shame and public ridicule.

After the story broke, I was intrigued by the way a number of African American athletes, including newscaster Cris Carter, came forward and said they too were beaten as children but decided not to do it to their own children. Aaron Gouveia, *Huffington Post* blogger and founder of the *Daddy Files*, posted a great commentary that challenged the notion of so many child victims and community members that "whoopings" and "beatings" are just a normal, healthy part of growing up.[15] Gouveia wrote:

> I've been told it's a southern thing. A cultural thing. A black thing. A religious thing. I've been told it's the only way to make sure children are raised to be respectful. I've been told if more kids were disciplined like this, there would be fewer school shootings and spoiled children. But mostly, I've been

told this kind of corporal punishment is acceptable because the parents who do it were raised this way themselves. And after all, they were whipped and they turned out just fine.

Want to know how I know they're wrong? Because they still think it's OK to take up weapons against children and beat them bloody.

If this is part of your southern culture, then your southern culture condones child abuse and needs to change. If this is because you're African American, then the black community needs some serious internal reflection and a change of heart, because this is wrong. And if this is how you were raised, well … I'm sorry for that. But just because your parents made a terrible mistake out of ignorance doesn't mean you have to continue the violent cycle. This isn't about spanking, because Adrian Peterson didn't spank his son. I can count on one hand the times I've given my oldest a swat on the butt, mainly because he was attempting to run toward the road or trying to tear off the electrical outlet cover after putting his hand in the dog's water bowl. And even then, it wasn't the force that made him cry—it was the stern "No!" that accompanies the light spank.

That's in stark contrast to Peterson, who reportedly took the time to fashion himself a switch and proceeded to beat his small child bloody with it by hitting him more than a dozen times. A grown man who smashes into offensive linemen and linebackers for a living whipping a small boy he's supposed to love and care for. How anyone can defend that is beyond me.[16]

Well said. Physical abuse of children causes post-traumatic stress (PTSD) and often plays a role in a lifetime of violent or broken relationships.[17] There is no doubt that abused children are at risk of engaging in criminal behavior earlier in life than non-abused children and at greater risk of continuing that criminal behavior into adulthood.[18] My strong bias is that we should *never* diagnose a child with the *D* in PTSD. My friend Dave Roberts, a member of the San Diego County Board of Supervisors, challenged me on this recently. He argued that labeling children with a "disorder" because of the way their bodies and brains have responded to trauma is wrong. Their bodies are reacting very normally to a very abnormal experience. I agree. It is a label, like many other labels put on children of trauma, which serves no positive purpose. They are suffering from post-traumatic stress (PTS). That is all the diagnosis needs to be and all the children need to be told. They are having a normal reaction to a very abnormal situation. "Disorder" is a label these children do not need or deserve. Hopefully this approach will become standard across the country as we work with those suffering from acute, chronic, and toxic stress.

Sexual Abuse as a Child

Research on the impacts of sexual abuse on the life of a child is incontrovertible. Whether the sexual molestation happens at the hands of a parent, a stepparent, a teacher, a coach, a youth leader, or another relative, the impacts are significant and often lifelong. My wife, Beth, has a friend who was molested as a child. At sixty years old, she still struggles with having been molested in a boarding school more than fifty years ago. I have a variety of dear friends, now in their fifties and sixties, who were molested as children and still deal with emotional and psychological issues related to this abuse.

Sexual molestation is a deep wound to the psyche and soul of a human being. It may be repressed for a time, but the impact is always deep and often lasts for life. There is little doubt in my mind that sexual abuse is the most heinous crime that can be committed against a child. My faith does inform my view. In the Bible, Jesus said, "Whoever causes one of these little ones who believe to stumble, it would be better for him if, with a heavy millstone hung around his neck, he had been cast into the sea."[19] In my version of this, I hope there is a special place in hell for pedophiles and child molesters. But we all must never forget that the vast majority of child sex abusers were molested as children and are acting out the same victimization they experienced.

Sexual abuse places children at high risk for PTS, suicide, sexual abuse of others, sleep disorders, substance abuse, and chronic health issues.[20] In my work over the years, I have met many child sexual-abuse victims and often have witnessed their sexualization at a very young age and their struggle to not act out sexually toward other children and adults. Dr. Bruce Perry tells a story in his excellent book *Born to Love* about meeting a young sexual-abuse victim for the first time. She wanted to sit in his lap, which he innocently allowed.[21] But no sooner did the little girl climb into his lap than she began unzipping his pants. A stark reminder of how much impact sexual abuse has and how quickly children will see sexual activity as normative, no matter what their age or their relationship with another child or adult. Research has documented this sexualization of children because of abuse over and over again.

Diana

On the opposite end of the spectrum is research stating that some children who have experienced sexual abuse struggle greatly with finding healthy intimacy or even being able to handle physical contact of any kind with others.[22] A number of years ago, our family had the opportunity to host a college-age young woman who was looking for a room to rent near the college she was attending. I will call her Diana. Diana came to meet us and was very emotionally protective during our first conversation. She declined to even shake my hand, though she did shake Beth's hand. She was cordial but not outgoing or emotionally "available" to us. We sensed some significant emotional issues, but we decided to rent her a room anyway. There was something about her that drew us in.

Diana lived with us for more than a year. I quickly figured out that she did not want to be alone with me or want me touching her in any way. As the months went by, we slowly learned more of her story.

Her father sexually molested Diana when she was a child. Later in life, she was raped by an acquaintance. Her mother was emotionally abusive. Diana had profound health issues connected to her childhood sexual abuse. Not until she moved out of our home more than a year later did she allow me to gently hug her. She told me what a big step it was to trust me with physical contact with her. We still maintain a relationship with Diana, who is now in her thirties. She is an amazing young woman who continues to struggle to overcome a host of emotional and physical challenges. It seems counterintuitive, but childhood sexual abuse can lead some to want no physical contact with anyone and others to engage in all kinds of inappropriate physical contact.

Divorce

Today, half of all marriages end in divorce. Given how many children now go through the trauma and pain of divorcing parents, the impact of divorce on children is always a sensitive subject. Many couples "stay together for the children" and end up causing the children even more pain through their unhappy marriage. And because so many people get divorced and life goes on for the children and the adults, it is hard to accept the research that says just how traumatic it can be for children to experience the divorce of their parents. Again, many who go through their parents' divorce do overcome it through other support and cheerleaders in their lives. But it is recognized in the ACE study as a trauma marker because the research is so clear.

Interestingly, the ACE research found no category in the ACE score to be clearly more damaging than another.[23] Divorce or abandonment by a parent produces one point in the ACE score, just as childhood sexual abuse does. I will say, however, that while administering the ACE survey last summer to teenagers at Camp HOPE, I noticed that children who had been sexually abused were more emotionally triggered by taking the ACE survey than those children who had to check a line saying that their parents were divorced.

Even if divorce is not as visibly impactful in trauma-exposed children, it does have a profound impact—particularly if the children are young when their parental loss occurs. Divorce causes children high levels of stress, and many still report trauma from the divorce years later.[24]

Often the trauma relates to the actions of one or both parents during the divorce. A number of years ago at Camp HOPE, I was talking to a young boy named Justice, who asked me what I did for a living. I told him I was a lawyer. He immediately asked if he could hire me. "What would you hire me to do, Justice?" Justice told me that his mom and dad were separated and soon to be divorced. He said one of the things that hurt the most was that his dad had taken every family picture with him when he left. "My dad took all the pictures. I don't have any pictures of myself at all. It makes me so mad. Can you just sue him to get the pictures back?" My heart broke for Justice, and I felt his pain from the separation and pending divorce of his parents. It wasn't just that his dad was gone. His dad stole his memories.

Witnessing Domestic Violence

Over the last twenty years, much has been written about children who grow up witnessing domestic violence in the home. While some children seem to overcome it without repeating the cycle as adults, a great deal of research confirms the increased likelihood that a child growing up in an abusive home will become an abuser as a teen or as an adult. There is also research that tends to say that girls growing up witnessing the abuse of their mothers are more likely to accept abuse as teens or adults. Boys witnessing their fathers' abuse of their mothers are more likely to become abusers, and girls watching the same abuse are more likely to view such violence as normative when they begin dating and looking for partners.

One of the most recent studies illustrates very clear findings on the generational nature of most abusers and victims.[25] Sam Houston University recently published a study based on the National Youth Survey Family Study, a national sample of 1,683 families, and followed 353 second-generation parents and their third-generation offspring over a twenty-year period. They tracked families with domestic violence and related child abuse and found that:

- 78.8% of children ended up becoming victims as adults.
- 76.2% of children ended up becoming perpetrators as adults.[26]

This is not something that many advocates in the domestic violence movement want to discuss. Early in my career, I was told that associating victimization with the home the girl grew up in was victim blaming, but the research is too clear. We cannot avoid it. While women who did not grow up in abusive homes can end up being victimized in domestic violence incidents, they appear to be the minority. The majority of victims of domestic violence grew up in homes with domestic violence.

In September 2014, I was honored to speak at the Silent Witness Exhibit at a conference of the Wyoming Coalition Against Sexual and Domestic Violence. The Silent Witness Exhibit has had a powerful impact across America by commemorating women, men, and children killed in domestic-violence-related homicides. The red silhouettes of homicide victims have been placed at so many community events and conferences to remind everyone of those we have lost because of failed prevention and intervention efforts. In Laramie, Wyoming, I was very moved to be there with three mothers—all of whom had lost their daughters in a domestic violence homicide in 2013. Each of them wept as the executive director of the Coalition, Jennifer Zenor, memorialized their daughters eloquently. After the ceremony, I spoke personally with each mom. Their pain was profound. As we talked, I asked each of them about their own homes growing up. I was not surprised to find out that each was a survivor of childhood abuse and each went on to marry or get involved with an abusive man in the home where her daughter was raised. Now their daughters were dead at the hands of another abusive man. And in each case, the killer too had grown up with domestic violence.

The research is consistent when it comes to assessing the impact on children who simply witness domestic violence between adults in the home but are never physically abused. Researchers estimate that between three and ten million children witness domestic violence every year in the United States.[27] Children who chronically witness violence between adults in their home face mental health, physical health, and behavioral issues. The ACE Study has examined this, and there are clearly short-term and long-term impacts. In my first book with Gael Strack, *Hope for Hurting Families*, we touched on the early research.[28] Children who witness or live with domestic violence are often burdened by a profound sense of guilt, believing wrongly that they should be able to stop it or that the violence is their fault.[29] Children who witness domestic violence often live in terror and fear for their mothers.[30] The research is clear that children live with uncertainty, grief, anger, and shame and often take these same feelings and patterns into adulthood without the opportunity to find hope and healing.[31]

Having spent nearly thirty years working in the field of violence prevention and crisis intervention, I have heard thousands of stories of children who have witnessed domestic violence and struggled through the consequences, both as children and adults. Statistics are significant, but every case represents a real child with real stories. Let me tell you one.

Lila

One of the stories still being untangled is of a now-teenager named Lila. I met Lila when she came to the San Diego Family Justice Center with her mom for help more than five years ago. Her dad was in jail for domestic violence, and her mom, Jillian, wanted a restraining order and counseling for herself. Lila seemed pretty together. I met her in the Children's Room at the Family Justice Center. She was ten at the time, and she was reading a book to her younger sister and brother. She seemed so responsible and mature. And even after many years in the field of violence prevention, I (and others at the center) missed Lila's needs. Jillian worked in the medical profession and really needed some emotional and mental health assistance. She was having trouble working and needed to work to provide for her children. Over the next couple of years, my wife and I spent quite a bit of time with Lila and her siblings. We hosted a number of pool parties at our home for a committee of survivors called VOICES, which supported the Family Justice Center, as well as for Lila and her brother and sister, who attended Camp HOPE San Diego a number of times. Lila was smart and was a voracious reader. Even at camp, we struggled to get her involved in activities because she loved to read so much.

It wasn't until one fall day when Lila was fourteen that I realized how much we had missed with her. I got a text message from her mom saying Lila was in the hospital and asking that we pray for her. I immediately called Jillian and found out the horrifying news that Lila had attempted suicide by cutting her wrists. Her mom confided in me that Lila was a "cutter" and that this was not the first time she had cut her arms and wrists. Looking back, I had never noticed her arms, but perhaps that was because she wore long sleeves so often that I had never seen her arms.

Lila had to be put in a lock-up unit at Children's Hospital in San Diego while they tried to provide the help she needed. A few weeks after she was hospitalized, I called Jillian to check on Lila, and she told me the latest disclosure from Lila to her therapist. During a recent counseling session, her psychiatrist had asked Lila what her first memory was in life. Lila responded, "It was the day my mom died." The psychiatrist was puzzled, as Lila's mom was very much alive. Lila, however, said she remembered standing over her mom when Jillian was pregnant with her brother and seeing her dad kill her mom. As Jillian became involved in the follow-up, the true story came out. Lila was only two and a half years old when her mom was pregnant with her brother and was strangled to unconsciousness by her dad. Lila found her mom unconscious on the ground and thought she was dead. This was Lila's first memory in life. It was never disclosed, never discussed, and never addressed before. Lila's brother was later born and diagnosed on the autism spectrum. Jillian would later leave the abusive relationship and go on to become a single parent of her children, but Lila would face profound and almost life-ending consequences from witnessing domestic violence at an age so young that no one ever would have asked her about it.

I don't know the rest of Lila's story. Cutting is often a high-grade marker for incest as well, so there might be more to the story than was ever disclosed. But Lila needed help long before she arrived at Camp HOPE. Lila did not have anyone to talk to about it. Lila didn't have a cheerleader until long after the impacts of witnessing the violence had played out for everyone to see.

Having a Parent Who Commits Suicide

Another large body of research has looked at the impacts on children who have a parent commit suicide. There is really no question that it is not a good thing, and there is much evidence that it creates major issues in the lives of children that linger into adulthood for them.

At Camp HOPE last summer, I saw the impacts of neglect, poverty, violence, and suicide in the life of a child all at one time during the first week of camp. On the second day of camp, we decided to have the children play Capture the Flag on the big grassy field. The children all ran to the field, and the counselors began dividing them up into teams. There was a lot of yelling, cheering, and anticipation. Soon the game was underway, with children running in all directions. But as I watched, I noticed a young boy named Zachary standing over by the fence a long way from all the playing children. I walked over to Zachary and asked if I could hang out with him. He did not respond. I suggested he sit down with me, which he did.

I asked him how he was doing, and he said he missed his dad and was feeling sad because he couldn't remember his mom. I asked him where his mom was, and Zachary said, "She breathed some bad air and died." Zachary said she had died four years ago, when he was five years old. He said he was saddest because he could not remember her, and his dad would always tell him that he should remember his mom. I asked him if he lived with his dad. He told me his dad was fifty-five years old and legally blind, and they now lived in a motel.

I put my arm around him and told him I was glad he was at camp. He said he did not really want to do anything. I asked him what he liked to do, and he said "only video games." I asked him to come play Capture the Flag with the other kids, but he did not want to play. No cajoling from me could get him up until a young Kidder Creek counselor (a sophomore at San Diego State University) named Cami came over, got down on Zachary's level, and said, "Zachary, we really miss you, and we would love to have you come play with us. It will be really fun. We love having you around with all the other kids, and they will all be happy to have you play." Zachary got up, took her hand, and joined Capture the Flag.

Camp HOPE started on Monday; my conversation with Zachary was Tuesday afternoon. On Tuesday night Zachary wet his sleeping bag, and then we saw him wet his pants during the tribal activities on Wednesday. Thankfully, none of the other kids even mentioned it, and we just got him a new sleeping bag. On Wednesday, we bought him some pull-ups (camouflage) for him.

At the time, I did not know Zachary's story, but I would later learn that Zachary had witnessed domestic violence between his parents and between his dad and other women. When Zachary was five, his mom killed herself. Child Protective Services had removed him multiple times from his home, both before and after his mom took her life.

By Thursday of that week of camp, Zachary was talking and engaging with the other kids. On Thursday night I talked to the kids about family violence and told my own family story. Zach cried along with many of the other children, but that night after our chanting time (I am strong; I am compassionate; I have hope; I am a leader), he asked if he could talk to the whole group while we were having dessert in the dining room. He said, "I see hope in all the tears tonight because we all love each other." Then he asked to sing a song. He stood on the chair and sang the theme song from one of his video games about Europe, the Russians, EA Games, Asia, and something about "Fortress Europe." It made no sense, and Zachary is no singer. But everyone cheered for him.It was just the fact he was doing it. Then he said, "Now, I have to tell you the most important thing. Listen. This is the most important. I am going to tell you the most important thing. Hope is spelled 'G-O-D.'"

On Friday morning Zachary told me Camp HOPE was the greatest week of his life. Zachary will be presented with many challenges due to the trauma he experienced, but the contrast between his life without cheerleaders and his life with cheerleaders was very clear in just one week of camp.

Being Raised by an Alcoholic Parent

The research is also clear regarding the impact on children who grow up with one or both parents who are alcoholics or drug-addicted. The ACE Study identified this issue, and many other studies have revealed difficulties that may arise from growing up in a home with an alcoholic parent.

More than twenty years ago, researchers first noted that children of alcoholics appeared to be affected by a variety of problems over the course of their lives. Such problems include fetal alcohol syndrome, which is first manifested in infancy; emotional problems and hyperactivity in childhood; emotional problems and conduct problems in adolescence; and the development of alcoholism in adulthood.[32] The only additional piece I will note here is that many children growing up in homes with alcoholic parents are also experiencing physical or sexual abuse, witnessing domestic violence, and suffering verbal and emotional abuse.

Witnessing Acts of Violence in the Media and the Community

One other set of impacts of traumatic experiences on children is worth looking at here before we move forward toward our efforts, strategies, and plans to cheer for the children. There is quite a bit of controversial research about the impact on children of witnessing real-life versus media portrayals of violence. One study found that children witness more than 186,000 homicides in video games and on television before the age of eighteen. Another study found that children witnessing acts of violence in digital formats are desensitized to the actual impact of such violence in real life and are therefore more prone to commit such acts in real life. My personal view is that media violence is not the true culprit. It is my view that media violence is not healthy or positive in a child's life, but the real issue is the witnessing of actual violence in their homes, in their neighborhoods, and in their schools.

I tend to think that experiencing bullying or witnessing violence toward others probably has far more impact than a television show or a video game. It makes sense to me that once this fertile soil in a child's life has been cultivated by true-life violence, neglect, and abuse, television or electronic portrayals of violence probably affect that child more. Children growing up in neighborhoods with gang violence, street violence, and related traumas do not fare well later in life.

The Attorney General's National Task Force on Children Exposed to Violence rightly focused significant attention on the issue of community violence and the impact on children of growing up with violence in the streets.[33] The complexity of community violence and its relation to child trauma, domestic violence, divorce, and other ACE categories should not be overlooked. High levels of community violence often correlate with poverty, historic oppression, and racial disparities.[34] Poor communities frequently lack the resources to protect children and address violence and abuse. Tribal and rural communities often lack the necessary social services, child-welfare support, and other infrastructure necessary to address trauma. As we dive deeper into this book, we will look at programs that successfully address trauma and abuse. We will look closely at the power of individual mentors and cheerleaders in helping children dealing with the impacts of trauma, abuse, and community violence.

Childhood Trauma and Homicide

I have believed throughout most of my career that the vast majority of domestic violence homicides are related to childhood trauma in the life of the killer. David Adams's recent work about men who kill their partners has only solidified my views.[35] Though Adams moves quickly past any strong correlation between high ACE scores and domestic homicide, the correlation in his raw data is very obvious.[36] While more than 50 percent of the murderers he interviewed actually corroborated child abuse and/or domestic violence in their homes, the more interesting number came from his interviews of female survivors of attempted domestic homicide. Ninety-four percent of the survivors of attempted domestic homicide described their partners as having grown up in a home with child abuse and/or domestic violence.[37] There is little doubt that childhood trauma plays a major role in later domestic-violence-related homicides.

The other key correlation recently documented by Alliance for HOPE through our Training Institute on Strangulation Prevention (www.strangulationtraininginstitute.org) is the relationship between law-enforcement officers killed in the line of duty and men with a history of domestic violence. Men with a history of violence against women—particularly men who strangle women—are the most dangerous men on the planet. While we know that childhood trauma produces high likelihoods of later violence against women, we have now discovered that men with a history of domestic violence, particularly those who have committed prior strangulation assaults against intimate partners, are far more likely to later be shot by a law-enforcement officer or to shoot a law-enforcement officer in an officer-involved critical incident.[38] In Riverside County, California, Deputy District Attorney Gerald Fineman has documented that men who strangle women are likely to be responsible for the majority of deaths of law-enforcement officers killed in the line of duty.[39] While more research is needed in this area, it is clear that childhood trauma—witnessing domestic violence, experiencing physical and sexual child abuse, abandonment by a father, and other ACE score factors—is highly predictive of homicidal conduct later in life.

Reflections

Life without a cheerleader is incredibly challenging. It is clear that short- and long-term outcomes are worse for children who experience trauma and abuse and do not have mitigating influences in their lives to counteract these powerful negative life experiences. Many children exposed to significant trauma do indeed overcome those impacts and avoid many of the ugly consequences of high ACE scores. Not all children end up repeating the abuse or engaging in destructive behavior as teens or adults. The reasons why some overcome and some do not make up most of the rest of this book.

So, let's move toward the heart of this book! The most interesting implication of the ACE Study and so much other research about children experiencing bad things is not the ugly, bad news of chapters 1 and 2. The most interesting questions are: How we can mitigate and ameliorate those impacts? What are the differences between children who suffer terrible lifelong impacts from childhood trauma and children who overcome those traumatic experiences and go on to do great things in life? The rest of this book points to the hope and healing that we can and must offer to children exposed to trauma.

There is hope for children. There is hope for adults who grew up in abusive homes and those who have made bad choices later in life. The hope for so many of us has everything to do with cheerleaders, passionate fans, and people who are willing to invest their lives in making sure that no one—no adult and no child—spends his or her life without cheerleaders. We don't need the pom-poms and the cheers from basketball or football games. We do need those positive, forward-focused, relentless cheerleaders that home teams thrive with and athletes long to see in the stands during their competitive efforts. We need cheerleaders in the lives of every child—whether trauma exposed or not—but we especially need them in the lives of children with the deck stacked against them. And we need to make sure that no child ever again says, like Jasmine from our early years of Camp HOPE, "No one has ever cheered for me before."

Three

Saving the Children of America

What isn't tried won't work.
— Claudia McDonald

IF WE WANT to change the world, we must focus on the children. There is no Plan B. There is no other better solution. But we have to develop a bigger vision and grander plan, and we must particularly focus on trauma-exposed children. Trauma-exposed children—children growing up with physical and sexual child abuse and witnessing domestic violence—are the most likely to end up perpetrating violence and abuse on others, populating our prisons, and experiencing violence and abuse themselves.

If you include an overlay of poverty, racism, or historic oppression, the problems are further magnified. The Ferguson, Missouri, tragedy and all the fallout from it have missed one piece. Michael Brown had trauma issues in his life and was acting them out minutes before he died, stealing from a store, assaulting the owner, and then physically engaging a police officer. This does not excuse the decisions of Officer Darren Wilson or ignore the issues of race, discrimination, and oppression playing out in interactions between law enforcement and boys and young men of color across this country, but it does help us look further into the tragedy of Michael Brown's death.

After the grand jury declined to indict Wilson, singer and music producer Pharrell Williams said, "It looked very bully-ish; that in itself I had a problem with. Not with the kid, but with whatever happened in his life for him to arrive at a place where that behavior is OK. Why aren't we talking about that?"[1] Pharrell went on to talk about racism and the injustice of Michael Brown being shot while unarmed, but I took notice of his comment. What was Michael Brown's journey before the day he died? There has been no meaningful conversation about his home life, his parents or stepfather, and the other factors that contributed to his internalized rage and the issues he was dealing with in his life at the time of his death. We are rightly troubled today by the racial, social, political, and economic issues grounded in hundreds of years of white supremacy and subjugation of people of color, but that conversation has drowned out a rational discussion of trauma and its impact on the lives of young African American men dying from guns held by white police officers.

We must identify these issues of trauma-exposed children and the origins of their delinquent or criminal behavior and talk about them whenever they come up. Recently I read a story about a major sex-trafficking sting operation in San Diego. The newspaper story in the *San Diego Union-Tribune* called the victims "runaways" and "girls from broken homes." What a terrible description for the public about who the child sex-trafficking victims are in this country. We do have foreign national women in the trafficking industry, but the vast majority of trafficked teens are American children coming from homes with domestic violence and child abuse.[2] They are runaways, but there is a reason they are runaways. They are running away from violence and abuse at home. They are the trauma-exposed children this book is focused on identifying and helping. It does a terrible disservice to the truth to simply say they are runaways or girls from broken homes.

In 2012, I was part of a team that made a documentary on child sex trafficking called *Indoctrinated*. The producer, James Ellis, did an excellent job of documenting the world of child sex trafficking in National City, California. My friend, Manolo Guillen, a leader in the trafficking prevention movement, identified more than ten young girls/women to be interviewed for the documentary. One courageous survivor, Nikki, poignantly told her story and gave context to the lives of the other child trafficking victims. At the premiere of *Indoctrinated*, I had the chance to interview Nikki and ask her some questions. One of the questions I asked her was this: "In your years on the streets in the prostitution industry, what percentage of the girls you met were victims of child abuse or witnesses to domestic violence before they ended up trapped in prostitution?"

Nikki paused when I asked her the question and then said, "I hate it when someone says 'always' or 'never,' and I hate it when people say 'a hundred percent' or 'nobody,' because there are always exceptions to everything." She paused again. "But in all the stables I was ever in and with *all* the girls I ever met ... every one of them was from a domestic violence home. One hundred percent." Nikki then went on to describe a series of girls who were molested by a parent or stepparent before running away to find love with someone they met on Facebook or at the mall. Those "someones" turned out to be men who would later become their "boyfriends" and then their pimps and traffickers. These are the children of sex trafficking in America. These are the trauma-exposed children we need to save across this country.

The mistake of ignoring the foundational issues with troubled children who might present as "child prostitutes" or "delinquents" is not unique to San Diego. Across America, when we talk about "delinquent" children or "truant" children, we rarely delve deeper into their trauma histories before they end up as wards of the court or being placed in foster homes.[3] There is virtually always a history of trauma, abuse, neglect, and violence. And if we are going to save the children of America and change the endings for millions of children, we need to be very clear on who they are and how they ended up where they are when we reach out to help them.

Many of the children are already identified, but our investment in them is far too small. This includes the children of domestic violence shelters, foster-care systems, alternative schools, truancy sweeps, child abuse cases, teen-pregnancy centers, homeless shelters, dependency and delinquency courts, domestic violence restraining order cases, and other intervention programs across the country. We need to be far more intentional about investing resources and creating mentoring support for each and every one of those children—those who are already identified in our agencies and systems.

But we also have millions of children we are not identifying: Children witnessing domestic violence that is not being reported; Children experiencing neglect and abuse without any intervention; and Children of divorce who never get any counseling, mentoring, or support. Agencies and system professionals may not know about these children, but their parents know, their grandparents know, and their relatives and neighbors know. Perhaps they don't consider what is happening to the children as "trauma." Perhaps they don't realize the impact of that trauma but do know that bad things are happening in the lives of children around them, and they are doing nothing about it. This book is a call to get educated about the impacts of trauma and then open your eyes to see it in the lives of children around you.

Saving the children requires macro and micro strategies. On the micro level, it involves knowing how to encourage and support trauma-exposed children. It involves understanding what works with children who have experienced painful and challenging things in their lives. It requires a personal commitment to become a mentor or support a Camp HOPE or other local program that is building resiliency in the lives of at-risk children.

On the macro level, saving the children requires major investments of time, talent, and treasure by individuals, corporations, city, county, and state governments, and the federal government. It requires complex re-allocation of resources to shift money from the back to the front end of the system. We will later dive into the micro-level of what we can each do. But the macro-level deserves focus here as policy makers, elected officials, philanthropic leaders, and others think strategically in the years ahead about how to invest more in children, how to invest more money earlier in the lives of trauma-exposed children, and how to spend more in the prevention arena.

Prevention is particularly challenging. How do we get to *before*? How do we get to before the trauma, before the abuse, and before the impact of witnessing domestic violence? How do we measure success in prevention? It is hard to measure a negative. It is hard to show that you prevented something bad from happening. Our systems are all reactive and not preventative. The criminal justice system is as reactive as virtually any institution ever invented. It reacts to bad things people have done. It deals with trauma-exposed children after they have acted out in rage and pain. The prison system, where we spend billions, is completely reactive. It simply waits to warehouse people long after the trauma has transformed them into criminals. It is the ultimate example of a reactive institution that provides no healing, no resiliency building, and no redemption. This all makes it hard for us to focus on initiatives for children that will *prevent* instead of *react* to the impacts of trauma and abuse.

What major new initiatives should we as voters and policy makers pursue then if we are going to truly save the children of America? What are the biggest brush strokes? What are some of the smaller initiatives we should be piloting in communities across the country? While this discussion may not appeal to readers who simply aspire to be better parents or mentors to children, it is important to identify the major policy initiatives and strategies we need in this country to truly change the way systems operate in addressing trauma issues with children. Let's spend some time on those major policy areas.

Mentoring Across America

We have thousands of mentors in America—in nonprofit organizations, in court-appointed special-advocate programs, in faith-based organizations, and in youth programs. However, we need *millions and millions* of mentors. We don't need government programs to solve every problem and to address every element of trauma exposure. But we do need greater policy leadership, more substantial corporate and philanthropic resources, and larger, earlier government investment in the work to mitigate trauma and create resiliency in children exposed to violence. Elected officials at the local, state, and federal level should be spending more time engaging in policy discussions about how to challenge more Americans to invest time in children.

Mentoring efforts in local communities have been evolving for decades, and they do produce positive results in the lives of many children. We simply need far more agencies, organizations, corporations, churches, synagogues, and government entities investing in mentoring initiatives. And don't buy the lie that we don't have the money. We have the money. We just spend it on different things. One F-22 Raptor fighter jet costs about $150 million. We spend more on one plane to kill people in other parts of the world than we spend on all the mentoring programs in America combined.

I recently read a story in the *Washington Post* about a NASA weather satellite that was supposed to cost $3 billion but was $4.5 billion over budget. It was a two-paragraph story on about the fourth page of the paper—no scandal or controversy because weather satellites are important. They are always wrong, but they are important. So don't buy the argument that we don't have the money to provide far greater investment in supporting outreach, education, training, and awareness around the need for mentors in the lives of every trauma-exposed child. If NASA ran mentoring programs, we would be all set, but it doesn't. The programs that need the money have a tough time competing with our current military, economic, and corporate priorities in this country.

Connect Existing Mentoring Programs to High-ACE-Score Children

If the first issue in expanding mentoring in America is about the allocation of resources, the other significant issue is about connecting existing mentoring programs with organizations working with severely trauma-exposed children. Some of the children coming to

Big Brothers Big Sisters and existing mentoring programs might have high ACE scores. But the largest number of children with high ACE scores are currently receiving services in domestic violence shelters, family justice centers, foster-care systems, alternative schools, truancy programs, child-welfare system interventions, teen-pregnancy centers, family resource centers, homeless shelters, dependency and delinquency courts, domestic violence restraining order clinics, and other intervention programs across the country. And they are not actually getting connected to mentoring resources. Mentoring programs seem to operate independently of all those agencies seeing high ACE score children. I have been unable to find strong collaborative mentoring partnerships between any of these major intervention agencies and the established, formal mentoring programs anywhere in the country.

Institutions operate in silos. Agencies operate in silos. It appears that most of the current mentoring movement has not yet been formally linked and partnered with many of the children witnessing domestic violence or experiencing child abuse who likely have ACE scores of three or higher. The Court Appointed Special Advocate (CASA) Program has probably come closest to matching advocates with children with high ACE scores through the juvenile court system, but the CASA Program is not a pure one-on-one mentoring program. Not all children get a CASA, and most children are getting them very late in their journey if they have already been removed from their home or separated from their parents. We need domestic violence shelter directors, family justice center directors, and other agency and system leaders to build relationships with existing mentoring programs or prioritize the development of their own mentoring programs to support the tens of thousands of trauma-exposed children currently passing through their agencies.

If you are reading this book as an individual simply trying to learn more about what you can do, you need to invest in an existing mentoring program and build a relationship with a hurting child. There are so many opportunities in many good mentoring programs. We need millions more mentors in this country. And if you join an existing program, challenge the executive director to connect with a local domestic violence shelter or family justice center. Agencies working in silos don't change the world. The future needs to be all about collaborating agencies, coordinated responses among government and nongovernment agencies, and faith-based organizations getting serious about investing in the lives of trauma-exposed children in much larger numbers.

On a national policy level, I would like to see five hundred million dollars invested in camping and mentoring programs focused on children exposed to violence and abuse. If you want to reduce the prison population by 50 percent in twenty years in America, invest the money now in every child we know of with high ACE scores. It will change the destinies of a whole generation of children experiencing the pain, heartbreak, and tragedy of growing up with trauma—destinies they do not deserve or choose.

Peer Mentoring

Mentoring is not simply about adults. We also need far more investment in peer-counseling programs. One of the powerful elements of Camp HOPE has been the investment of teens and college students in the lives of young children. We have teens as young as seniors in high school (seventeen years old) serve as assistant counselors at Camp HOPE. We recruited our first counselors for Camp HOPE San Diego out of Granite Hills High School in El Cajon, California. Danny Root, a teacher at Granite Hills, was the advisor for Eagle Link, a peer-mentoring program. Peer mentoring, which has shown promise across the United States, is an excellent way for older high school students to encourage and become cheerleaders for incoming freshman.[4] Teens need to be challenged to invest in the lives of others. It is an excellent way for young people to make a difference in the world and to keep them from simply focusing on themselves.

Community-based domestic violence agencies, family justice centers, and other nonprofits must also prioritize ways to engage youth. When I speak at conferences across America, I am always amazed that there is virtually no one in the room under the age of thirty and very few under the age of forty. Those of us in the field need to invest in the next generation. Those not working professionally in the field of domestic violence and child abuse, however, need to pursue the same strategy. How can you engage your own children in the work to change destinies for children exposed to violence and abuse? I am passionate about engaging each of our children in the work to help trauma-exposed children. How can you challenge other teens and college students to engage in helping those less fortunate? The sooner we engage young adults in caring about children who have experienced violence and abuse, the sooner we will change the priorities created by the next generation of policy makers, government leaders, and business professionals.

Shift Resources to the Front of the System

Perhaps the most significant impact of saving the trauma-exposed children of America will come from leadership at the state and national level moving far more resources from the back of the system to the front of the system. In my first book with Gael Strack, I talked at length about the costs of the criminal and juvenile justice systems in America.[5] We spend tens of billions of dollars unsuccessfully every year in this country on the processing and incarceration of adult and juvenile criminals. Influential industries have risen up around the incarceration of criminals and the processing of criminals in the criminal justice system. A number of years ago, I was pushing some legislation in California to define family justice centers in state law and create some standards around the operation of these amazing centers, where all the services are provided under one roof. After California State Assembly Speaker Toni Atkins introduced our legislation, one of her aides told me that we better get the support of the California Correctional Peace Officers Association.[6] I asked why they were so important. The answer? They had enormous influence over any criminal justice initiative in California. How did prison guards become so powerful and influential? The answer is that we have become a state and a nation that has very few solutions to serious criminal offenders except to lock them up. We are not changing their lives and solving any problems by locking them up, but that has been our primary strategy for decades.

According to the International Centre for Prison Studies, the United States locks up more individuals per hundred thousand people than any country in the world.[7] We have states that are leading the way in locking people up as well. Louisiana, Mississippi, and Alabama lead all fifty states in the country in the number of incarcerations per hundred thousand people.[8] And there is *no* evidence that locking people up is solving any of our major social issues.

Public policy favoring incarceration as the primary solution to crime is slowly changing in America. Attorney General Eric Holder helped lead a national effort to reduce nonviolent offender populations in federal prisons during his tenure and advocated for prison to be used to "punish, deter, and rehabilitate" instead of "convict, warehouse, and forget."[9] In California in 2011, Governor Jerry Brown successfully advocated for AB 109 (known as "Public Safety Realignment") to reduce prison overcrowding. The goal of the historic legislation was to help California close the revolving door of low-level (nonviolent) inmates cycling in and out of state prisons. It was the cornerstone of California's solution for reducing the number of inmates in the state's thirty-three prisons to 137.5 percent of design capacity by June 27, 2013, in response to a federal court order resulting from a lawsuit initiated by the American Civil Liberties Union.[10]

Lost in the discussion about AB 109, Proposition 30 (offenders with drug-related offenses), and Proposition 47 (reduced penalties for nonviolent offenses), however, was the reality of whom we lock up in California and across the country.[11] As we touched on in the beginning of the book, the vast majority of criminal offenders we lock up in this country for all crimes came out of homes with some mix of domestic violence, child abuse, and/or drug and alcohol abuse. This includes violent and nonviolent offenders. So the effort at the federal level, in California, and in a number of other states to avoid using prison beds for nonviolent offenders is still missing the point of this book. Potential prison inmates, whether violent or not, need help long before we get to the debate of what kinds of offenders we should be putting in prison in this country. Investing money in mentoring, camping, and other early-intervention initiatives is *far* less expensive than juvenile justice facilities, jails, and state prisons. It is *not* a close call.

Most of us support the notion of prevention. We were all raised with the adage that "an ounce of prevention is worth a pound of cure"? Prevention, in broad terms, encompasses a wide range of interventions aimed at getting in front of a problem or getting to *before*. In the health context, prevention is aimed at reducing the incidence of disease and disability or slowing the progression and exacerbation of illnesses. In the context of trauma-exposed children with high ACE scores, I would say that prevention is about mitigating the impacts of the trauma before children begin to suffer the long-term consequences. Some from the child-welfare world might call this "secondary prevention" because the problem has already occurred, but it is hard to imagine anyone being against this effort, whatever you call it, as a public-policy priority.

The real questions are: How do you shift resources from the back end to the front end of the system? How do you get from the bottom of the cliff to the top of the cliff? It is a complicated topic, and we should be investing major public-policy expertise into it right now. Some say that prevention and early intervention are not always cost effective, while others rightly acknowledge that reactive approaches are generally always more expensive.[12] My view is that when you consider both the economic cost and moral cost of trauma and abuse, prevention is always the better strategy. Getting to the top of the cliff and helping people stay away from the edge is *always* better than waiting at the bottom of the cliff to try to help people after they have fallen over the edge. Entrenched interests make it difficult to move money from a reactive back-end approach to a preventative front-end approach. Nevertheless, we need to challenge the public, policy makers, elected officials, and philanthropic funders to *all* start spending more time focused on how to mitigate the trauma of children, rather than waiting for their health and criminal justice issues to play themselves out in our systems.

This shift includes advocating for far more funds to be spent on all the evidence-based practices discussed in this book. As is true in any public-funding advocacy effort, the money must come from somewhere else. Public funding for most of this work is a zero-sum game. Money must be reallocated from one place in order to be spent in another place. This book is a clarion call to shift resources from the back end of the criminal and juvenile justice systems to the front end.

Implement the Recommendations of the Attorney General's Task Force

In 2012, the Attorney General's National Task Force Report on Children Exposed to Violence, co-chaired by Joe Torre (former New York Yankees manager) and Robert Listenbee Jr., the director of the Office of Juvenile Justice and Delinquency Prevention, made a series of recommendations to help address the epidemic of children exposed to violence in this country.[13] There are a host of recommendations, many of them focused on government policies and the procedures and protocols of federal agencies. But some of the recommendations need to be heeded by local communities, by government and non-profit community-based agencies, and by those reading this book that want to help make a difference in the lives of children.

Let me highlight ten of the recommendations relevant to all caring members of every community.

1. *Engage youth as leaders and peer experts in all initiatives defending children against violence and its harmful effects.* This is so important. As I touched on earlier, when I attend conferences, workshops, and forums on violence and abuse, I frequently find there is no one in the room under the age of thirty. We

recently had a forum on domestic violence in San Diego, hosted in partnership with San Diego State University, and filled the room with college students. How did we do it? Normally, only professionals working in the field and a few survivors willing to be identified in public attend community forums on domestic violence. How did we engage so many college students? We recruited college professors and their departments at San Diego State and asked them to provide college credit to the students for attending—simple, easy, effective! The forum was so much more powerful with all the students in the room helping us look at solutions.

2. *Ensure universal public awareness of the crisis of children exposed to violence and change the social norms to protect children from violence and its harmful effects.* This is no small undertaking, but it highlights our challenge. We need much greater public engagement. When a school shooting occurs, who is challenging everyone to look at the trauma history of the shooter? When police officers are killed, who is challenging everyone to look at the family history of the killer? This is not to excuse the killer's behavior. Adults committing adult acts of violence should be held accountable for them. But we must start looking at the history of the violent abuser to find the origins of the violence. We will know we are making progress when every media outlet in America knows about the ACE Study and every elected official keeps the ACE research in mind when developing public policy and spending taxpayer dollars.

3. *Launch a national initiative to promote professional (and public) education on the issues of children exposed to violence.* We need far more focus on the impact of trauma on children than we have now. Every police officer, prosecutor, social worker, teacher, pastor, priest, imam, and rabbi and every agency focused on gangs, bullying, and after-school programs should

be learning about the effects of trauma and the availability of related services. I speak across America to diverse audiences. When I ask them if they have heard of the ACE Study or know the statistics on the relationship between childhood exposure to violence and later abusive behavior, very few hands ever go up in the room. We have so much further to go.

4. *Galvanize the public to identify and respond to children exposed to violence.* This is somewhat related to the recommendation above, but it goes further. We need an informed citizenry to advocate for higher levels of services and support from policymakers for both prevention and early-intervention efforts. We cannot counteract the pessimism of a public immersed in the apparent inevitability of violence and abuse unless we demonstrate that it is not inevitable. It is predictable. And if something is predictable, it is preventable; it is only a question of resources and priorities.

5. *Ensure that all children exposed to violence are identified, screened, and assessed.* The Attorney General's task force said it this way: "Every professional and paraprofessional who comes into contact with pregnant women and children must routinely identify children exposed to (or at risk for) violence, provide them with trauma-informed care or services, and assist them and their families in accessing evidence-based trauma-specific treatment."[14] I support this recommendation, though I don't believe this responsibility lies only with "professionals and paraprofessionals." It is the responsibility of every caring adult. And I don't believe every child needs professional intervention. Children need the village. They need all of us to realize what has happened to them, acknowledge the potential impacts, and invest the time and love necessary to help them find hope and healing.

6. *Provide individuals who conduct services and treatment for children exposed to violence with workforce protection to prepare them for the personal impact of this work and to assist them in maintaining a safe and healthy workplace.* This recommendation particularly focuses on professionals, but it is clear that anyone working with trauma-exposed children needs to learn about vicarious trauma. Many working in the field professionally do not take care of themselves, process the trauma of others that they are hearing about every day, and make sure they get the care and support they need to stay healthy. Mentors, cheerleaders, youth workers, and even parents trying to help their own children recover from past violence and abuse need to learn to take care of themselves. You cannot be constantly emptying your own gas tank of empathy and compassion and then expect that gas tank to naturally refill unless you are taking time off, processing your struggles with trusted friends or professionals, and regularly assessing your own mental health.

7. *Increase collaborative responses by police, mental health providers, domestic violence advocates, child-protective-service workers, and court personnel for women and children who are victimized by intimate partner violence.* This is a crucial part of the effort to protect children and adult victims of violence and abuse. We must do prevention and early-intervention work simultaneously. Gael Strack, CEO of Alliance for HOPE International, often says: "Prevention and intervention are not mutually exclusive. You cannot do one without the other. When you do prevention work, you will always find current victims. When you are working with current victims, you are still trying to ensure that you prevent future abuse."[15] The continuum of work necessary to create collaborative responses to victims and their children is not the focus of this book, but it is worth mentioning. Local task forces and coalitions are often an important starting point to get everyone on the same sheet

of music about intervention efforts. Then, communities need to develop a coordinated response that focuses on how each part of the system is going to do its work with policies that are consistent. Family justice centers and other types of co-located multidisciplinary teams are the next level of collaborative work—when agencies actually move staff members in together, and police officers, prosecutors, advocates, doctors, nurses, civil legal service providers, and others work with each other day in and day out.[16]

8. *Ensure that parents who are victims of domestic violence have access to services and counseling that help them protect and care for their children.* We know that children growing up with violence and abuse tend to repeat the cycle into the next generation as either victims or perpetrators. This means that adult victims need support to help them be effective parents after the violence and abuse has ended, and they need to be able to mitigate the impacts of the trauma they have suffered as victims.[17] This does not have to be formal government or nonprofit-program work. Many parents need mentors, just like children need mentors. Parenting classes are the standard "go-to" programs for improving parenting skills, but I look forward to a day when we connect non-abusive parents with parents who have significant trauma histories in order to provide positive modeling. We have seen the benefits of peer-to-peer mentoring in the family justice center movement. Whenever parents without major trauma get to encourage and affirm parents struggling from their own trauma, good things result.

9. *Make trauma-informed screening, assessment, and care the standard in juvenile justice systems.* The juvenile justice system has evolved in this country as a mini criminal justice system. In so many ways, it seems to be failing to fully understand the trauma of the children and teens coming into the system. Every

child coming into the system, whether for a minor violation like curfew or truancy or a significant violation like alcohol/drug abuse or violence, should be screened for trauma history. There are very few children coming into the system who do not have high ACE scores, but no one is screening for their ACE scores or even looking deeply at their trauma histories.

10. *Whenever possible, prosecute young offenders in the juvenile justice system instead of transferring their cases to adult courts.* In the 1990s, a wave of aggressive criminal justice reforms swept across the country in an effort to deal with what the San Diego County sheriff used to call "thugs" and "animals" who "will kill you and then go eat a hamburger."[18] This resulted in many states, led by California, passing laws to treat juvenile offenders as adults in order to enhance penalties for violent crimes committed by juveniles.[19] I opposed such an effort then and still do today. A personal experience shaped my view nearly twenty years ago.

In 1995, I had the opportunity to meet with nineteen boys, ages eleven to sixteen that were in juvenile hall in San Diego. The boys were incarcerated for murder, rape, armed robbery, or other related violent offenses. I was at the time trying to create a program for the parents of children who were engaged in the juvenile justice system. The most stunning realization after getting to spend two hours with these boys was that all nineteen of them had a child abuse and/or domestic violence history before ending up in juvenile hall! At one point, I asked them if any of them had ever had a mentor or an adult really spent time with them in life. No one raised a hand. I wondered if they knew what a mentor even was, but then a young boy in custody for murder raised his hand: "I had an uncle who took me fishing once." They did know what mentors were—they just did not have mentors in their lives. Society's solution: Wait until they commit a serious crime, lock them up, and then prosecute them to the fullest extent of the law. What happened to the boy who answered me? At the age of fifteen, he got life in prison without the possibility of parole.

Demand Greater Collaboration, Coordination, and Ultimately Integration

For children exposed to violence to truly get the help they need, it is absolutely critical that there be greater collaboration between government and nongovernment agencies. This policy push will also have to include an effort to bring together closely related issues, as we have seen throughout this book, child abuse, domestic violence, sexual assault, elder abuse, stalking, and human trafficking.

Today, all sectors talk about the need for collaboration and coordination of services. Most members of the public think it already happens—agencies must be working together in all these areas related to children and trauma, right? Child abuse and domestic violence professionals must work together, right? Police, prosecutors, and social service providers must work together, right? Surely the court systems—family court, juvenile court, and criminal court—must work together, right? *Wrong.* All these systems rarely coordinate. In dealing with child abuse, sexual assault, domestic violence, human trafficking, and elder abuse, most of these entities don't work together at all. They all work separately. They all raise money separately. They all develop different protocols, policies, procedures, and approaches.

Recently, Charles Wilson, the former director of the National Child Advocacy Center in Huntsville, Alabama, (and now director of the Chadwick Center for Children and Families at Rady Children's Hospital in San Diego) and I called for the co-location of child advocacy centers and family justice centers across America.[20] There are approximately seven hundred child advocacy centers in this country focused on investigation, documentation, and prosecution of child physical- and sexual-abuse cases. There are hundreds of domestic violence shelters and community-based agencies and approximately a hundred family justice centers with a primary focus on serving victims and their children. Yet, with a few exceptions, these child abuse agencies and domestic violence agencies and centers operate independently of each other. They operate independently even though the co-occurrence of child abuse and domestic violence in abusive families is anywhere between 50 to 75 percent, depending on the study you read. Why do they operate separately? The child-welfare and domestic violence movements are two very different social-change and intervention movements with very different philosophies and histories. But they must come together if we want to change the way America provides support to trauma-exposed children.

The silo issue is not unique to child abuse and domestic violence organizations. Across America there are hundreds of rape crisis centers that attempt to serve victims of sexual assault. With a few exceptions, they generally operate separately from both child advocacy centers and family justice centers. They operate independently even though many perpetrators of sexual assault also assault other women and children. Many victims of sexual assault also have trauma histories dating back to childhood. Why don't these agencies work together? Because the sexual assault movement in this country has its own origins, policies, procedures, and approaches as well. I could go on and on. The separate agencies, policies, procedures, funding sources, and approaches also exist in the elder abuse and the human trafficking movements.

We can even pick other topics. Bullying now is a focus area in and of itself in communities, organizations, and government initiatives. But where do bullies come from? Bullies are most often children coming out of violent and abusive homes. Children don't become bullies without a role model! Usually, that role model comes from their home. An abusive and controlling parent is often the most important shaper of bullies on the planet. We talked earlier about the relationship between gangs and child trauma. Yet most gang intervention and prevention programs spend very little time focusing on the families of origin that current or former gang members came from. Philanthropists, private foundations, corporations, and government funders must all demand much greater collaboration, integration, and coordination among all of these deeply interrelated public health issues.

Let's look at one more area of national media focus to make the point about our failure to make critical connections. Today in this country we are deeply focused on our failures in meeting the needs of members of the military returning from combat. The Veterans Administration has been rightly criticized for systematic failures in meeting the needs of veterans, but the issue of trauma-exposed children who later join the military is at the foundation of many of these issues and has been ignored by the media and in virtually every other forum.

I was honored to serve on the congressionally created Department of Defense Task Force on Domestic Violence a decade ago. Members of the task force and I visited military bases across the country and around the world. We had a variety of conversations with military professionals, and it was clear that trauma-exposed children who later joined the military faced greater impacts from being in combat than military members with no trauma in their backgrounds. One of the things we are learning more about is post-traumatic stress (PTS) in soldiers returning from Afghanistan and Iraq. It appears that veterans who have experienced these violent scenes of blood, terror, and warfare react differently depending on their level of previous childhood trauma. Initial research from the Iraq and Afghanistan wars seems to show much more significant PTS issues in war veterans with a history of childhood trauma than in war veterans with no history of childhood trauma.[21] Yet we don't talk at all about the childhood trauma of war veterans when they return and commit suicide, kill a spouse and children, or end up in SWAT standoffs or armed confrontations with law enforcement.[22] We should be dealing with childhood trauma in young men and women joining the military instead of waiting until their stress becomes toxic and deadly because of the cumulative impact of war trauma on top of childhood trauma.

Philanthropic and corporate donors and foundations must help us build bridges between these disparate agencies and movements. The government must begin seeing all these issues as far more related, and federal agencies must be forced to collaborate more. Lynn Rosenthal, the White House Advisor on Violence Against Women during the Obama Administration, did a tremendous job of bringing together agencies of the federal government that all tended to work independently and promote initiatives without regard for other agencies. Lynn was a tremendous advocate for collaboration, team building, and alliances. During her leadership of the National Network to End Domestic Violence, she did the same thing for many years. But many more federal, state, and local leaders and corporate donors need to engage in this approach. Organizations are beginning to head down this road but the effort is still spotty. The No More Campaign (www. nomore.org), which has focused on ending domestic violence and sexual assault in America, grew out of a strong partnership approach among many national and local domestic violence and sexual assault organizations.[23] But most of these organizations were still unable to convince the National Football League (NFL) to truly engage in a massive social-change campaign after the national scandal around domestic violence among NFL players. Too many national agencies had their own agendas, operated out of their own silos, and could not truly come together to influence major cultural change around violence against women.[24]

Pursuing True Integration

After thirty years spent working in the areas of domestic violence, child abuse, elder abuse, and sexual assault, I have begun to talk more about the differences between cooperation, coordination, collaboration, and integration. Many use those four terms interchangeably. But they are not the same. **Cooperation** is usually between individuals, does not take into account the mission or vision of each organization, and does not require changes in the way any organization actually operates.[25] It is usually informal, does not require strategic planning or the sharing of resources among organizations, and generally has minimal impact on the way organizations interact with each other. Cooperation is usually based on an informal arrangement in which the individual agencies or stakeholders maintain their separate mandates and responsibilities but do some work together in order to meet a common goal.

Coordination establishes formal and informal relationships. It exists when multiple organizations work together for a period of time to achieve a mutual goal. The missions, visions, and goals of organizations generally must be reviewed to ensure compatibility but do not generally change in the process. Coordination tends to be time limited, and though more connected to the core operation of participating agencies, it still tends to vary depending on the commitment of leaders of the organizations involved.[26]

"Coordinated community response" (CCR), a model in the domestic violence world, grew out of early work in the 1980s in Duluth, Minnesota. CCR approaches were later replicated in various forms in communities across the country. Our work in San Diego around CCR was modeled after the work in Duluth, Minnesota. It produced a short-term task force of agencies, then a series of policies and procedures, and eventually a permanent coordinating body called the San Diego Domestic Violence Council that I was honored to lead for more than ten years (1989-1999). CCR has been hailed as a powerful, positive level of interaction among agencies. In 2014, the Duluth Coordinated Community Response to Domestic Violence won the 2014 Future Policy Award for Ending Violence against Women and Girls from the World Future Council, the Inter-Parliamentary Union (IPU), and UN Women.[27]

The Duluth Model won the Gold Award for effectively prioritizing the safety and autonomy of survivors of domestic violence while holding perpetrators criminally accountable through a coordinated response involving the whole community. Ellen Pence, one of the matriarchs of the domestic violence prevention movement in America, referred to Duluth's CCR as "a system of networks, agreements, processes and applied principles created by the local shelter movement, criminal justice agencies, and human service programs that were developed in a small northern Minnesota city over a fifteen-year period."[28] She always referenced the Duluth CCR as a "project in the making" that was never finished and never permanently accomplished. But there are two more substantial levels of interaction that we should all aspire to in communities truly wanting to address violence and abuse and desiring to change the destinies of trauma-exposed children: collaboration and integration.

Collaboration is a much higher level of interaction than cooperation or coordination. Agencies tend to pool resources and are able to accomplish far more than they would have accomplished without collaboration. The mission, vision, and goals of participating agencies must be aligned. Often agencies tend to interface their personnel much more in true collaborations and become actual business partners, whether in a for-profit or nonprofit context.[29] The family-justice-center movement I have talked about throughout this book is a collaborative model that moves beyond simple cooperation or even a coordinated community response. Family justice centers attempt to co-locate government and nongovernment professionals in order to allow the agencies to actually pool resources and to make it easier for victims and their children to come to one place to get their needs met.[30] Collaboration is about professionals working closely together. In a child advocacy center, family justice center, multidisciplinary team, or rape crisis center, it generally means professionals work closely together in the same location—at least part-time. But there is an even higher level or partnership we should be demanding if we truly want to change the world for trauma-exposed children. We must move toward integration.

Integration is our highest aspiration. Integration creates a single organizational framework even if there are multiple organizations—government and nongovernment entities—involved in the effort.[31] Integration requires collaboration, but collaboration does not require integration. Children growing up in homes with child abuse and domestic violence need agencies to help them in an integrated framework. The complexity of dealing with both abuse between adults and abuse of the children is challenging enough when agencies are all working within a single framework. Imagine how difficult it is for children to get the help they need when government and nongovernment agencies work in separate locations, operate in different system frameworks, and act out of different philosophical approaches!

If we can create a single framework among all the diverse agencies and professions that can help trauma-exposed children, we will truly begin to see systems change at the local, state, and national levels. Single frameworks will require paradigm shifts in many agencies. Single frameworks will make it difficult for silos to survive. Truly integrated models in communities will not just help agencies provide better services, but also have the potential to change the way major systems operate—the court system, the child-welfare system, the criminal justice system, faith communities, the school system, and other major social constructs that interface with trauma-exposed children. Integration in local communities must be our ultimate vision and our ultimate goal. Children lacking cheerleaders need the entire system cheering for them, providing trauma-informed interventions, and working collaboratively in ways that begin to transform society's understanding of how to help trauma-exposed kids before they end up in juvenile halls, jails, prisons, mental health facilities, and the health care system struggling with major, chronic illnesses.

Invest Far More in Prevention-Focused Initiatives and Policies

We should all be spending more time and money at the top of the cliff instead of the bottom of the cliff. Building a fence at the top of the cliff is always less expensive than sending ambulances to the bottom of the cliff. The problem is that most systems are reactive. Law enforcement is reactive. They usually get involved after the crime has happened. Prosecutors are reactive. They engage after the crime has occurred. Courts as well are reactive. We need far more focus on how to prevent major childhood trauma, but there are some very clear priorities that need to be established for this to happen.

First, we need to invest far more in raising national public awareness and changing the norms. Norms and values that facilitate or enable circumstances where childhood trauma continues are well established. These include parents' right to use violence with their children, the right of people to protect their home from government intrusion, and the unfettered ability of anybody to parent a child without any responsibility, training, or accountability. We need more strategic, broad, and sustained work around the creation of social norms. Most of our focus here should be on children. Thirty years ago, we decided to try to get people to wear seatbelts. We quickly realized we could legally require it, but that did not necessarily push us over the top to major social change. Educating the children and getting them to educate their parents were perhaps the most influential part of the seatbelt movement that has saved so many lives in the last thirty years. We need this same effort with children today around child abuse, domestic violence, verbal and emotional abuse, and other causes of childhood trauma.

Second, we need to focus on getting supportive-parenting principles much deeper into the social fabric of the country. Home-visitation programs using nurses or social workers to help educate and support pregnant mothers have shown tremendous prevention potential. Interactive parenting programs very early in the lives of new parents appear to be very helpful.

Dr. Felitti and I love the idea of developing a television series that juxtaposes healthy, supportive parenting up against unhealthy, abusive parenting. The series could create two parallel story lines with the same actors playing in both of them but could illustrate the long-term outcomes for children and adults when supportive parenting is used and when abusive parenting is used. It would not be hard to make the series consistent with the research. Children in the abusive-parenting track would end up dealing with profound consequences in adolescence and in adulthood. Children in the supportive-parenting series would enjoy lives filled with safety, security, and joy with all the attendant benefits of an ACE score of zero. My personal view is that such an approach could be commercially viable television. I have begun brainstorming with a Hollywood producer and friend about this very concept.

Public service announcements (PSAs) are great. Futures Without Violence, a national violence-prevention organization, has done some great ones over the years. The No More Campaign has run a host of PSAs with funding from the NFL. But PSAs don't produce change in and of themselves. We need a more comprehensive and sustainable approach that will begin to impact the social consciousness of children and adults nationwide.

Third, we need to engage faith communities in a much more national way. The faith community is not the enemy in reducing childhood trauma. Faith-community leaders and members can be a powerful ally, but we must enlist them, engage them in developing strategies and approaches, and then work side by side with them toward social change. Too often faith and religious teachings are distorted or manipulated to condone violence and abuse of children. Too often domestic violence is tolerated or ignored by spiritual leaders in this country. All of us can play a role in challenging our own pastors, priests, rabbis, imams, and faith-community lay leaders to read *Cheering for the Children,* speak to their congregations about the research on childhood trauma and abuse, and call for supportive-parenting modeling in homes across America.

Fourth, we must reengage in the battle to address childhood trauma in schools and universities across America. We have lost the battle to include outreach and education about healthy relationships and abusive relationships in the school system in recent years. The public and many political leaders have demanded that schools focus on education only and not spend significant time on "social issues." But children should be learning about major public health issues in schools. Childhood trauma is one of the most pressing public health issues in America. It should be front and center if we are going to raise healthy, functional, well-educated children. Personally, I think by middle school, every child in America should be recording his or her ACE score in order to help communities support those already in need and educate children about trauma and abuse, even if they do not have trauma markers on their ACE scoring sheets. Character Counts and similar character-development programs have been gaining ground in school curriculums in order to increase resiliency. Why can't the ACE Study be used more and profiled more in school curriculums? It is possible and it is desperately needed if we are going to get to the *before* of childhood trauma.

Reflections

Saving the at-risk and high-risk children of America requires personal, political, social, and economic commitments that do not currently exist in this country. We have made the commitment to deal with them as adults when their profound impacts play out in the social services industry, the prison system, the health care system, and elsewhere. But we have not made an effort to move our resources from the bottom of the cliff to the top of the cliff. We have not made the personal commitment to ensure that every child with high trauma levels gets connected to a mentor and supportive programs and services.

We need to change the dialogue. We need to change the media's approach to reporting on crime and violence and those who commit violent acts against others. We need to start asking more questions about societal and community failures to invest in the children who have such high likelihoods of facing difficulties later in life due to childhood trauma and abuse. We need to care about children of color long before they get shot and killed by a police officer. We need to focus on the needs of a killer long before he kills.

But above all, we need to SEE the children before we can help them. When we see those who have been paralyzed in a car accident, physically diminished by ALS, or disabled by losing an arm or leg in the war on terror, our hearts of compassion go out to them. But we do not readily recognize children paralyzed by trauma, diminished by abuse, or disabled by witnessing domestic violence. Their wheelchairs, walkers, and prosthetics are invisible. Our hearts do not easily go out to them because their injuries and disabilities are not obvious. We must change that. We all need to start SEEING the children amidst the wreckage of violence and abuse in the home. Only then can we heed the call of this book to save them

Four

The Camp HOPE Story

Camp HOPE is where you really learn what hope is. It is a place to get rid of all those hard feelings you have inside you.

—Zach, 10

THIS CHAPTER FOCUSES on Camp HOPE, the first dedicated camp in the United States focusing on children exposed to domestic violence. We have talked about life without cheerleaders and the negative impacts of high ACE scores and major trauma exposure. We have talked about major policy initiatives and funding priorities. Camp HOPE is a great example of a program that can change the endings for children with high ACE scores and major childhood trauma. Camp HOPE is focused on using camping and mentoring with high-ACE-score children. The average ACE score for Camp HOPE children in 2014 was six—300 percent higher than the average ACE score for other children and adults who have been evaluated in the United States. Remember, an ACE score of six reduces life expectancy by nearly twenty years. These are the children facing a premature death because of childhood trauma. This chapter is central to the book for two reasons. First, working with at-risk and high-risk children dealing with varying levels of childhood trauma should be our greatest passion. Second, we have learned lessons from Camp HOPE that will help everyone aspiring to be a cheerleader for children—lessons that connect to many of the strategies and recommendations included throughout the rest of the book.

The Beginning of Camp HOPE

Camp HOPE started in 2003 in San Diego, California. It was the first dedicated summer camping program in the country focused primarily on children exposed to domestic violence. We did not start it with a statewide or national vision. We had just opened the San Diego Family Justice Center, the first collaborative model in the country to bring together staff members from twenty-five agencies under one roof to try to help victims of domestic violence and their children. No community had ever co-located 120 professionals and 120 volunteers from both government and nongovernment agencies in one place with the goal of addressing as many of the needs of victims and their children under one roof. In San Diego we had started co-locating police, prosecutors, and advocates in 1990, but in 2002, our vision for the most comprehensive center ever created became a reality. In January 2003, Oprah Winfrey profiled and endorsed the family justice center model on the Oprah Winfrey Show, and the model began to garner national and international attention. Within two years of appearing on the Oprah Winfrey Show, we had site visitors from seventy-seven countries at the San Diego Family Justice Center. Oprah had stunning reach around the world!

But even as the San Diego Family Justice Center operated under the shared leadership of the elected city attorney (my role from 1996 to 2004) and the police chief at the time (David Bejarano), I was troubled that we were too focused on adults and on the crisis-intervention piece of family violence. In February 2003, as I took a Harley ride one Saturday afternoon into East San Diego County, a question nagged at me: What do we have to offer the children of domestic violence homes? If all we had to offer to children was intervention—we will arrest and prosecute your dad, we will send you and your mom to a shelter, and we will get you a therapist—where was the hope in that? What did terrified, traumatized children have to look forward to after coming to the center with their moms (or in some cases, dads)? And that Harley ride became a divine appointment. East of the rural community of Ramona, I saw a sign for Lake Sutherland. It was one of those brown signs that always intrigued me when out for aimless Harley rides. I had never heard of Lake Sutherland since moving to San Diego in 1985. As I followed the narrow two-lane road toward the lake and over the crest of a hill, I saw a beautiful valley below with a small sparkling body of water and scattered oak trees, boulders, and Manzanita bushes. The winding little road headed down the mountain, and eventually I ended up at a closed gate that said, "Lake Sutherland, City of San Diego, No Trespassing, SD Municipal Code Section 52.30." I was stunned. I was nowhere near the City of San Diego out in this part of East San Diego County, but here was one of the city's nine water reservoirs!

As I turned off the motorcycle, only the ticking of the hot Harley engine and the sounds of birds, the wind, and water lapping on the shore were distinct. A whole group of wild turkeys went wandering by me as I sat in my black leathers on my bike. I did not hear an audible voice, but in my heart, God said, "You are going to run a camp at this lake." Camping was not even on my mind that day! But here I was with the answer to the question—what will the center offer that will give children something to look forward to when they come for help? We would give them a camping experience that would cause these hills and the shoreline of Lake Sutherland to ring with laughter, squeals, and happy children for the next seven years.

I came home that day with a profound sense of calling, but I was scared to tell my wife, Beth. Was it real? Was it my own hallucination? I decided not to share the details of my day with her. But the next day, I asked Beth if she wanted to go for a motorcycle ride after church. She said yes, so we headed toward the mountains. As we approached the turnoff for Lake Sutherland, I put on my blinker and we turned. Beth asked where we were going, but I knew she knew nothing of Lake Sutherland. Just twenty-four hours earlier, I too had been completely ignorant of the existence of the city-owned lake. We headed along the two-lane road, and as we crested the hill and saw Lake Sutherland sitting in the valley below, Beth did not even hesitate. "We're going to run a camp at this lake, aren't we?" she asked. I smiled. There was no need to answer. It was obvious to both of us.

Two months later, I had the support of former City Manager Mike Uberauga, then-mayor Dick Murphy, Water Department Director Larry Gardner, and three city council members to start Camp HOPE at Lake Sutherland. But I still lacked one vote to make the camp a reality. I did not know which council member to focus on, but I knew that City Councilmember Donna Frye was the most environmentally conscious and generally the most opposed to any type of development in undeveloped areas. I decided I would meet with her and pursue her support. She had supported the creation of the San Diego Family Justice Center. And even though she was a Democrat and I was a Republican, I felt that she might support the vision to help abused children. I called and got an appointment with her for lunch at a small coffee shop across from City Hall. Donna and I did not know each other well, and since my election as city attorney, we had not had a lot of positive interaction. I knew she was married to famous surfboard maker Skip Frye, and I knew she didn't really like me. But the vision and dream was strong in my heart, and I decided to share my heart with her.

Donna and I met for lunch on a Thursday. We ordered some food, and then I made my pitch. I told her how the San Diego Family Justice Center was already getting national attention from Oprah Winfrey and how I felt the model of bringing all the agencies under one roof might spread across the country. And then I told her of my dream for Camp HOPE. I told her the whole story of the Harley ride and the sense of divine calling to develop the camp. Donna listened and asked a few questions, but she remained very reserved throughout our lunch. As we began to wrap up lunch, my excitement was waning. I could not read her, and she was not sharing her views at all. But after she finished her lunch, Donna leaned back and said, "Casey, you don't know me, but you need to know that before I was married to Skip, I was married to someone else. My first husband abused me. When I finally left him and showed up on my parents' doorstep, I was so badly beaten that my mother did not recognize me when she opened the door. I remember thinking two things that day: I wanted to feel safe, and I wanted to feel free. If you promise to develop a camp where children feel safe and free, I will support Camp HOPE." I shook Donna Frye's hand that day, and the Camp HOPE vision became a reality.

By that summer, we had the city council create a lease for land at the lake and we raised money, hired a part-time coordinator (Tiffany Mills), and built a wilderness camp complete with platforms and tepees near the shore of the lake! Our first children from the San Diego Family Justice Center attended Camp HOPE in the summer of 2003. We developed a program with a host of volunteer police officers, prosecutors, local church volunteers, and community members. The first Camp HOPE program included fishing, canoeing, a skit night, art, campfires, archery, tubing, wakeboarding, and hiking along the beautiful grounds surrounding Lake Sutherland.

We did not do any formal evaluation during that first summer, but the faces of the children, the transformation in them from the first day of camp to the last, and the joy and laughter ringing out across the lake gave us a sense that we were on the right track. These children—so traumatized, scared, angry, and closed off when they arrived at camp—flourished over the course of a week. We saw hope in their faces. We saw hope in their interactions with each other. We saw the power of taking them out of their every day lives and providing them a safe place where they were accepted and honored for who they were and what they had experienced. They shared their stories, tried new things, learned campfire songs, looked at the stars, sat around the campfire, sang, laughed, and cheered for each other. Something powerful was happening, and we could all see it. It was the humble beginning of what would later become a statewide and now national dream.

The Power of Nature in the Lives of Children

Richard Louv, a San Diego author, writes in *Last Child in the Woods* of the power of nature in the lives of children.[1] When I read his book, the first thing that jumped out at me was his point about the electronic nature of children's lives today. Never far from a TV, absorbed in video games, connected to a cell phone, smart phone, or gaming console as if it was a bodily appendage, the children of this generation are never fully quiet, never disconnected, and virtually never in a place to hear only birds in the trees, water lapping on the shore of a lake at night, or the crackling of a campfire. So at the camp, we took seriously Richard's writings and the growing body of research pointing toward the healing power of nature and the outdoors. We eliminated all cell phones from camp, we did not have video games, and we made sure there were no radios, iPods, or laptops. If children brought them, they had to turn them in at the beginning of camp. There were no exceptions. No headphones and no cable or satellite TV were permitted.

In those early years, Beth and I never imagined that Camp HOPE would grow into something bigger. We saw it as our San Diego program and our way to give children something to look forward to in their lives. We knew the kids loved it, but we did not fully understand what was happening to them. It took a few years to see children starting to feel better about themselves, about their lives, and about their futures. They would come back from camp, and their moms would comment on how different the children were when they came home. A mom would say, "He is so much kinder to his sister now," or a dad would say, "She listens to me when I talk now."

We were not sure which part of camp was most impactful for the children. Was it the recreational activities? Was it the water sports? Was it the peer interaction and realization that they were not alone? Was it the art, music, and drama? Was it having youth counselors (high school and college students) to talk to and bond with over the course of the week? Was it the fun of being praised every day, cheered for by others, and encouraged for a whole week by staff and volunteers? We did not know, but it worked.

Camp HOPE operated from 2003 to 2008 as a program of the San Diego Family Justice Center Foundation, the nonprofit we had created to help raise money and support for the San Diego Family Justice Center. Then, in 2008, we made a decision to break Camp HOPE off as a separate nonprofit and create the National Family Justice Center Alliance (www.familyjusticecenter.com) to focus on our national and international work of developing and supporting multiagency family justice centers. Camp HOPE was briefly operated by another nonprofit but then faltered and shut down in 2010. It was one of the great heartbreaks of my professional life to see Camp HOPE end seven years after it began.

In early 2012, Beth and I felt a strong sense that the children of San Diego deserved this kind of adventure and fun in the midst of pain, trauma, and heartbreak. We prayed about it, we talked about it, and then, with the help of our daughter youngest daughter, Karianne, we decided to bring Camp HOPE back to life. Our first camping session was a winter weekend with thirty-six children in the snow east of San Diego. We rented a YMCA facility called Raintree Ranch and raised the money with the help of County District Attorney Bonnie Dumanis and former San Diego Police Chief Bill Lansdowne. We followed that up with another weekend in June and a week in August of 2012 at Camp Marston, a large YMCA camp in East San Diego County. The children loved it, and we were inspired by their joy, laughter, and sense of safety and freedom. Camp HOPE had a heartbeat again.

The Camp HOPE Dream Gets Bigger

But the real inspiration for a national vision for Camp HOPE did not come from us in San Diego. It came in June 2012, from two passionate domestic violence advocates from Redding, California—Michael Burke and Angela McClure. In the spring of 2012, Michael was serving as the executive director of the Shasta County Family

Justice Center and Angela was the director of the Victim-Witness Program in the Shasta County District Attorney's Office. Angela had been the visionary behind the Shasta Family Justice Center and was the first FJC professional outside of San Diego to take on the challenge I had been putting out since 2003 for other family justice centers to develop a Camp HOPE for their children. Even though our vision for Camp HOPE had struggled to survive in San Diego, they believed in the power of the vision and decided to create their own version of Camp HOPE. Michael and Angela asked Beth and me to join them for their first week of Camp HOPE at Whiskeytown Lake outside of Redding in 2012. They organized the camp entirely by themselves and recruited volunteers from churches, businesses, and other nonprofits in Redding to help them.

We arrived two days after they had started camp at a county-owned camping facility. I immediately felt their passion and determination. They had brought eighty-three children to camp for a week! They had recruited local high school students to serve as cabin counselors for the children, enlisted the help of Walmart Heart (the truck drivers of Walmart) to donate food and supplies, and brought in the Inter-Tribal Council of California to help the children learn about Native American culture. Nearly a quarter of the children had Native American blood, and the cultural piece was very meaningful for many of the children. I got the opportunity to speak to the children a couple of nights at the campfires, but Beth and I mostly just observed, cheered for Angela and Michael, and spent time with the children. They taught the children to fish, took them wakeboarding and tubing, let them experience kayaking and canoeing, hosted campfires every night, and used our general curriculum from Camp HOPE in San Diego, including arts and crafts and skit night.

They added a few components we liked as well. They brought in the Shasta County Public Health team to do games with the kids focused on health and teamwork. They brought in the Youth for Christ Equestrian Rescue Program, which teaches children how to love and respect abused horses that have been removed from their owners. It was so poignant to see abused and neglected children learning to love and care for abused and neglected horses.

Michael and Angela learned that week that planning and operating Camp HOPE is not for the faint of heart. Children with trauma in their backgrounds trigger at camp and often have major behavior issues. You need a lot of adults and counselors to maintain control and be able to invest in each child. And a full week of camp is exhausting for adults, counselors, and campers. There were really too many children for the number of adults and counselors, and we had a few moments in which we feared the leadership team was losing control! But their passion, heart, and love for the children were so obvious and transformational in the lives of the children. It was clear that children were experiencing activities and relationships they had never before enjoyed. They were happy, safe, cared for, and affirmed by everyone around them. And with that affirmation, encouragement, and support, the children shined. The children of Camp HOPE rose to the expectations of the leaders, and they quickly embraced the affirmation, encouragement, and support of the staff members. The Shasta Family Justice Center's Camp HOPE week was life changing for me.

*Casey Gwinn and friends at the Shasta Family Justice
Center Camp HOPE*

By the last night of camp, there was no doubt in Beth's or my mind—we needed to invest far more of our time and energy in this vision. Camp HOPE had a powerful impact on trauma-exposed children in San Diego, and a similar model was quickly and visibly transforming the children of the Shasta Family Justice Center— now known as One Safe Place Shasta. If Camp HOPE worked in San Diego and in rural Shasta County, it could probably work in other communities. If the power of nature changed the outlook and personal sense of self for these angry, hurting children, it could do the same for thousands of other such children. We just had to figure out how to do it and how to fund it.

During the evolution of Camp HOPE in Redding and San Diego, I met a volunteer who I will call Laura. She was passionate for Camp HOPE. At first, I did not know why. Today, I know her story. She inspired me and still does. One of her quotes began the first chapter of this book. Her story is a poignant reminder of why both children and adult survivors of childhood trauma can play a powerful role in a Camp HOPE vision.

Laura's Story

I stood next to my mom, securely attached to her leg as she hung out the clothes. I was two, and this is my earliest memory. A sense of comfort and safety consumed me. That was the last time I recall feeling cared for and safe.

Raised in a middle-class family in a small, predominantly white Northern California town, I had an upbringing that was fairly typical of most families of the 1950s. Gender roles were clear, and women were expected to be subservient to men. Once in grammar school, I can remember telling my mom that one boy and I were the fastest runners in the school. She immediately responded by saying, "Oh, Laura, you have to let him win because he is the boy."

Many of my early years were spent outside. There were oak trees and ponds to explore, and I had my dog by my side.

Nature and my dog became my sources of security. My dog knew my pain and loved me through it.

My father began molesting me when I was three years old. When my parents divorced, I was eight, and they lived in separate houses. When at my dad's, my molestation increased. I recall vividly many mornings when he would take me from my bed to his. The furniture, the ceiling light, his smell, his behavior, asking if I liked this or that, were all part of the scene I learned to dissociate myself from. Afterward he would take me into the shower with him and hold me up to wash off my genitals. I remember him saying, "Don't tell your mother about this," and when I asked why, he said, "Because she wouldn't like it." So I didn't.

By the time I began dating, I always felt I was obligated to service males, even if I had no interest in them. This carried through to college and beyond.

In my early twenties, I met my husband and fell totally in love with him. For the first time, I felt a sense of completeness with a man. Unfortunately, buried deep in my being was the premise that I was still supposed to respond to male advances. Distressed by my internal anguish, I became consumed by disgust and shame for who I was. At age forty, I was so distraught I thought I only had two choices left: suicide or counseling.

Through my employee-assistance program at work, I was assigned a male counselor and began my journey. My counselor came to know all my vulnerabilities and triggers, making me an easy target. He violated all ethical standards, abused his power, and sexually abused me. In hindsight, I realize he had been grooming me all along. Broken and devastated, I tried once again to get help, and this time I found a competent female counselor who started me on the right path. It took six years to complete individual, marriage, and family counseling and considerable time to rebuild my marriage and regain my husband's trust in me.

Once I was strong enough, I hired a female attorney, educated her about abuse of power, and filed a suit against the counselor who abused me. In time the case was settled out of court. This counselor was the first to lose his certification in the state of Arizona, and I won a $210,000 settlement. I didn't want money, I wanted to expose him so others would not be victimized. Therefore, I refused to sign the gag order and openly named the perpetrator as Thom Cooper. Much of the money went to my attorney, and the remainder was used to help other victims of abuse of power.

Today I speak my truth and have overcome years of self-loathing and shame. My love for the outdoors and my pets continues to this day. One of the things that brings me the most joy is volunteering for Camp HOPE. These children get to experience an array of exciting activities, including swimming, fishing, horseback riding, rafting, archery, and ropes courses. But more importantly, youth leaders and staff receive extensive training in affirmation and encouragement techniques. They learn how to love these precious children.

Most of us have some form of trauma in our lives. I was fortunate enough to have the support and resources to find hope and healing, but earlier intervention could have saved me from a lifetime of misery. There is nothing more rewarding for me today than seeing children overcome difficulty and become empowered to change their lives forever.

Anyone who reads Laura's story and has grown up in the camping world already knows the truth of our conclusions about the power of camp. Boy Scouts, Girl Scouts, YMCAs, Outward Bound, Young Life, Christian camps, secular camps, special-population camps, and so many other models have impacted millions of children and adults for generations. As I touched on at the beginning of the book, I grew up at Mount Hermon, a Christian camp in the Santa Cruz Mountains of Northern California, and experienced the power of God's creation and nature for the first eighteen years of my life in ways that most people only experience for a week from time to time. Some kids only get the chance to go to camp for one week with outdoor science in fifth or sixth grade. Other kids get to go to a camp of some kind every summer. But most inner-city children and children growing up in violent and abusive homes never get to experience organized camping. Since we began Camp HOPE in 2003 in San Diego, we have been amazed how many of the children have never been to a camp, seen a horse, eaten a S'More, rafted on a river, gone tubing behind a boat, or simply enjoyed the adventure of being away from home for a week surrounded by nature, love, and laughter.

It was clear from the beginning, though, that Camp HOPE would have to be different from other camps. Your typical camps have a counselor for every seven or eight campers. Most camps have only a small number of adult staff members around the kids all day. At Camp HOPE, we have always wanted a counselor for every two to three children and an adult for every five to six children. Abused, neglected, and traumatized children often struggle in traditional camps. They may trigger and face discipline when what they need is love and support. They may feel all alone because of what has happened to them, and most of the children at a regular camp have not experienced what they have gone through. So much might be bubbling up inside them at camp, but the staff may not be specially trained to talk with sexually abused children or children who have witnessed chronic and regular violence in their homes.

We needed to have a specialized camping program just for abused and traumatized children. We needed them to meet other children just like them. We needed a specially trained team of counselors, adults, and professionals to join us in this effort. Perhaps most significantly, we needed to give children things to look forward to when they came back from camp. We realized early on that we could not give them this "mountaintop experience" when they would have nothing after camp for them to look forward to and get excited about.

The Camp HOPE Dream on Steroids

After our amazing week with the children and staff of the Shasta Family Justice Center in June 2012, I knew that Camp HOPE needed to become a statewide and perhaps even a national project. It was not a little camping program unique to the San Diego Family Justice Center. It could be so much bigger.

In July 2012, I flew from San Diego to Northern California to look for a camp for sale. I invited Angela McClure, Michael Burke, and Laural Park from the Shasta Family Justice Center to join me in the search. We spent two days looking at various pieces of property for sale in Shasta County, including a couple of camps that had closed down during the recession. But nothing got us excited, and as we wrapped up for the second day, I was a little discouraged. My plane ticket home to San Diego, however, was not for another day, so I decided to go see a camp that Mount Hermon owned up near the Oregon border in northern California. It was called Kidder Creek. I had met Kidder Creek Camp Director Pete Morrill a few months earlier while visiting Mount Hermon, and he had encouraged me to come visit sometime. Mount Hermon had acquired ownership of the camp a few years earlier, but I had never been there to see it. Kidder Creek is six hours north of the main Mount Hermon property in the Santa Cruz Mountains. I invited Angela, Michael, and Laural to join me, and we headed north of Redding to Siskiyou County to see Kidder Creek Camp the next morning. On the way up, Michael and Angela were inquisitive. "Is the camp for sale?" I told them it was not. "Then why are we going to see it?" I told them I just had some extra time and thought it would be good to see an operating, healthy adventure camp so we would know what we were looking for when we found the camp we wanted to buy.

Two hours north of Redding on Interstate 5, we came to Yreka.

Yreka is hot, dry, and not very appealing. But as you head south from Yreka on Highway 3, you climb over some mountains and then drop down into a large, peaceful valley—the Scott Valley. It is beautiful, with thousands of acres of wheat and ranch land sitting below the Marble Mountain Wilderness Area and thousands of acres of forests of pine, Douglas fir, and Manzanita. Kidder Creek Camp sits up against the hills above the floor of the Scott Valley near a seasonal creek called Kidder Creek.

We turned on South Kidder Creek Road, and as we approached the gravel road at the edge of the 330 acres of Kidder Creek Camp, we saw a large, beautiful meadow filled with horses grazing on the lush grass. In the distance, I saw an apple orchard and a small office building. As we pulled up to the office, I wondered where the camp was.

But we went into the office and met Pete Morrill. Pete is a stocky, five-foot-ten-inch mountain man with a strong smile, even stronger handshake, and a wry sense of humor. He welcomed us into his little office, pulled in a few extra chairs, and began telling us about Kidder Creek. I knew some of the history already. Kidder Creek Camp was an operating apple farm in the 1960s and 1970s. Dick Jones, a rancher from Grass Valley, California, purchased it in 1976. Dick's vision was to create a camp for at-risk children and Christian kids, with the goal of letting them experience a working ranch and the power of nature. I had heard that in 2006, the Kidder Creek Camp board began talking to Mount Hermon about possibly merging. Kidder Creek is a long way from any population center, and the camp always struggled with getting children to come to camp in large numbers. It was not easy to get there, and most parents did not want to drive their children many hours to camp. Pete told us the story and then looked at me and said, "Your dad was part of the vision for Kidder Creek Camp." It stopped me dead in my tracks.

My dad, Bill Gwinn, was the director of Mount Hermon from 1957 to 1978. He was a giant in the Christian camping world. In 1977, he served as the president of Christian Camping International

(CCI). He was a dreamer, and he was a visionary. He also grew up in a violent and abusive home and struggled in much of his early adult life with undiagnosed bipolar disorder. The reason my dad left Mount Hermon in 1978 was because of mental health issues he was experiencing. Weeks later he would have a major mental breakdown and end up hospitalized in a mental institution. He was unemployed for a year after his breakdown. I did not know much about his life during that year. I left home and went off to Stanford University for my freshman year of college after my dad lost his job. I did not come home much during that time, and my dad was heavily medicated for most of that year because no one yet knew he was bipolar or how to deal with his major and deep depression.

Pete, however, told me something that day I never knew. "Casey, in 1978 after your dad lost his job at Mount Hermon, Dick Jones invited him up to Kidder Creek to help him dream about Kidder Creek Camp and what it could be for at-risk children. Your dad came up here and spent quite a bit of time with Dick, walking the property and helping him dream about the future of Kidder Creek."

Pete gave us a tour of Kidder Creek that day and showed us the rustic cabins (with no electricity), the swimming pond, the ropes course, and horseback arena. But as we finished the driving tour, Pete said he wanted to take us down to see the kennel (Marble Mountain Kennels), where he and his wife breed and raise Labrador retrievers. And then he said, "I want you to meet my wife, Julie. She is the real reason you are all here." The last statement caused us all to look at each other. "The real reason" was to meet his wife? It sounded very odd to all of us.

We soon pulled up to Pete and Julie's house, and Pete got out one of the litters of puppies. They were worth the trip from Redding! As we played with the labrador retriever puppies, though, I saw Julie come out of their house and walk over to us. I got up to meet her, and she hugged me and said, "I have been praying for you to come for two years." I did not know what that meant. As Julie told us her story, it all became clear. Pete was her second husband. She had previously been married, and her husband was abusive to her and to her daughter. Julie did not know how to get out or how to get help. In 2006, she said she went on www.amazon.com and bought a book that saved her life. As she talked, she raised up a dog-eared copy of my first book, *Hope for Hurting Families: Creating Family Justice Centers Across America*, written with Gael Strack, and said our book had helped her find the courage to leave and figure out all the places she needed to go to get help. Julie said, "Two years ago, Pete and I got married, and I told him that I believed Kidder Creek Camp should be used to help the children of domestic violence homes. Pete said we did not have the expertise to do that, but if that was going to happen, we needed to wait for the people who know how to run a camp like that." So Julie Morrill started praying in 2010 for people to come to Kidder who could help them run a camp for children exposed to domestic violence. As we stood there listening in July 2012, Angela, Michael, Laural, and I were all stunned.

The vision for Camp HOPE Kidder Creek was born that day. By September 2012, the Mount Hermon board and the National Family Justice Center Alliance (now Alliance for HOPE International) Board had blessed a partnership between our organizations. We then reached out to family justice centers across California, developed a program model, and started the planning process for the first state-wide camping model in the country for children exposed to domestic violence.

The program that developed is now an evidence-based curriculum that will be used with thousands of children in California (www.camphopecalifornia.com) and around the country in the years ahead (www.camphopeamerica.com). We learned the power of affirmation, encouragement, and praise in the lives of traumatized children. *You can cheer for them and love them at ten and give them hope and a future, or your can lock them up at seventeen or eighteen and say you are tough on crime. It is the choice that every community in America must make.*

Adult staff, counselors, and campers

Gemma and Yesenia on the High Ropes Course

The Camp HOPE Program

The Camp HOPE Program, developed in partnership with Kidder Creek Camp, is a values-based, "Challenge by Choice" camping model with a focus on praising children for observed and developing character traits through the course of a six-day program. "Challenge by Choice" refers to challenging children to try new activities and activities with perceived danger or risk but allowing them to opt out of those activities if the challenge creates unmanageable stress or fear.

Camp HOPE is operated in collaboration with Kidder Creek Camp/Mount Hermon, Inc. Trained Kidder Creek Camp staff members, who also operate weekly summer camps that are not focused on children exposed to domestic violence, supervise all recreational activities for Camp HOPE. *Hope* is defined throughout our weeklong camps as three things: believing in yourself, believing in others, and believing in your dreams.

Using a trauma-informed camper/counselor approach, Camp HOPE focuses primarily on providing affirmation and encouragement. During the nightly campfire sessions, campers receive character awards from their youth or adult counselors. Everyone cheers for each child receiving an award after the observed character trait is specifically and contextually described to the entire group.

Camp HOPE Kidder Creek program activities include rafting on the Klamath River, high and low ropes courses (age specific), horseback riding, arts and crafts, recreational hiking, field games, skits, camp songs, nightly campfires, journaling, KBAR (Kick Back And Relax) time in the cabins each day with counselors and campers, group discussions each night ("Where did you see hope today?"), three family-style meals each day (eating with their own cabin group), and other relationship-oriented times. Each day at Camp HOPE begins with a theme word for the day. These words include *hope, kindness, courage, friendship, respect,* and *leadership.* Children have "structured free time" at Camp HOPE but are never without an adult mentor, youth counselor, or adult volunteer.

*Raeanne Passantino from the Alameda County Family Justice Center
teaching girls to swim*

Camping sessions at Camp HOPE Kidder Creek in Etna, California, currently include five separate weeks each summer, and now camping weeks are beginning at a second venue, Camp HOPE Bethel Ranch in Arroyo Grande, California. The bigger vision is to operate for more weeks in the summer and even add parent-child weekends in the spring and fall. Camp HOPE Kidder Creek weeks involve children ages seven to eleven in one program and children ages eleven to sixteen in another program. Campers have the opportunity to be assistant counselors after they turn seventeen. In the first year of Camp HOPE Kidder Creek, children came from family justice centers in California, where many of the children were already receiving some level of trauma-informed care. The participating family justice centers in 2013 and 2014 included Shasta One Safe Place (Redding, CA); Nampa Family Justice Center (Nampa, ID); A Safe Place Family Justice Center of Clackamas County (Oregon City, OR); Sacramento County Family Justice Center (Sacramento, CA); San Joaquin County Family Justice Center (Stockton, CA);

San Diego Family Justice Center (San Diego, CA); Imperial County Family Justice Center (El Centro, CA); Orange County Family Justice Center (Anaheim, CA); Solano Family Justice Center (Fairfield, CA); Yolo County Family Justice Center (Woodland, CA); Alameda County Family Justice Center (Oakland, CA); West Contra Costa Family Justice Center (Richmond, CA). All the children attending Camp HOPE had been exposed to/witnessed domestic violence prior to coming to Camp HOPE. Some had been physically and sexually abused. About 20 percent of the children had been sexually abused, 50 percent had been physically abused, and virtually all the children had witnessed domestic violence in their homes.

Riding the "Stagecoach" at Kidder Creek

As Camp HOPE continues to expand, more family justice centers across California will be added, and more states are beginning Camp HOPE programs with the support of our organization, Alliance for HOPE International (www.allianceforhope.com). At the writing of this book, the vision for Camp HOPE has spread to Oregon, Idaho, Oklahoma, Texas, Georgia, and Connecticut. There is little doubt it will spread across the country as communities begin to understand the power of changing the way abused children see themselves and their futures through camping and mentoring. It is far less expensive than prison—the likely home of so many abused and traumatized children as they repeat the abusive patterns of their parents as adults.

Camp HOPE Evidence-Based Outcome Research

The reason Camp HOPE is gaining momentum is based on our early outcome research. We can prove that camping is not simply a "feel-good" experience for trauma-exposed children. Dr. Chan Hellman and the Center for Applied Research on Non-Profit Organizations at the University of Oklahoma agreed to help us develop a five-year longitudinal evaluation program once we started operating Camp HOPE California. Chan Hellman is one of the leading hope researchers in America today, and the early evaluation of Camp HOPE has been significant. Last year, at our International Family Justice Conference, Dr. Hellman stated, "Camp HOPE is clearly changing the way children exposed to domestic violence see themselves and their futures."[2]

Camp HOPE counselor Nate Johnson guiding his cabin down the Klamath River

Running Dragon's Tooth on the Klamath River

The research, currently pending publication, has found significant increases in Hope scores for children attending Camp HOPE. The powerful findings establish Camp HOPE as an evidence-based program that increases hope in the lives of children exposed to domestic violence and other challenges in their lives. The OU Research Team concluded that Camp HOPE helps children exposed to domestic violence find the motivation and pathways to pursue their goals. As discussed in the next chapter, Hope scores are highly correlated with children overcoming the trauma of abuse in their lives.[3]

HOPE scores for the five weeks of Camp HOPE 2013 increased from an average of 25.5 before camp to an average of 27.6 after camp.[4] The research team concluded in 2013, "Camp HOPE exists to give children experiencing family violence hope. These children are often characterized as living in high-stress environments that leave them at a greater risk for such things as poverty, substance abuse, crime, lower educational attainment, intimate partner abuse, child abuse, etc. Camp HOPE is a pathway of hope for the children exposed to domestic violence."[5]

The Faces of HOPE

Hannah and Paola floating together during the rafting day of camp

HOPE scores for the five weeks of Camp HOPE 2014 increased from an average of 25.67 before camp to an average of 27.09 after camp. On two other key measurements in our research—children feeling like they are part of a group of people who care about each other and children believing they can achieve their dreams—there were significant increases in scores from pre-camp to thirty days post-camp.[6] Programs working with children and adults should be measuring hope in the lives of trauma-exposed children before they help them and after they help them. It is the best way to know if you are truly helping children find the strength to change and giving them the pathway to new lives free of trauma and violence.

The Biggest Dream of All

As the Camp HOPE dream has evolved, the long-term vision for California has focused on two camping venues. Camp HOPE Kidder Creek will serve children from Northern California and Southern Oregon. We hope to raise two million dollars to help build permanent, winterized cabins at Kidder Creek. Camp HOPE Village will allow camping programs year-round at Kidder Creek. A second venue, however, is now under development. In 2013, Beth and I sold our home in San Diego and purchased 50 percent of Bethel Ranch, a 612-acre property in San Luis Obispo County, California. Our vision is to develop a for-profit ranching operation in partnership with a local real estate developer, Barbara Bethel, with all our profits going to fund Camp HOPE Bethel Ranch. Bethel Ranch is a very different venue from Kidder Creek but includes property adjacent to Lopez Lake, a beautiful recreational area near Arroyo Grande, California. With support from the San Luis Obispo County Parks Department and a dynamic, visionary park ranger by the name of Kristin Howland, Camp HOPE Bethel Ranch will be able to include sailing, windsurfing, tubing, and wakeboarding in its activity list, along with all the other traditional activities of Camp HOPE. We are seeking to raise two million dollars in donation funds for this vision as well along with program-related investment funds (social venture capital) to help develop the revenue stream necessary to operate Camp HOPE Bethel Ranch in perpetuity.

Lessons Learned from Camp HOPE

After thirteen years, we have learned lessons from Camp HOPE that will help everyone aspiring to be a cheerleader for children—lessons that connect to many of the strategies and recommendations included throughout the rest of the book.

- **Everybody deserves and needs to be loved**. Children with high ACE scores don't know what real love is, and they don't believe they deserve to be loved. They mistake unhealthy attention for love. They act out for attention, and adults can easily focus on the misconduct and miss the need for love. They may not know how to express their need for love, but it is there, crying out through their anger, pain, and shame.

- **Call children by their name**. It has always bothered me when people call children "buddy" or "sweetheart," usually because they don't know their name. Take the time to learn a child's name, and then call him or her by name. If you don't remember, ask the child, and then use his or her name in sentences and conversation until you remember it.

- **Caring conversation and active listening are healing**. Children don't need fancy programs, a lot of material gifts, and complex activities to begin to heal. They need to be listened to. They need to be asked what happened to them. They need a loving, caring adult to ask good questions and listen to the answers.

- **Children need to celebrate their childhood**. So many trauma-exposed children have grown up too fast. They have been forced to experience adult power and control. They have been forced to struggle with emotions and physiological responses to trauma that they are not prepared to handle. They need to be children, and we need to give them their childhood back in every way possible.

- **Fun is therapeutic.** Camp HOPE is focused on letting children laugh, play, and be kids together. The therapeutic power of fun, laughter, joy, and freedom is immeasurable. Programs and agencies that work with children or offer them services should also ensure that the children are having fun and have enjoyable things to look forward to in their lives.

- **Children can live without technology.** Children struggle to give up their technology when they come to camp. Once we have taken it all away, however, their senses come alive, they engage more with other children and adults, and they have little interest in their electronic toys.

- **Nature is therapeutic.** We have seen children find their sense of wonder in nature. Fascinated by the simplest of sounds or smells, children come alive in nature. Most have never seen a creek, touched a horse, smelled a campfire, or gazed at the stars.

- **Celebrating differences in children builds up all children.** Children can move beyond the biases of their parents, racism, and intolerance if we help them celebrate and appreciate differences. At Camp HOPE we celebrate Native American culture, music, and dance. Though most of our children are not Native American, they come to enjoy and celebrate the culture. Children can be helped to realize their differences in culture, ethnicity, life experience, gender, and sexual orientation and find self-esteem and friendship in the process.

- **Celebrating children for who they are and who they are becoming is transformative**. Character awards and the celebration of observed and developing character traits have special significance to trauma-exposed children. It is not competitive. They are not winners and losers when we celebrate character instead of accomplishments.

- **Music, art, writing, and drama unleash creative, healing energy**. Singing silly songs around a campfire, writing in a journal, drawing pictures of hope, kindness, courage, and compassion, dressing up for a skit, playing a role in a skit, and telling stories to others all produce creativity and healing energy in the lives of hurting children.

- **Children long for a sense of community**. Children love to belong to a group of people who care for each other. They love to feel like they are part of a family. If they don't have a healthy family, we need to give them other groupings of people who can be a family or provide a loving, supportive environment. Just giving them a sense of being loved and then taking it away does not give children that enduring sense of belonging to a community of caring people.

- **Creating norms around safety, respect, and kindness brings healing**. Children live so much of the time with danger, uncertainty, fear, and unkindness. They stop knowing what it is like to feel safe at home and safe around other children. They see disrespect and dishonor between adults in their lives so often that they forget what respect even is or how it feels. We can and must create norms at camp or in other environments so they can know what safety, respect, and kindness feel like and look like.

- **Children need things to look forward to**. Bringing children to camp for one week does not solve the problems in their lives. No matter how powerful and positive something is in their life, they need other things to look forward to when they come back. We need to constantly be giving children things to look forward to, plan for, and get excited about.

- **Every child has things to celebrate and be grateful for**. Gratitude, however, needs to be taught, facilitated by adults, and practiced by children. It does not always come naturally.

- **Fancy programs and facilities aren't necessary for children to feel loved**. You don't need a fancy camp or fancy home or facility to help children feel loved. You need loving people to help children feel loved. Special surprises are great. It is great for them to feel warm, safe, and secure. But you don't need to spend enormous amounts of money on facilities or programs to provide a loving environment filled with joy and happiness.

- **Some children do need professional help**. We consistently see children who have deep wounds, major triggering, and need professional help.

- **Help children see that counseling is not a stigma.** Children who need professional help should be getting it. We can help change brain development and brain function with evidence-based interventions. We can model the need for counseling by getting it as we need it, and we can let children know that it is a good thing to have someone help us work through things that have happened to us in the past.

- **Competency creates self-esteem.** We teach children how to do so many things at camp: how to swim, ride a horse, paddle a raft, go down a waterslide, navigate a ropes course, hit an archery target, roast a golden-brown marshmallow, perform in a skit, or find the Milky Way. As children learn to be good at activities, they develop a sense of competency and competency increase the self-esteem that children need to overcome the impacts of trauma and abuse.

Last summer, we administered the ACE Index to nearly one hundred teenagers at Camp HOPE on the recommendation of Dr. Vincent Felitti. I did not imagine the average ACE score would be nearly six, nor did I think I would see a score of ten from any child. Ally, a beautiful young seventeen-year-old woman, scored a ten on the ACE Index.[7] Ally had it all. She had witnessed domestic violence, was molested as a child, was physically, verbally, and emotionally abused, and had a mother with mental health issues who later died and an alcoholic father who is now in prison. Ally was bounced from foster home to foster home and later placed in a group home by child-welfare services. When she arrived at camp, she fascinated us because of her hard exterior, an enormous amount of makeup, and the beanie always pulled down over her forehead. By the end of one week of

Camp HOPE, the makeup had come off, the beanie was gone, her smile was gorgeous, and her favorite thing to do was just sit with the adult volunteers and talk to us about our lives and our dreams. She shared her dream of going to college, one day having a family, and raising healthy, happy children. Every child deserves having dreams like that come true.

The Camp HOPE Goodnight Song

My daughter, Karianne, the coordinator of Camp HOPE California, wrote a "Goodnight Song" for Camp HOPE two years ago. We gather in an enormous circle with the children, the counselors, and the adult volunteers and sing it under the stars every night. We sing it through twice. Throughout the year, the campers sing it at parties and reunions. It is the story of Camp HOPE, and the power of it in the lives of every child.

> *The sun's gone down; it's time to go*
> *Tomorrow will be great, I know*
>
> *Let's celebrate and give God thanks*
> *For all that we have done today*
>
> *Tonight I'm safe, I am at peace*
> *And look at all these friends surrounding me*
>
> *Let's go to sleep and dream sweet dreams*
> *Tomorrow HOPE will rise again.*[8]

Reflections

Cheering for the children, through the vision of Camp HOPE, is going to change the destinies of thousands of children in the years ahead. It is my dream that all people who read this book will get excited about how a similar vision can develop in their community and in their state. As I noted in the introduction, all proceeds of this book will go to supporting the operation and development of Camp HOPE California (www.camphopecalifornia.com) and our rapidly developing vision for Camp HOPE across the United States (www.camphopeamerica.org). I long for a day when we invest more money in giving children mentors and sending them to camp every year than we invest in funding juvenile justice facilities and prisons across this country. Prisons and juvenile justice facilities will *never* cost less money than camp and will *never* produce hope in the lives of those who experience them. Camp HOPE will *always* cost less than prison and will *always* produce more life-changing, life-giving outcomes for childhood trauma victims.

Five

HOPE Heals

We want to create hope for every person ... we must give hope, always hope.

—Mother Teresa

WE CAN MEASURE trauma using the ACE score. The ACE Study has shown us the potential consequences that others or we are facing based on childhood trauma. The challenge of our generation now, in saving the children of America, is how do we mitigate the trauma? How do we change the ending for childhood trauma survivors? The answer is hope. The answer has always been hope. Abraham Maslow called it "self-actualization" in 1953 in his famous "Maslow's Hierarchy."[1] I call it hope. Camp HOPE is one example of how we can give hope to children. If you have hope, you can survive almost any trauma and move forward. If you lose hope, you lose your way and struggle to move at all in life. The rest of this book is devoted to creating pathways to hope for children impacted by trauma. Hope is what every adult needs. Hope is what every child needs. But can we quantify hope? Can we measure it in our own lives or in the lives of others we are trying to help? Two years ago I did not believe there was any way to measure hope. I was wrong.

Our Goal Is HOPE

The validated Children's Hope Scale, discussed briefly in the

Camp HOPE chapter, allows us to focus on the key elements of hope in the lives of children. If we want children to grow up with high levels of hope—whether they have experienced abuse or not—and to have high levels of motivation to pursue healthy pathways to productive lives, then we need to know what beliefs produce high hope in children.

I love the power of hope. I love that we now have strong research that allows us to understand what hope looks like in the lives of children and adults and shows us how to measure it. ACE scores and Hope scores will let us measure trauma in the lives of children and, more importantly, benchmark their level of hope before we begin to work with them.

Though our focus here is on the Children's Hope Scale, there is also an Adult Hope Scale.[2] Hope researchers are beginning to administer the Adult Hope Scale survey to professionals in many fields working with trauma survivors. It allows researchers to look at the level of hope in those working with trauma-exposed children and adults. Burned-out, hopeless people don't have much to offer. My friend Chan Hellman, who works at the University of Oklahoma, recently shared with me how he administered the Adult Hope Scale survey to service providers for the homeless in Tulsa, Oklahoma.[3] The people working to help the homeless population were stunned to find out that their Hope scores were barely above the scores of the homeless population they were serving every day! If you are in the serving professions, you still need to take care of yourself.

Hope Theory is a cognitive process related to a child's expectation toward achieving a future goal.[4] Indeed, on the basis that we are driven by our goals, Hope Theory argues that if we can establish clear strategies or pathways to achieving the goal and are willing to direct mental energy (agency) toward pursuing these pathways, we are experiencing hope. Those who have a pathway but low energy and motivation (agency) are considered low hope. Similarly, those with high mental energy but no mental pathways toward goal attainment are considered low hope. In order to be high hope, the child must have both pathways and agency toward their goal. But can you really measure "hope"? The answer is yes.

Hope in children has been successfully assessed and measured using the Children's Hope Scale. It examines the extent to which children believe they can establish pathways to their goals and develop and maintain the will power to follow these pathways.[5] Both pathways and willpower are required to establish hope. The Children's Hope Scale is a widely used measure with over two hundred published scholarly studies to back it up.[6]

The basic elements in the validated Children's Hope Scale allow children completing it to rate themselves on the following series of statements:[7]

1. I think I am doing pretty well.

☐	☐	☐	☐	☐	☐
None of the time	*A little of the time*	*Some of the time*	*A lot of the time*	*Most of the time*	*All of the time*

2. I can think of many ways to get the things in life that are most important to me.

☐	☐	☐	☐	☐	☐
None of the time	*A little of the time*	*Some of the time*	*A lot of the time*	*Most of the time*	*All of the time*

3. I am doing just as well as other kids my age.

☐	☐	☐	☐	☐	☐
None of the time	*A little of the time*	*Some of the time*	*A lot of the time*	*Most of the time*	*All of the time*

4. When I have a problem, I can come up with lots of ways to solve it.

❑	❑	❑	❑	❑	❑
None of the time	*A little of the time*	*Some of the time*	*A lot of the time*	*Most of the time*	*All of the time*

5. I think the things I have done in the past will help me in the future.

❑	❑	❑	❑	❑	❑
None of the time	*A little of the time*	*Some of the time*	*A lot of the time*	*Most of the time*	*All of the time*

6. Even when others want to quit, I know that I can find ways to solve the problem.

❑	❑	❑	❑	❑	❑
None of the time	*A little of the time*	*Some of the time*	*A lot of the time*	*Most of the time*	*All of the time*

Any professional reading this book can use this validated Children's Hope Scale to measure hope in the lives of children and then keep measuring it over time. Scoring is simple and straightforward. Each question has a potential minimum score of one and a maximum score of six. The maximum Hope score on the six questions is thirty-six.

None of the time = 1
A little of the time = 2
Some of the time = 3
A lot of the time = 4
Most of the time = 5
All of the time = 6

Kara's Story

A Camp HOPE camper, who I will call Kara, said it so well last year:

"Hope means to trust in other people, to believe in yourself, and to work together so you can conquer whatever you are going after."

We had Kara fill out the ACE Index at camp. Kara scored a six, but she is learning about her normal reactions to the bad things that have been done to her. She is finding a pathway to hope. Before camp last summer, she scored a twenty-one on the Hope Scale. After camp, she scored a thirty on the Hope Scale. We must create hope for every child with high ACE scores if we are going to change destinies and mitigate the ugly, long-term impacts currently documented in all the research from Chapters 1 and 2.

We can measure hope in the lives of trauma-exposed children both before and after we invest our lives in them. Statistically significant increases in Hope scores during our work with children tell us that we are creating pathways to hope. If scores don't move, we need to try other things.

We want to move children from the left end of these spectrums to the right end of these spectrums on each question.[8] We also know from a great deal of work with trauma-exposed children that the more trauma they have experienced, the more they tend to show up on the left side of each spectrum and the harder it is to facilitate movement over time toward the right end of the spectrum.[9]

So, how is it that these questions actually mean something and are able to measure hope in the lives of children exposed to trauma? It may help to know a little more about Hope Theory and the research.

Hope Theory assumes children:

- Are goal oriented and that their thoughts focus on agency (motivation to act) and pathways (how to get where they want to go);
- Can initiate and sustain action toward their desired goals;
- Need to recognize and pursue pathways to those goals; and
- Act based on the combination of agency (motivation) and pathways (how to get there) thinking toward their goals.

This is how it evolves:

- How children think about their goals makes a difference in how they handle stressors and trauma in their lives.
- Children who can think hopefully can imagine and embrace goals to overcome their stressors and trauma.
- Children's hope is defined as a cognitive set involving the beliefs in one's capabilities to produce workable routes to goals (the pathways component), as well as the self-related beliefs about initiating and sustaining movement toward those goals (the agency component).
- Hope therefore connects to a child's sense of control. A child's self-perception of competence is based on the child's belief that they can accomplish certain goals through identifiable pathways.

Once we understand the basics of hope (agency and pathways), we can dive a little deeper into other findings from hope researchers:

- How children learn to think about themselves (self-esteem) in relation to barriers they encounter is an important part of hope.
- Children become upset when encountering obstacles to their goals.
- In the context of the present Hope Theory, impediments to goal pursuits elicit negative emotions; conversely, the successful pursuit of goals, especially in spite of impediments, results in positive emotions. In other words, positive or negative emotions in children are theorized to reflect, respectively, instances of successful or unsuccessful goal achievement.[10]

It is very clear that self-esteem is an important part of healthy living and being able to truly care about others and overcome trauma and abuse.

So, how does Hope Theory help us in understanding how self-esteem develops in children?

- Hopeful thoughts precede self-esteem.
- The extent to which children perceive that they can successfully attain their desired goals serves to guide their felt self-worth.
- The hopeful children who sense that they can attain goals then feel positively about themselves; conversely, children who sense that they cannot attain goals then feel negatively about themselves.

Learning to Be HOPE Givers

Once we fully understand Hope Theory, we know what we must do as cheerleaders in the lives of children. We must become *hope* givers. We must help inspire and motivate children to have dreams and goals, and then we must help to create and identify pathways to help them achieve the goals they have set for themselves. We must also be sure that we focus on helping them to develop character on this journey instead of simply focusing on materialistic or education-related goals.

We can see in Hope Theory and in the key questions in the Children's Hope Scale that children need the power of positive thinking in these key areas. Let's look at the key elements of the Hope Scale. It can and should inform our focus areas when working with trauma-exposed children individually or in formal programs.

Thinking of Many Ways to Get Things in Life that Are Important to Me

A child's ability to think of many ways to get things in life that are important to him or her is another key element. This means that we need to help children develop problem-solving skills to ensure they do not give up easily when confronted with obstacles to things that are important to them. This might be achieving something in school. This might be addressing a difficult situation at home or school. This might be actually acquiring a material object, though I prefer a focus on more significant goals than material acquisition. I often find that brainstorming with children does help stir their mental processes, and often this involves having someone to talk their goals through with or to bounce ideas off of in order to figure out difficult challenges.

Doing Just as Well as Other Kids My Age

Children's view of themselves in relation to their peers connects to the level of hope in their lives. Children who feel alienated, alone, and like they have fallen behind in life have less hope and therefore less motivation to move forward.

Things Done in the Past Will Help Me in the Future

This element focuses on children's ability to feel that what they have been through has made them stronger and more able to navigate issues in the future.

Children who feel their past has crippled them or made future success impossible are more likely to give up. It is, by the way, why we should not be labeling children with a "disorder" at a young age as we talked about earlier.

When Others Quit, I Can Solve the Problem

A sense of self-efficacy and the motivation to persevere are both important in their level of resiliency. The motivation to keep striving to solve problems even if others might quit is foundational to finding the pathway forward.

Doing Pretty Well

This element focuses on the existence of positive thinking even in the face of significant trauma or abuse. It is important to note that all the key elements may vary over time. This element could have a significant range depending on the current issues in a child's life.

Coming Up with Many Ways to Solve Problems

This element connects to creativity, motivation, and the ability of a child to continue navigating challenges in their lives. Creative problem solving also appears to mitigate the rage and anger that can come from seeing no way out of a traumatic situation.

Reflections

We can all be hope givers. Some of us might need a little more training. Some of us might need to unlearn bad habits, like I did, because of childhood trauma and abuse. But we can all do it. We can all learn how to measure hope and then help increase it in the lives of children. Now it is just a matter of our own motivation and agency! The power to change the destinies of every child we come in contact with does not lie only with the professionals. We *all* have the power to become cheerleaders for children, give lifesaving and life transforming hope to them, and impact the culture for generations to come.

Six

Be a Mentor to Other Children

The best way to not feel hopeless is to get up and do something. Don't wait for good things to happen to you. If you go out and make some good things happen, you will fill the world with hope, you will fill yourself with hope.

—President Barack Obama

Every child needs one adult in his or her life that passionately supports, believes in, and loves him or her. Every parent should intentionally work to become that adult. All the research says that if trauma-exposed children have that one person in their lives who truly cares about them and encourages them, they are much more likely to develop resiliency, overcome the trauma they have experienced, and become healthy, functional adults. President Obama added another element in his quote above. We are all healthier if we serve others, invest in others, and work to help others. It is better for us to be mentors than sit on the sidelines and it is far better for children if we provide mentors for them. Parents feel better about themselves when they practice a plan to affirm and encourage their children. We all feel better being mentors for and cheerleaders to children than simply living focused on ourselves and the children benefit almost beyond measure.

Yet in America we still will not spend the money to ensure that every trauma-exposed child, every at-risk child, has a mentor. It is *less expensive* than sending trauma-exposed children to prison, *less expen-*

sive than juvenile justice system intervention with troubled kids, *less expensive* than dealing with the health issues adults experience after childhood trauma, *less expensive* than dealing with a teen pregnancy, and *less expensive* than dealing with sexual assaults, alcohol and drug abuse cases, chronic health issues, or a host of other likely outcomes for untreated and unsupported trauma-exposed children.

President Barack Obama and Attorney General Eric Holder have both played critical roles in encouraging a national focus on mentoring programs for children, with a particular focus on children of color and at-risk children. Building on nearly a decade of advocacy for these causes before he took office, President Obama has focused on volunteerism and mentoring as two key pieces of individual engagement in making a difference in the lives of children.[1] First Lady Michelle Obama has used her powerful pulpit to push the Corporate Mentoring Challenge, which seeks to engage corporations and their employees in the effort to mentor children.[2] The Harvard Mentoring Project also has played a major role in helping the public to think of mentoring as a "job" and a profound responsibility for caring adults in changing the future for children.[3]

The primary focus of this chapter is a personal challenge to all those reading this book. What are the options for you if you want to personally engage? What programs have evidence-based outcomes with proven track records? What types of approaches would have an impact if you were to invest yourself in them? What programs are worthy of your financial support? My focus here is on a limited number of programs. There are many more beneficial and committed programs across the country. But hopefully this chapter will help you learn the kinds of questions you should ask of any organization focused on mentoring at-risk children. I hope it will help you invest in children in your life, with or without a formal mentoring program. I hope it will also help you ask the right questions about outcomes in faith-based programs you are interested in supporting as well.

Before we look at some of the highly recognized programs,

including those with evidence-based outcome research, let's look at the history of mentoring as a movement.

The History of Mentoring

New York developed one of the first major statewide pushes back in the 1980s, led by the wife of then-governor Mario Cuomo, Matilda Raffa Cuomo. The early work in New York led to the creation of the first statewide, school-based, one-to-one mentoring program in the country. The first lady of New York's work led her later, in 1995, to found Mentoring USA, a national nonprofit focused on developing mentoring programs and recruiting mentors. The first major push on a national level around mentoring came from Colin Powell in 1997 in his National Summit on Volunteerism. Powell called for a major engagement of adults in the lives of children. While mentoring programs had existed in formal and informal structures for decades, Colin Powell's voice was powerful and large. This certainly helped spur participation across the country in existing and developing mentoring programs. The Clinton and Bush presidencies included some focus on mentoring approaches with at-risk children, but President Barack Obama has clearly put more focus into the issue through the Defending Childhood Initiative and a host of other strategies. President Obama has said, *"Every day, mentors in communities across our nation provide crucial support and guidance to young people. Whether a day is spent helping with homework, playing catch, or just listening, these moments can have an enormous, lasting effect on a child's life."*[4]

The Office of Juvenile Justice Delinquency Prevention (OJJDP) in the US Department of Justice and the visionary leadership of Bob Listenbee has helped shape the focus on mentoring for the Obama administration. OJJDP recently selected a national nonprofit, MENTOR: The National Mentoring Partnership, to serve as a technical-assistance provider to local communities seeking to develop mentoring programs. MENTOR has been doing national work around mentoring for almost twenty-five years. MENTOR has

now launched The National Mentoring Resource Center to serve
as a comprehensive resource for mentoring tools, information, and
technical-assistance support. Their work includes an annual Summit
on Mentoring.[5] The National Mentoring Resource Center uses
evidence-based national standards for quality mentoring programs.
The standards are known as *The Elements of Effective Practice for
Mentoring.*[6] The goal of the National Mentoring Resource Center
is to improve the quality and effectiveness of mentoring across the
country by helping youth-mentoring practitioners to more deeply
incorporate evidence-based practices.

I share this history to help us all better understand the growing
momentum around the age-old concept of one person investing his
or her life in another person. My pastor, Mike Quinn, always challenges us to try to have "one person behind you to encourage and
mentor and one person ahead of you to help mentor and encourage
you." Our focus here is on that person we can encourage and mentor
who might need a hand up, help finding a pathway to hope, or just
someone to believe in and cheer for him or her.

Mentoring relationships, of course, are only as good as the
mentors involved in the program. Most of the research has found
dramatic differences in the impact of mentoring programs based on
what the mentor says and does in the relationship with a mentee.[7]
But there are key characteristics of successful mentoring relationships, including:

- Enduring relationships between mentor and mentee;
- Consistent, reliable contact between mentor and mentee;
- Strong emotional connections and feelings of closeness
  between mentor and mentee;
- A developmental, or youth-driven, approach to mentoring;
  and
- Mentors who are genuine, understanding, affectionate, and
  supportive, and who challenge their mentees.[8]

Research on the success of mentoring programs is relatively recent, but some key elements of successful programs have been identified:

- The focus is on youth at the highest risk.
- There are clearly defined goals and expectations.
- The diverse personalities and needs of mentors and mentees are acknowledged and addressed.
- There is a requirement of at least twelve months of participation.
- There is a set length of time, understood by everyone.
- There are activities that promote relationship building.
- The mentees' parents and families are involved.
- There is a structured matching of mentors and mentees.
- The mentors are well trained.
- Mentors are screened to ensure children's safety.
- Mentors receive ongoing support and training, and there is oversight of mentors.
- The program is consistently monitored and evaluated to determine if any changes are warranted.[9]

Let's look at a few of the oldest and most established group and individual mentoring models, and then we'll look at some of the newer models and options that include camping—the passion of my work. Group impacts are great. Coaching a team of boys or girls is important. I loved coaching teams with my kids growing up. Some coaching models have profound mentoring impacts, and we will touch on those in this chapter. But the primary focus of this chapter is one-on-one relationships. We cannot look at all the existing programs. There are thousands of programs across the country. In San Diego County, for example, more than twenty-five mentoring programs have developed over the last twenty years.[10] But let's look at some of the models and options and what is known about the outcomes of these programs.

Friends of the Children

An adult survivor of childhood trauma and abuse named Duncan Campbell founded Friends of the Children, a 501(c)(3) nonprofit organization, in 1993. Duncan faced many disadvantages as a child, overcame them, and became a successful entrepreneur. After his financial success, Duncan turned his attention to equipping disadvantaged children with the tools to become successful despite their challenging circumstances. He created what is now considered one of the leading mentoring models in the country to help children in the neighborhood where he grew up. He based this groundbreaking program on the best available research for helping children with multiple risk factors overcome those obstacles. The Friends of the Children model has now grown to seven chapters in seven cities nationwide.[11]

The Approach

Friends of the Children is based on the principle that the most vulnerable children can become healthy, productive adults if they have a consistent, caring adult in their lives. In this book, I call them cheerleaders. Friends of the Children calls its mentors "friends." Friends of the Children is the only mentoring organization in the nation that pairs children from distressed neighborhoods with paid, full-time professional mentors for twelve and a half years!

How Friends of the Children Operates

Friends of the Children selects children who are beginning to experience issues related to trauma, neglect, poverty, a poorly performing school, or other issues. The program begins in kindergarten or first grade, and each mentor then spends four hours a week with his/her assigned child—every week through high school graduation! This consistency ensures that each child has an unwavering resource, advocate, and friend no matter what. It is, far and away, the longest mentoring commitment in a child's life of any program in America.

Friends engage in a wide variety of activities with the children to foster their school success, enhance their emotional and physical health, and expose them to new places and experiences. The combination of these activities nurtures each child's passions and talents and prepares them for their future.

Outcomes of Friends of the Children

Friends of the Children is currently part of a longitudinal study looking at the impacts of the organization's mentoring model. But research has already established significant impacts. Friends of the Children has three main goals for children, including achieving success in school with a minimum of a high school diploma or GED, avoiding involvement in the criminal justice system, and avoiding early parenting.[12] Since beginning formal evaluations in 2007, the organization has found that 91 percent of participating children are attending school regularly and 83 percent of program graduates have obtained a high school diploma or GED.[13] Additionally, 93 percent have avoided any juvenile justice system involvement, despite the fact that 50 percent have an incarcerated parent. And finally, 98 percent of the children have avoided becoming early teen parents, though 85 percent had a teenage parent.[14]

Friends of the Children is now operating in Portland, Klamath Falls, Seattle, Boston, and New York City with more chapters in the planning stages. Early investors included the Robert Wood Johnson Foundation, the National Institutes of Justice, and the Edna McConnell Clark Foundation. The challenge in the Friends of the Children model is the cost per child. The cost is estimated at $8,000 per year, per child based on the program's professional-mentor model—using paid mentors with salaries and benefits. President Terrie Sorenson argues that this cost is still far less expensive than the costs of the juvenile or criminal justice system, where so many of the children are likely to end up without intervention.[15]

I love the Friends of the Children model. If it interests you, perhaps your first step would be to reach out, either as a financial supporter or perhaps as a prospective full-time professional mentor.

The scalability of the model is still a question mark, but there is no doubt that paid, salaried mentors are an effective approach to putting cheerleaders in the lives of at-risk children. The disadvantage of the model is that Friends of the Children in Portland, for example, is only impacting a hundred children at any given time. The need is clearly far greater.

To learn more about Friends of the Children, go to http://www.friendsofthechildren.org.

Big Brothers Big Sisters of America

Big Brothers Big Sisters (BBBS) is another excellent mentoring model. Perhaps one of the longest-standing mentoring programs in America, BBBS puts mentors into one-on-one relationships with at-risk children—mostly in inner-city neighborhoods. BBBS has five hundred local agencies within its network, maintaining more than 145,000 one-to-one relationships. It is the largest and most well-known mentoring program in the country.

The Approach

BBBS has two major mentoring program models—its community-based program and its school-based program. Each program includes basic elements of most mentoring programs, such as orientation, background checks, and mentor training. The expectation for mentors is that they will commit for at least one year to be a "Big" to a "Little." The "Little" is, of course, the child the adult will engage with in a one-to-one relationship. The mentors generally meet with their match three to four times per month.

A BBBS match is carefully administered and held to the strictest standards of accountability and tracking. Each BBBS agency or branch strives for matches that are safe and well suited to each child's needs. The entire matching process, from the initial screening to the final pairing, requires supervision, staffing support for the mentor, and ongoing interaction with BBBS. Programs without this significant infrastructure appear to have shorter mentor-mentee relationships than BBBS. I also like the fact that BBBS provides training and context to the child's family so the family members do not see the mentor as a threat to their own relationship with their child.

Outcomes of Big Brothers Big Sisters

Big Brothers Big Sisters has conducted major evaluations of its program model with Public/Private Ventures.[16] In the largest study, Public/Private Ventures, an independent Philadelphia-based national research organization, looked at over 950 boys and girls from eight BBBS agencies across the country selected for their large size and geographic diversity. The study, conducted in 1994 and 1995, is widely considered to be foundational to the mentoring field in general and to the Big Brothers Big Sisters community-based program in particular.[17]

Approximately half of the children in the study were randomly selected to be matched with a Big Brother or Big Sister. The others were assigned to a waiting list. The matched children met with their Big Brothers or Big Sisters about three times a month for an average of one year.

Researchers surveyed both the matched and unmatched children and their parents on two occasions: when they first applied for a Big Brother or Big Sister and again eighteen months later. Researchers found that after eighteen months of spending time with their "Bigs," the Little Brothers and Little Sisters, compared to those children not in the program, were:

46 percent less likely to begin using illegal drugs;

27 percent less likely to begin using alcohol;

52 percent less likely to skip school;

37 percent less likely to skip a class; and

33 percent less likely to hit someone.

They also found that the Littles were more confident in their performance at school and getting along better with their families.

The research team found that children in single-parent families particularly benefited from the program.[18] According to the study, BBBS programs were found to "focus less on specific problems after they occur, and more on meeting youths' most basic developmental needs."[19] The matched Bigs and Littles who were observed shared everyday activities: eating out, playing sports or attending sporting events, going to movies, sightseeing, and just hanging out together. But what mattered most to the children, as in many mentoring programs, was not the activities. It was the fact that they had a caring adult in their lives. Because they had someone to confide in and to look up to, they did better in school and in relationships at home.

Big Brothers Big Sisters publishes a National Youth Outcomes Survey that reflects changes in children and teens after being matched with a mentor for one year in the community-based program or one academic year in its school-based (site-based) program.[20]

The National Youth Outcomes Survey measures youth impact in eight areas: social acceptance, scholastic competency, grades, educational expectations, attitudes toward risk, parental trust, truancy, and presence of a special adult. By measuring changes in three strategic areas—school-related performance, risky behaviors, and socio-emotional competency—the survey builds on two longstanding research studies conducted by Public/Private Ventures that found youth enrolled in BBBS experienced positive improvements in all of those areas.

Highlights from a recent BBBS Youth Outcomes Survey Report include the following:

- 83.5 percent of youths in the BBBS community-based program and 73.4 percent in its site-based program maintained an average or above-average score or improved in all three targeted areas (education-related success, avoidance of risky behaviors, and socio-emotional competency).

- Statistically significant improvement was found in six of eight outcome measures for the BBBS community-based mentoring program and five of eight outcome measures for its site-based program.

- 97.9 percent and 96.6 percent of youths maintained an average or above-average score or indicated improvement in the area of socio-emotional competence for BBBS community-based and site-basedprograms, respectively.

- 88.8 percent and 83.4 percent of youths maintained an average or above-average score or indicated improvement in the area of avoidance of risky behaviors for BBBS community-based and site-based programs, respectively.

- 94.5 percent and 95.2 percent of youths maintained an average or above-average score or indicated improvement in the area of educational success for BBBS community-based and site-based programs, respectively.

- 91.5 percent of youths showed improvement or maintained an average or above-average score across at least three of eight outcome measures in BBBS community-based programs, as did 89.4 percent in its site-based program.

There are two observations that jumped out at me in studying the tremendous work of BBBS from the big-picture perspective. First, the largest mentoring program in America is still only impacting a *very* small percentage of the children needing a mentoring relationship. Second, BBBS does not appear to be partnered anywhere with domestic violence shelters, community-based domestic violence intervention agencies, family justice centers, or child advocacy centers, where the largest percentage of trauma-exposed children are identified. This is not a criticism of BBBS as much as a call to create collaborations and partnerships between the organizations working most often with trauma-exposed children.

To learn more about Big Brothers Big Sisters, go to http://www. bbbs.org.

4-H

For much of my life, I only saw 4-H programs at county fairs and associated them with helping children raise animals. But 4-H is a much more diverse and robust group-mentoring organization with programs spread across the country and a host of target populations, including at-risk children. 4-H is one of the largest youth-development organizations in the country, and its origins date back more than a hundred years. And though it began with a focus on agriculture and animals, its influence now spreads into working with youth in rural, urban, and suburban communities.

It is hard to describe in a few sentences all that 4-H now focuses on. The organization challenges young people to learn about many topics, including global food security, climate change, sustainable energy, childhood obesity, and food safety. 4-H out-of-school programming, in-school enrichment programs, clubs, and camps also offer a wide variety of opportunities—from agricultural and animal sciences to rocketry, robotics, environmental protection, and computer science—to improve the nation's ability to compete in key scientific fields.[21]

The Approach

4-H does excellent work in developing both programs and mentoring relationships for young people. Life-skills development is built into 4-H projects, activities, and events to help children become contributing, productive, self-directed members of society. Some programs focus on one-on-one relationships, while others focus on group support and dynamics.

It is fair to say that most participants in 4-H programs do not appear to fit the definition of at-risk or high-risk children. This does not reduce the importance of the organization or the benefits of the organization. But it is very clear that most of its programs, with the exception of its dedicated mentoring programs with at-risk children, do not face the same challenges as organizations working predominantly with children with high ACE scores

Outcomes of 4-H

4-H was evaluated in a large longitudinal study between 2002 and 2010.[22] Children participating in 4-H were found to be

- four times more likely to make contributions to their communities (grades seven to twelve);
- two times more likely to be civically active (grades eight to twelve);
- two times more likely to make healthier choices (grade seven); and
- two times more likely to participate in science, engineering and computer-technology programs during out-of-school time (grades ten to twelve).

Additionally, 10th grade girls were found to be two timesmore likely and 12th grade girls nearly three times more likely to take part in science programs compared to girls in other out-of-school activities.[23]

The basic findings of the longitudinal study showed that compared to non-4-H participants, 4-H youth participants:

- Excel academically and pursue higher levels of education;
- Make healthier choices, andavoid drugs and alcohol abuse; and
- Contribute to their communities in more ways.[24]

We should all aspire to see improvements in the lives of children because of our engagement. In the years ahead, we should also be aspiring to measure more significant outcomes than those listed above. I want to see all programs look for children with potentially high ACE scores and then work to reduce the negative impacts of those ACE scores through intentional-intervention models.

For more information about 4-H, go to www.4-h.org.

Boys and Girls Club of America

Boys and Girls Club of America (BGCA), now more than a hundred years old, is one of the leading group-mentoring and youth-engagement organizations in the country. BGCA has almost fifty thousand employees across the country and nearly four thousand clubs where young people come after school and on weekends. Volunteers play crucial roles in building relationships with youths participating in clubs and programs. BGCA estimated its volunteer base at over two hundred thousand! This allows BGCA to impact approximately four million children every year. The organization also hosts many programs within its clubs.[25] BGCA estimates that more than fifteen million children are left unsupervised after school every day and that forty-three million children don't have access to critical summer learning programs.[26] While children with severe trauma histories are not the specific focus, it is clear how great the need is that BGCA is trying to address.

The Approach

BGCA's primary impact is connected to its four thousand clubs and the programs and activities it offers to children during after-school hours. Without question, it is one of the most impactful after-school programs ever created. All the research confirms it is better for children to be in a positive, nonviolent, learning- and activity-oriented environment than on the streets after school. While BGCA does not focus on the specific trauma of children connected to child abuse and domestic violence, it clearly can have positive impacts on the lives of trauma-exposed children.

BGCA primarily functions without strong, close partnerships with other organizations working with at-risk youth. I recently saw a family justice center threatened with eviction from a building it shared with a Boys and Girls Club in Wyoming because the club wanted more space. The family justice center is serving victims of domestic violence and sexual assault and their children. The Boys and Girls Club is focused on meeting the needs of at-risk children in after school programs. Why are they not totally partnered and joined at the hip? They should be fully integrated with each other—not in conflict. We have a long way to go with the BGCA and other mentoring and youth-development organizations in truly establishing partnerships, coordinated services, and integrated social-change collaboratives.

Outcomes of BGCA

BGCA is one of the most evaluated and researched youth-engagement organizations in the country.[27] Though much of its work focuses on group engagement and peer connections versus one-on-one mentoring relationships between staff members and participants, BGCA's research does confirm that instilling a sense of competence, usefulness, belonging, and leadership improves short- and long-term outcomes in the children's lives.

To learn more about Boys and Girls Club of America, go to www. bgca.org.

The National Association of Police Athletics/Activities Leagues

The National Association of Police Athletics/Activities Leagues (National PAL) focuses on building relationships between police officers and youth across the country.[28] With the profound tensions between law enforcement and communities of color, we have never needed a more vibrant National PAL than we do now. Local PAL chapters vary in their activities and structures, but I love their mission. I love their tagline: "It is better to build youth than mend adults." It is one of the major themes of this book. It is morally superior to invest in children, and it is far less expensive than trying to heal them as adults!

The Approach

The list of activities and programs offered by National PAL are too extensive to cover in detail but include AAU basketball, after-school sports of all kinds (National Youth Sports Program), arts and crafts, drama and music, horseback riding, camping, educational field trips, karate, tutoring, junior golf, junior police explorer, and so much more.[29] The primary focus is group engagement and peer support.

National PAL has 416 local chapters. Local law-enforcement agencies, retired law-enforcement professionals, or committed community leaders have started most of the chapters. National PAL is always looking to expand its work and supports the creation of small local chapters in order to establish additional programming. Each chapter is responsible for raising its own money and support for local programs. The local PAL chapters depend heavily on volunteers, including many local law-enforcement officers.

Outcomes of National PAL

There is not a lot of evidence-based research specifically focused on the impact of PAL programs, but all the general research on the power of mentoring clearly demonstrates that close relationships between police officers and children, particularly in communities of color and high-crime-rate communities, are a good thing. Many years ago, I participated in a variety of sporting activities connected to the local San Diego PAL and was impressed by the impact of police officers having fun with children.

In the early years of Camp HOPE, we recruited San Diego police officers to join us at camp for added security. The children loved spending time with the officers. They looked up to them as role models. In 2012, before Camp HOPE went statewide in California, a police lieutenant in San Diego, Bernie Colon, was serving as the director of the San Diego Family Justice Center, and he joined us at camp for a winter weekend. The children, particularly the boys, loved hanging out with Bernie and hearing about his career. It was very obvious that Bernie was acting as a mentor and role model, even without any official title or uniform.

To learn more about PAL programs, go to http://nationalpal.org/chapters.

MentorYouth

MentorYouth is the faith-based clearinghouse for mentoring and youth-outreach programs for the faith community. Through a cooperative agreement with the US Department of Justice, MentorYouth recruits and refers Christian adults and the community as a whole to local mentoring programs.[30] MentorYouth is hosted by the National Network of Youth Ministries (NNYM) and connects with hundreds of youth-outreach organizations in community-based and church-based ministries.

The Approach

MentorYouth is not a direct services organization has other mentoring programs listed in this chapter, but I include them here as a resource for many other community-based programs in churches and other faith-based organizations seeking to develop partnerships and alliances. The faith-based community in the United States is a powerhouse of youth-engagement and mentoring services for children in general and at-risk children in particular. If you are a person of faith and would like to find out about local opportunities to engage in mentoring with young people, you can go to http://www.mentoryouth.com or call the toll-free number at 1-877-500-MENTOR.

Coaching Boys Into Men

Another group and individual mentoring model is Coaching Boys Into Men (CBIM). Futures Without Violence started CBIM as a media campaign to engage men as fathers, uncles, teachers, and coaches to teach boys to respect women.[31] The success of the media campaign led to the creation of a sports-based violence-prevention tool called the *Coaching Boys Into Men Playbook*.[32] The playbook uses coaching as a metaphor to engage athletic coaches to help shape attitudes and behaviors of their young male athletes. The playbook and its principles—respect, integrity, and nonviolence—led to the creation of the CBIM Coaches Kit. The Coaches Kit is a complete toolkit to guide coaches in helping their athletes build respectful relationships and prevent violence.

The Approach

CBIM has developed into a program to be implemented by coaches in local communities. It is not a direct service organization but a set of tools to be used by coaches to help young athletes develop non-violent relationships.

The premise of CBIM is that men have a powerful role to play in stopping violence by other men against women and girls. In a culture in which sports play such a powerful role, CBIM is an excellent initiative around youth engagement and group mentoring. Coaches play a powerful role—for ill or for good—in the lives of those they coach. A few years ago, my son, Chris, graduated from California Baptist University in Riverside, California. Chris is a great athlete and grew up playing basketball, baseball, lacrosse, and water polo. By high school he focused on water polo and had a great high school and college career. After his graduation ceremony, we went out to eat and celebrate. While we were sitting at dinner, I posed a question for Chris: "How many coaches, teachers, youth ministers, or other adults communicated messages to you in your years growing up about respecting girls and women?" Chris listened to my question and then said, "Besides you, Dad?" I said, "Besides me." He reflected for another twenty seconds and then said, "I cannot think of one, Dad." Wow! If not for my role in modeling respect for women and girls for my son, there would have been no one! CBIM is committed to changing that reality in the lives of student athletes. We have a long ways to go.

To get more information about CBIM, go to www.coachescorner. org.

Court Appointed Special Advocate Program

The Court Appointed Special Advocate Program (National CASA) recruits and trains court-appointed special advocates to work on behalf of foster children in court systems across the United States.[33] The foundations of National CASA go back to the vision of Seattle-based Juvenile Court Judge David Soukup. Judge Soukup's vision has now produced advocacy support for more than two million foster children across the country. National CASA is not a mentoring program but is important to mention here. It is one of the most powerful voices in the juvenile justice system and gives foster children a non-attorney, non-systems-professional advocate to evaluate all the issues and make recommendations to a judge. The advocates are often simply referred to as "CASAs." It is a high calling to be a CASA. I worked with a variety of CASAs in my career as a prosecutor, and I was always impressed by their passion and love for children who were suffering. In San Diego, the CASA program is called Voices for Children.[34] There are nearly 950 similar chapters across the country, though many communities do not yet have a CASA program.

National CASA attempts to provide support for more than six hundred thousand foster children going through the juvenile court system in this country every year. CASAs (sometimes called "guardians ad litem") play a crucial role in the juvenile justice system. CASA volunteers are appointed by judges to advocate for the best interests of abused children and to ensure that they do not get lost in the overburdened child-welfare system or languish in an inappropriate group or foster home.

I have heard from many foster children over the years who

identify their CASA as one of the most important "cheerleaders" in their lives. The CASA volunteers work to know the child by talking to everyone in that child's life, including parents, relatives, foster parents, teachers, medical professionals, mental health counselors, attorneys, social workers, and others. They then use the information they have gathered to educate judges and others about the child's needs and recommend what they believe is best for the child. Though CASAs are not there to be the child's friend, they still build an important relationship with the child and can help encourage him or her to set goals with regard to school, relationships, and the future. I regularly hear children talk about their CASAs and the way their advice helped point them in the right direction in dealing with all they have experienced.

One of my dreams is to see a closer working relationship between the National CASA model and community-based domestic violence programs, family justice centers, and camping and mentoring programs. Foster children represent trauma-exposed children who have been removed from their parents either temporarily or permanently. They need enormous support, many cheerleaders, and far more help than they are getting now.

To learn more about the CASA program, go to www.casaforchildren.org.

Royal Family Kids Camp

Royal Family Kids Camp is a faith-based camping and mentoring model that began in Orange County, California.[35] The visionary behind Royal Family Kids Camp was a pastor by the name of Wayne Tesch. Wayne had a heart for foster children and felt called to do something about it more than twenty-five years ago. He began in Southern California. The original model was simply focused on encouraging local churches to raise money and recruit volunteers and then offering a week of camp at a rented Christian camping facility for foster children. The camper-counselor ratio is close to one-to-one. Though it initially began as a one-week mentoring relationship,

Royal Family Kids Camp is now developing clubs and mentoring approaches to allow ongoing contact between the "camp counselors" and their campers.

Activity centers, games, sports, hiking, swimming, fishing, and horseback riding are all part of the program, depending on the activities of the local Christian camp being used by a Royal Family Kids Camp.

I love the Royal Family Kids Camp model because it allows a single compassionate church in a local area to be responsible for each Royal Family Kids Camp. Strict measures are in place to ensure the camps are safe for the children.

Camp administrators and counselors go through intensive training, including a study of the dynamics of child abuse and neglect, using recognized professionals in the field to train all volunteers. There is an intensive screening process for counselors and staff.

There are strict policies about the behavior of campers, counselors, and staff, and this ensures that there is never an opportunity for an unsafe or questionable situation. The campsite itself has been specially selected to provide a safe, fun place for the camp experience.

Outcomes of Royal Family Kids Camp

There are no published outcome studies of Royal Family Kids Camp, but Dr. Chan Hellman, director of the Center for Applied Research on Non-Profit Organizations at the University of Oklahoma (OU), has begun looking at it. Dr. Hellman is leading the research team studying our Camp HOPE program, as well. OU will be assisting in using the validated Hope Index to measure outcomes for Royal Family Kids Camp. But strong anecdotal evidence exists to conclude that Royal Family Kids Camp has a profound impact on trauma-exposed children now living in foster homes. The program is a Christian, faith-based approach that seeks to address the spiritual needs of the children while also helping to address self-esteem through Challenge By Choice activities, Bible study, prayer, music, and a host of other activities. The relationship component seeks to develop short-term mentoring relationships between local church members and foster children in the same community.

For those with an interest in mentoring and camping from a faith-based perspective, Royal Family Kids Camp would be an excellent resource.[36] Royal Family Kids Camp, in partnership with local churches, now hosts more than two hundred camping weeks per summer across the United States in partnership with local foster-care programs and agencies. There is no doubt in my mind that bonding with a foster child at camp, away from all the daily routines of life, and then maintaining an ongoing relationship with the child can have an enormous impact on that child for life.

To learn more about Royal Family Kids Camp, go to: http://www.royalfamilykids.org.

Camp HOPE

We have discussed my passion for Camp HOPE. Camp HOPE is not a faith-based camping model like Royal Family Kids Camp, but Camp HOPE California has developed in a partnership with a Christian camp called Mount Hermon, as I noted earlier. Mount Hermon owns the adventure camp (Kidder Creek) that Camp HOPE California uses for all Northern California and Southern Oregon communities. Camp HOPE Idaho has also partnered with a Christian camp called Trinity Pines. Camp HOPE Texas has partnered with a Campfire Girls Camp. Other Camp HOPE operations across the country are using a variety of partners. The key notion is connecting community-based family justice centers or other types of multiagency, multidisciplinary collaboratives that work with children exposed to domestic violence or abuse with an existing camping operation to develop a camping model.

Our vision for Camp HOPE California includes eventually having two major venues: Camp HOPE Kidder Creek (Etna, CA) and Camp HOPE Bethel Ranch (Arroyo Grande, CA). Camp HOPE Kidder Creek will operate in partnership with Mount Hermon Camps, and

Camp HOPE Bethel Ranch will operate as an independent camping facility. Camp HOPE Bethel Ranch is based on a social-enterprise model. My wife and I have purchased an ownership interest in 612 acres of land near Lopez Lake in Arroyo Grande, California, and hope to develop successful business enterprises that will help fund Camp HOPE Bethel Ranch in the distant future.

Outcomes of Camp HOPE California

Camp HOPE California, our statewide initiative, has strong outcome data gathered by Dr. Chan Hellman at the University of Oklahoma's Center for Applied Research on Non-Profit Organizations using the validated Hope Index. Two years of evaluation data have demonstrated statistically significant increases in the HOPE scores of trauma-exposed children attending Camp HOPE from across California. Increased HOPE scores are highly correlated with improved educational outcomes and decreased delinquency behavior in trauma-exposed children.[37] Early increases in HOPE scores have been significant with the program used by Camp HOPE California. Other camping programs, with significant variations from the Camp HOPE California program, have not yet documented the same statistically significant outcomes.[38]

If you are interested in getting involved with Camp HOPE, there are now camps in five states, with more under development. Adult volunteers play significant roles in Camp HOPE.

To learn more about Camp HOPE, go to www.camphopecalifornia.com or www.camphopeamerica.org.

Reflections

So, why don't we just do it? Why don't we have mentoring programs in every community in America? Why isn't Camp HOPE already happening in every state in the nation? Why don't we have the necessary investment at the national, state, and local level to make sure children with major trauma exposure in their lives get a mentor? Why is there no outcry for mentoring for all children growing up with an incarcerated parent, a violent and abusive parent, a drug- or alcohol-addicted parent? Why don't we have hundreds of millions of dollars of state and federal funding flowing into programs to focus on such efforts? Why do mentoring programs beg for money, beg for mentors, and struggle to fund their activities? Why are good programs only impacting small numbers of children on a local, state, or national level?

The answer is pretty clear. We don't have critical mass in social-change theory. We have never reached a tipping point on these issues. Existing mentoring programs, like Friends of the Children or Big Brothers Big Sisters, don't have a high-profile platform. Funding for jails, juvenile justice facilities, and prisons dwarfs funding for mentoring, education, and prevention programs. No national presidential candidate or gubernatorial candidate has run on or been elected on such a platform. No significant federal leader in the House or the Senate has run on or been elected on such a platform. When mentoring has been prioritized, it is a "flash-in-the-pan" issue that quickly moves from the front burner to the back burner.

This book is a call for such a movement. As the founder of the rapidly developing family-justice-center movement, I would like to see every family justice center in America make developing and implementing a mentoring program a top priority. Every community-based domestic violence program should invest in developing mentoring programs. Every child advocacy center in America should invest in or build a partnership with a mentoring program. I would like to see pastors, priests, and rabbis across America challenge their congregations to support mentoring programs. Every church in America should be hearing about MentorYouth and its work in the faith community.

I would like to see every state in the nation develop a Camp HOPE program that includes a mentoring component. What if every talk show host in America called for support for mentoring programs? What if major philanthropic and corporate foundations all prioritized evidence-based mentoring models? The president has called for it, as have his predecessors. Major corporations and philanthropic organizations have invested some resources in creating more cheerleaders for children. But it is still such a small drop in a very big bucket.

If the vision of this book became a reality, crime rates would decline, fewer children of color would end up in prison as teens or adults, fewer girls would become pregnant as teens, and fewer children would end up in sex trafficking. What if we had millions of cheerleaders for children across this country? What if we could develop critical mass in social-change theory? It would change the world for millions more children than our good programs and outcome-based initiatives are impacting now.

So, where do we start? I want to challenge every reader of this book to become a mentor to more children than your own. In communities like Portland, Boston, and Seattle, this might mean engaging with organizations like Friends of the Children. In other communities, this might mean reaching out to your local family justice center and helping to start or expand a mentoring program for FJC children. If you want to know if you have a family justice center near you, go to http://www.familyjusticecenter.com and look for one in your area. In communities with Big Brothers Big Sisters, this might mean volunteering to become a mentor. If your passion is children in the foster-care system or children who become wards of the court, you could become a Court Appointed Special Advocate.

We need people to reduce television watching by four hours a week and become a mentor to a child in need. We need people to give up a week in their summer to volunteer at a Camp HOPE somewhere in America. If you are a member of a faith-based community, you could engage with Royal Family Kids Camp in your community or connect with MentorYouth and find out what other youth-engagement programs you could support in your area. By the end of this book, I hope that you will personally engage in some role. That is a start.

If you have not been enough of a cheerleader, it is not too late to start. Your children need you, but the rest of the children in America need you too. So many children without that cheerleader in their lives need you. What might it mean to a struggling single mom dealing with overcoming violence and abuse in her own life to have a mentor come along for her children? How many children living within thirty minutes of you need you to become their cheerleader? How many more children will end up in jail or prison because we are all "too busy" to personally help a child find hope?

Seven

The Power of Affirmation in the Life of a Child

The best way to cheer yourself is to try to cheer somebody else up.
—Mark Twain

MANY YEARS AGO I read the story of a famous artist who late in life was asked how he became an artist. He was clearly gifted as a young child, but early on things could have gone in a different direction. He came home from school one afternoon, and his mother was not home. He found food coloring in the kitchen, found paper, and decided to draw a picture of his sister, Sally. The carnage in the kitchen was fully complete by the time he finished his sister's portrait. When his mother came in nearly an hour later, he saw a stunned look on her face; then she gathered him up in her arms and said, "Why, it's Sally!" She told him what an incredible picture he had drawn and what a gift he had. Then she kissed him on the forehead and told him to go get cleaned up for dinner. Years later he never failed to give credit to that amazing woman. His name was Benjamin West, and his clear recognition of his mom's affirmation should never be forgotten: "My mother's kiss made me a painter."[1]

Now, let's play this out another way. His mom came in, saw the mess in the kitchen, grabbed a wooden spoon or a paddle, and beat him on the backside until he could not walk. Or how about his mom came in and said, "Benjamin, how dare you! What were you thinking? You stupid, stupid boy! Wait until your father gets home and you will answer for that!" I can imagine a host of scenarios that might not finish with a kiss and words of affirmation. Perhaps you as a parent have had a few of those moments. I too have failed to respond to the stressful moments of parenting with the right words and actions. Hopefully, I am having less and less of those types of responses as I grow older and wiser. But I do remember one when our two oldest girls were very young.

Kelly and the Kite String

One Saturday, my wife, Beth, decided to run some errands, leaving me at home with our two young daughters and son in our tri-level house in the suburbs of San Diego. My wife and I had three kids in rapid succession, so our kids are close in age. At the time, Kelly was about three and a half, Karianne was two and a half, and Christopher was about one. I had herded the kids from the backyard into our downstairs family room so that I could try to make them some lunch in the kitchen. As I was in the kitchen, I heard Kelly whispering to Karianne and saying, "I am cleaning it up. Shhhhh. Be quiet so Dad doesn't hear you." Being a prosecutor by training and always interested in finding crimes in progress, I left the kitchen and went downstairs to the family room. As I entered the room, all eyes turned toward me. Christopher was on the floor with an empty bucket and remnants of sand around his mouth. Karianne was frozen in place, waiting for me to react. And Kelly was pushing her plastic pretend vacuum cleaner and smearing a whole bucket of sand all over the new Berber carpet in the family room. I was beside myself as Kelly quickly explained that Christopher had brought the sand in from the backyard and then dumped it on the carpet after I brought them inside. I had missed that little piece of the children's trek into the house.

I told Kelly to stop immediately, told her she was ruining the carpet, and asked them all to step back so I could clean it up. I went and grabbed the real vacuum out of the closet, plugged it in, and started vacuuming. There was only one problem. I did not see the roll of kite string. Within seconds, fifty feet of kite string was in the vacuum! The vacuum started to smell of burning kite string, and I moved past simmer to boil. Trying to avoid saying anything I would regret to my children standing ten feet away, I told them to leave the family room and go wait in the living room while I tried to get the kite string out of the vacuum. My voice was tense; my body was rigid. I was on the edge of exploding in frustration. I found a screwdriver and began taking apart the vacuum and unwinding the half mile of kite string!

As I was slowly removing the kite string from the vacuum, I heard the girls whispering in the living room. I could not resist listening in on their dialogue. Kelly was saying, "Karianne, close your eyes."

Then I heard Karianne say, "My eyes are closed. How can you see my eyes if yours are closed?"

Still looking for an outlet for my frustration, I headed to the living room to intervene. As I arrived, I said, "Girls, what you are doing?"

Kelly said, "We are praying."

I said, "Girls, what are you praying about? Praying is not a game."

Kelly's eyes started to well up with tears as she said, "We are praying you will be a good dad about the sand and the kite string." Zing! Wow! A knife straight to my heart! First, I was all amped up about nothing that really mattered. Second, I was scaring and hurting my children for no good reason. And finally, I was missing an incredible opportunity to affirm Kelly for being kind, helpful, and supportive as a big sister—a missed opportunity to be a cheerleader but a poignant reminder of how easy it is to miss the mark as a parent.

Why Affirmation Matters

We need to become experts in affirmation in order to become life-changing, society-changing cheerleaders for children. Child psychologist and author Linda Chamberlain says it so well:

We know more than ever before about how to help children exposed to domestic violence. Positive, supportive relationships are at the core of recovering from trauma. We need to instill hope while helping children to understand and express their feelings, validating their experiences, and helping them to recognize and build on their strengths. Affirmations that help children to believe in themselves (confidence), recognize that they are good at something (competence), and encourage them to share their gift/skill with others (contribution) are essential building blocks of resiliency.[2]

Research on the power of affirmation in the life of children has been rolling out for many years.[3] There is little dispute. You can be too negative. You can be too critical. You can be too angry. But you can rarely be too positive. You can rarely provide too much affirmation. Affirming a child is an action—the verb—but affirmation is the noun; it is a statement that speaks truth into your own life or the life of another. Martin Seligman, the father of the positive-psychology movement, has argued that words of affirmation have the ability to reprogram the subconscious through the habit of positive thinking: "Habits of thinking need not be forever. One of the most significant findings in psychology in the last twenty years is that individuals can choose the way they think."[4]

My dad used to talk about "stinking thinking" and always challenged me to replace my negative thoughts with positive thoughts. It is a concept the Bible teaches as well—whether you are speaking truth into your own life or speaking it into another person's life. In Philippians 4:8, the Apostle Paul challenges followers of Jesus with these words: "Finally, brothers and sisters, whatever is true, whatever is noble, whatever is right, whatever is pure, whatever is lovely, whatever is admirable—if anything is excellent or praiseworthy—think about such things." In Ephesians 4:29, the Bible says, "Let no unwholesome word proceed from your mouth but only what is good for edifying that it may give grace to those who hear."(New International Version).

Affirmation is critical to all children. Affirmation and edification (building children up) are two of the most impactful strategies that any parent can use to build up healthy, confident, and happy children. Children long for the affirmation of parents and adults in their lives! We all have a built-in need for affirmation and words that build us up, inspire us, and motivate us to be our best. The power of affirmation connects to the power of positive thinking.

Nearly 150 years ago, Abraham Lincoln said, "Most folks are about as happy as they make up their minds to be." Seventy years after that, Norman Vincent Peale advocated for the power of positive thinking in the lives of human beings in his *New York Times* best seller, *The Power of Positive Thinking*. Mental health experts at the time did not accept his views, and many challenged the lack of empirical evidence for most of his claims. Peale was before his time, but soon research would confirm the truth of his approach. Positive thinking has been linked to a wide range of health benefits, including:

- Longer life span
- Less stress
- Lower rates of depression
- Increased resistance to the common cold
- Better stress management
- Better coping skills
- Lower risk of cardiovascular disease-related death
- Increased physical well-being
- Better psychological health
- Reduced frailty in old age[5]

The positive-thinking movement later paved the way for the positive-psychology movement.[6] Martin Seligman once stated that a positive attitude "allows people to rise to life's challenges, overcome adversity, resist illness and depression, and lead happier, more successful lives."[7]

Though some have criticized the positive-psychology movement

for being unrealistic about the reality of mental illness and the neu-
robiology of trauma and its physiological impacts, I strongly support
the movement toward the power of affirmation and a person's ability
to respond to the negative impacts of trauma and abuse.[8] I have never
seen a child struggling in life because he or she is receiving too many
words of affirmation.[9] There is always a danger with affirmation that a
child can become self-centered and develop an unhealthy self-image.
But little research has found this to be true.[10] In fact, affirmation is so
powerful that it can create resiliency in the life of a child, even when
the affirmation is coming from a parent or adult guardian who might
also be abusive.

As I was growing up, I experienced physical abuse and emotional
abuse at times from a father who used some of the same abusive parenting techniques on me that his father had used with him. Nevertheless, my father also made a decision with me to be affirming and
encouraging a large percentage of the time. "You are smart. You are
gifted. You can be anything you want to be when you grow up. I am
proud of you. I love to see how determined you are to excel at that.
Great job. Well done." I heard it all from my dad, from my earliest
memories until well into adulthood. Even in the midst of physical
and emotional abuse, my father's affirmation made me believe I could
overcome any challenge, be anything I wanted to be, and achieve
almost anything I set my mind to accomplish.

Strengths-Based Approaches

Just as the positive-thinking movement paved the way for the
positive-psychology movement, the positive-psychology movement
paved the way for strengths-based approaches to working with trauma
exposure. Strengths-based approaches focus on what children do
well, instead of what they don't do well. If you focus on the positive
in a child and build that up, you will be far more successful than if
you focus on their negative behavior and try to eliminate it or hold
it down. In social work practice, professionals distinguish between a
"deficits" approach and a "strengths" approach. Deficit approaches

focus on problems, while strength approaches focus on what the child does well. It does not ignore the problems, but it seeks to build on strengths instead of directly focusing on the weaknesses or problems. Let's look at a personal-assessment analysis contrasting a strengths approach with a deficits approach with a child living in a home where there is domestic violence and child abuse.

Strengths	Deficits
Loves math in school	Acts out near the end of school day
Very athletic	Rage in conflict situations
Protective of siblings	Verbally abusive with siblings
Perseveres	Defiant in the face of authority

We can choose to build on the left column, or we can focus on the coping mechanisms of the child because of the violence and abuse he or she is experiencing at home.

The deficits above are all pretty normal reactions to growing up in an abusive home. They are not really abnormal reactions at all. Children tend to react very similarly to abnormal situations that they don't deserve to experience. If we focus on their deficits, we are essentially making the problems of others the problems of the children. If we focus on their strengths, we can help them develop better coping mechanisms. We can build up (a positive approach) the strengths in the left column. We can only try to eliminate or condemn (a negative approach) the items in the right column. If we focus on building on strengths, we are helping a child build resiliency—the most important concept of all in the work of helping children cope with trauma and abuse. One of the greatest goals of cheerleaders should be building resiliency in the lives of children.

Resilience

Resilient people are able to utilize their skills and strengths to cope with and recover from trauma, challenges, and the setbacks of life. Whether the challenge is loss of a job, financial problems, physical illness, natural disasters, medical emergencies, divorce, death or loss of a loved one, or violence and abuse, children and adults with higher levels of resilience tend to navigate the short-term issues and the long-term psychological consequences more effectively.

Throughout my career as a prosecutor, I was always amazed at how some people became overwhelmed by their victimization and others seemed to be able to move past it relatively quickly. I did not know why the differences were so stark at the time, but it was all about resilience. Some victims of domestic violence, sexual assault, and other abuse were much more resilient than others. Those with low resilience tended to use unhealthy coping mechanisms (drugs, alcohol, bad relationship choices) and seemed to be much slower to recover from their victimization. I did not see the low resilience as the cause. I did not see the trauma in their lives. I just saw their bad choices and focused on what was wrong with them. But it was all about low resilience levels, and I did nothing to help increase their resilience. I didn't know how.

Resilience does not wipe out stress or end life's difficulties, but it does give a person the strength to deal with problems more directly. Resilience helps us overcome adversity and move forward in life. Over the last seven years, I have been honored to work a great deal in New Orleans, Louisiana. Our organization, Alliance for HOPE International (formerly the National Family Justice Center Alliance), was brought in by the US Department of Justice after Hurricane Katrina to help develop the New Orleans Family Justice Center to meet the needs of victims of domestic violence, sexual assault, and related child abuse. I fell in love with the people of New Orleans. They have been through so much in the way of natural disasters, but they also struggle with high poverty rates, complex challenges in the criminal justice and social service systems, and challenging racial dynamics. But I have met many individuals who have demonstrated incredible resilience in the face of unimaginable struggles and who muster the strength to survive and even prosper.

Some resilient people come by resiliency naturally—it connects to key personality traits, such as perseverance, courage, acceptance, patience, self-awareness, mindfulness, and optimism. The research on resilience has found these character traits in people demonstrating resilience.[11] However, character traits and protective factors (discussed below) are not just inborn traits. Most experts today agree that resilience can be developed, learned, and enhanced. Affirmation, encouragement, edification, and other strategies have the power to increase resilience in adults and children, particularly in children struggling from trauma and abuse.

Much of the resiliency research has focused on children born into or growing up in high-risk conditions. The most intriguing finding from most of these long-term studies is that 60 to 70 percent of these children and teens growing up in really bad situations did develop social competence as adults; this means the vast majority did overcome their issues and went on to lead successful lives. Why? Why did most of the children dealing with child abuse, witnessing domestic violence, living in poverty, or growing up in war-torn countries come through it and overcome their exposure to severe trauma? The answers were found in both their own resilience and in the nature of the environments and relationships that helped them develop resilience.

We are all born with innate resiliency. It is in our genes. Resilient survivors of all kinds of stress and trauma demonstrate certain traits—problem-solving skills, autonomy, belief in a bright future, social competence, and a sense of purpose including goal direction, educational aspirations, optimism, faith, and spiritual connectedness.[12] For the majority of children and adults dealing with major stressors, the inborn capacity for self-righting and the desire for transformation and change help them move through and beyond their situation.[13] But another factor is at play here: resiliency created or enhanced by people's environments. In most of the research, these are referred to as "protective factors."

Protective Factors

Protective factors are important to focus on here because they form a nest in which affirmation can thrive and grow in the life of a child. Characteristics of environments with protective factors that mitigate or even reverse the negative outcomes of stress and trauma fit into three broad categories: caring relationships, high expectations along with a belief in the ability of the child to meet those expectations, and opportunities for participation and contribution in a community.[14]

We can all play a role in the first category—caring relationships. When we act with kindness and care, we send a message of compassion, understanding, respect, and genuine interest. We must listen actively, earn trust, and make sure children feel safe in order to have them sense our care for them. The second category is equally important. High-expectation messages communicate guidance, create structure and boundaries, and, most importantly, help children find their own strengths instead of focusing on their problems or weaknesses. Finally, giving children responsibility to make decisions and then challenging them to participate and contribute to others plays a role in creating resiliency.

An affirmation is a positive statement that is repeated over and over. Through repetition, the designated words trigger the subconscious mind to change in a positive direction. Parents have found that children who are exposed to positive affirmations become stronger and more confident in their abilities. Various disabilities that hold children back from reading, thinking, and concentrating can be improved through positive affirmations.

When my children were growing up, I made a commitment to find ways to affirm and edify them. Sometimes it wasn't easy. I would have to work hard to find something to affirm or edify, especially if the children or I were in a particularly cranky mood. I remember one time trying to find something to affirm in my son, Chris, after he had drawn on a number of pieces of furniture and thrown things all over his room. The only things I could think of to affirm were his creativity and free spirit in making a mess in his room, and his smile was priceless. I could have come down on him hard and told him to clean up his mess, but instead I chose to go with the positive, and it even made me feel slightly better about his messy room!

Sometimes being affirming means keeping your mouth shut. I remember Chris being really loud while playing the drums when he was twelve. I almost burst in to his room to beg him to stop. But that still small voice in my throbbing head said, "You should be thankful he is in his room, at home, and happy." I went for the Advil instead of coming down on him. Chris went on to love music, rhythm, and the spoken word. The nonprofit I work for runs a program called the Training Institute on Strangulation Prevention. Last year, I was preparing for a session for expert witnesses on how to testify in court, and my presentation seemed quite boring. At 11:45 PM the night before the presentation, I texted Chris and asked him if he could come up with a rap or rhythm for it. Less than twenty minutes later, he e-mailed me a rap song on expert witnesses in strangulation cases that brought the house down the next morning! Sheer musical genius from the now-grown drummer boy who gave me the headache of my life when he was twelve!

Affirmation, in both words and actions, is the power to let your children know they are accepted, loved, and supported. Children with affirmation in their lives tend to achieve at higher levels in school, have better interactions with peers, and ultimately develop a stronger self-image. On the contrasting side of life—life without affirmation—there is no research that finds children without affirmation have any beneficial outcomes.

Life without Nurture from the Beginning

The research and the evidence are clear on the negative consequences of growing up with abuse and trauma. But what happens if you simply don't get enough affirmation or nurturing from birth on? Without affirmation, loving touch, and edification, children grow up at a severe disadvantage. It seems fairly straightforward and clear. But given how many children still grow up without affirmation, perhaps more parents and policy makers need to hear the obvious.

First, let's look at the worst extreme—no loving touch, no nurture, and no affirmation of any kind in a child's earliest moments of life. In *Ghosts from the Nursery*, Robin Karr-Morse describes a young boy named Ryan born to an unmarried mother who gave him to an adoption agency at birth. Ryan had an irregular heartbeat at birth due to the anesthesia administered during his mother's cesarean section. Ryan was placed in foster care for the first thirteen weeks of his life in a home caring for nine babies under the age of three. In those first critical weeks of his life, Ryan was left alone on a crib mattress with little to no human touch or affection. He was fed regularly by bottles propped up in his crib, without anyone holding him, talking to him, or providing any kind of loving nurture. By the time Ryan was adopted, his adoptive parents found he was covered with infant acne and had oozing infections in both his ears and a bleeding diaper rash. Ryan fought human touch and seemed to try to throw himself out of his adoptive mother's arms when she tried to feed him or cradle him. Karr-Morse described the consequences in Ryan's life—despite the fact that he'd grown up in a loving adoptive home—when he was an adolescent: "He has been diagnosed with Asperger's syndrome along with anxiety and depression and has never fully outgrown his isolation and unsureness about people. He is withdrawn and is overly stimulated around people. He becomes anxious and lacks confidence in a social group and has a high need for solitude."[15]

In her next book, *Scared Sick*, Karr-Morse goes on to talk about children like Ryan in more clinical terms and connects such early deprivation with later diagnoses on the autism spectrum, anxiety, depression, and reactive attachment disorder.[16] Ryan would likely be a candidate for medication as a child in order to attempt to keep him focused in school, mitigate the autism symptomology, and address the depression. But Ryan's issues trace back to completely preventable neglect and lack of attachment. And the cost of addressing his issues much later in life will dwarf the cost of giving him the love, nurture, and affirmation he needed from birth to thirteen weeks of life.

Mental health professionals refer to this deep need in children as "secure attachment." But in lay terms, I would argue it is the first opportunity for loving, affirming, affectionate interaction with the smallest of babies. We need it in utero, at six weeks old, six years old, sixteen years old, and sixty years old.

Perhaps the ugliest research on the impact of a lack of affirmation, nurture, and loving, caring touch comes out of the Romanian orphanages as the West gained access to these desolate, inhumane, and ugly holding cells for abandoned and disabled or disfigured children in the 1980s. The children were virtually never touched at all. Lack of all loving touch is really devastating to the developing brain of a child. The Romanian orphanage research documented that the children had much smaller brains than normal children do.[17]

Life without affirmation becomes uncertain and even scary. Children don't know who they are, and they don't know how to behave. Life without any affirmation often motivates children to act out in negative ways because it becomes the only way that their parents or other adults in their lives give them any attention. A boy without affirmation questions who he is, questions his self-worth, and even questions whether he is loved. A girl growing up without affirmation will become starved for it and will look elsewhere for affirmation and value if she does not receive it from her parents or other healthy adults in her life. Girls particularly need it from their fathers. A girl growing up without a father or strong father figure invariably has a hole in her life that she will try to fill with affirmation, praise, or flattery from some other male. With same-sex lesbian parents and single parent homes without a father, this need for male role modeling can be addressed in other ways, but I still believe in the importance of affection and affirmation in the lives of young girls.

Many times children who have grown up without healthy affirmation and encouragement appear arrogant and prideful. Inside, however, they are scared and insecure and harbor a very poor self-image. That chip on their shoulder or their brash outward arrogance masks their internal pain and emptiness. I have always believed that arrogance is how insecure children imitate confidence. They don't believe in themselves, so they have to fake it. Without affirmation, insecurity grows instead. Many abusive men I have prosecuted over the years struggled from deep insecurity that played itself out as jealousy, controlling and condescending verbal abuse, and physical violence. Putting another person down verbally or physically helped the abusive man, in the short term, to feel better about himself.

It is rare to find a healthy, functional adult who grew up without affirmation from his or her parents. If you do find such an adult, you will invariably find that he or she received such affirmation from someone else or multiple "someone elses." In a recent focus group conducted with survivors of sexual assault and domestic violence at the San Diego Family Justice Center, we asked each of the women in the group how many of them grew up with a strong male role model in their lives who was affirming on a regular basis. Only one out of eleven adult women in the group could describe that male role model in her developing years, and she lost that affirmation at the age of eleven because of a divorce. She quickly looked elsewhere for such support and ended up in an abusive relationship as a teenager, as she picked the wrong guy to find the affirmation she longed for in her life. Pregnancy by age seventeen created more complex consequences as she began a journey through a series of abusive relationships. It was true for every woman in the group.

To avoid much of this heartbreak and pain, every child should have one affirming person who is passionately committed to loving, cheering for, and supporting him or her. Ideally, this should be a parent. But if it is not or cannot be a parent, every child, especially those exposed to trauma and abuse, needs that one passionate cheerleader, mentor, and supporter. *If we as a nation invested the money and time necessary to give every trauma-exposed child a cheerleader, we would empty our prisons and mental health facilities within two generations. We would dramatically reduce intimate partner violence and see stunning drops in crime rates across all categories of crime. We have the resources, and we know what to do. It is only a question of our priorities and commitment.*

Reflections

We have now seen the fundamental problem and the fundamental solution: High levels of trauma and abuse in childhood create negative, often lifelong consequences. Most children have natural or environmental resilience that helps them overcome the trauma and abuse. But many other children don't have the same level of natural or environmental resilience. Cheerleaders put that resilience in the life of a child or help trigger the child's own innate resiliency characteristics. But at the heart of resilience is the power of affirmation—believing in oneself, believing in others, and believing in something outside of oneself. Resilient people do not let adversity define them. They don't become professional victims living underneath the weight of the trauma all the time. We all need to be strong enough to overcome the difficulties of life and then be able to affirm, support, and speak truth into the lives of children to help them define themselves as capable, confident, and loved. Relentless affirmation is a game changer for hurting children. Benjamin West experienced the power of affirmation more than two hundred years ago. His legacy as one of the greatest artists of his time was made possible by his mom. She chose to focus on his strengths and, I have no doubt, changed the destiny of his life.

Eight

Praising Children for Who They Are and Not What They Do

We often confuse "doing" and "being." When we focus on doing only, we feed ourselves the misconception that what we do is who we are. When we focus on being, we find ourselves more connected to others and more fulfilled in relationships. It is a gift we can give the children in our lives and ourselves to focus on being as much as we focus on doing.

—Casey Gwinn

I WAS RAISED IN a home with a high premium on achievement and performance. There were certainly many good things in my home growing up, but I rarely remember being praised for anything that did not involve achievement, appearance, or accomplishment. "You are so handsome." "You are so smart." "Congratulations, Casey. Straight As! Well done." "You went three for three in the game today. Great hitting." "You just played the best basketball game of your life. You were unstoppable." I could go on and on. But if you asked me to list all the times my mom or my dad said something about my character or my character traits, I would be hard pressed to name more than a couple. I don't write this to be hard on my parents. I am so thankful for having a mom *and* a dad, and I am thankful that my parents worked through many issues and stayed married for fifty-eight years. I know they did the best they could and used techniques and strategies learned from their parents—whether good or bad.

The more painful admission is that I raised our children with an enormous amount of praise for what they did instead of who they were. I loved to praise them for achievement in school, accomplishments in athletics, and even for appearance and hygiene more than anything else. This is not all bad. Rewarding and acknowledging good behavior in any of these areas reinforces positive behavior and discourages negative behavior. It is no coincidence that all my kids graduated from high school, did well in college, and have become healthy, productive adults. But they have wounds and scars from growing up in a performance-based environment, and ultimately, I am responsible for the home environment they grew up in.

This past Christmas, we had a special time as a family up in the Sierras, and I had the opportunity to ask each of my grown children about the impacts they saw on their lives of too much emphasis on performance and achievement instead of character and content. The interview with my youngest daughter, Karianne, was the hardest. She is keenly attuned to spiritual truth and human emotions. She always has been the child with the most insight into what lies beneath the surface in our own family and in the lives of others. She quickly honed in on the expectations and performance pressure that existed with regard to sports and school. Karianne felt that I praised her for things that mattered to me and were connected to my giftedness instead of really studying what she was good at and cheering for her in those things. She has strong memories of feeling that I did not want to process her emotions with her as a young child, which sometimes left her sad and alone in her room. I had to own up to that shortcoming. I was not raised to be emotionally vulnerable to my parents and siblings. I was raised to lock up my emotions and certainly not let them out. This, combined with a performance focus, left Karianne feeling very isolated and frustrated at times. Karianne also had many good things to say about our home growing up, but her sensitivity to the performance-based culture of our home was fair and honest. It is one of many things I have to forgive myself for and try to be better at in the lives of my children, my grandchildren, and other children I have the opportunity to impact in the years ahead.

In contrast, my oldest daughter, Kelly, said that she was aware of the performance-based culture but believed it was good for her as a driven, motivated girl and teen. She remembered the phrase "Don't settle," and it helped her effort in school, in sports, and in picking boyfriends and, eventually, a husband. Kelly saw setting high expectations as a positive in her life. She was not traumatized by it or hurt by it. This has led to much self-reflection. Why was Karianne more troubled by high expectations and performance-based praise than Kelly? It clearly has to do with personality types and maybe even birth order. It was a reminder that one size does not fit all and that we need to be attuned to how different children receive love and affirmation.

During my interview with my son, Chris, he agreed with Karianne that he sometimes felt praised more when he performed well in some sport but said he did not get anything from me when he did not do well. I would get very quiet and have little to say on the way home from sporting events. I asked him how that made him feel, and he said it seemed like I was disappointed in *who he was*. I told him during the interview that I had been really disappointed in how he had played, but Chris said it did not feel like that at the time. He said that my talking about every play when he did well and then not talking at all when he did poorly made it seem like I was disappointed *in him,* not just in his poor play. It was tough to hear that from my son. All I could do was apologize.

I don't intend to make the argument that praising children for who they are and who they are becoming is the *only* thing that matters. But I want to challenge any adult who has not praised their children for who they were at least an equal amount of times as they have for what their children achieved. It is a "do" or a "be" syllogism. Are we more concerned about what our children do or who are children are?

Performance-based parenting does not exist in the absence of profound cultural influences and norms. We are a performance-based culture. Employers rarely reward employees for their character traits. They reward them for performance, achievement, and accomplishment. Schools have not historically given major awards or honors to children who are good friends, trustworthy in keeping their word, or who are kind to others. They give recognition to—indeed they cheer for—those who do well in school. The valedictorian, the salutatorian, the summa cum lauds, and the magna cum lauds are not handed out for integrity, or honesty, or compassion, or courage. They are handed out based on grades that rank children, teens, and college students on their performance in comparison to others. I am pleased with school programs that are focusing more on character and rewarding strong character traits in students, but we have a long way to go in putting this high on the list of priorities in every school in America.[1]

On an even more superficial level, the advertising industry in America rarely builds commercials around character. They pick attractive actors and actresses and focus on the importance of outward appearance and beauty. It would not cross the mind of beer advertisers in America to audition potential commercial actors based on their character for industriousness, diligence, determination, or passion for a cause! They want them to pretend to be happy—ecstatic, even—drinking that beer because they want the message to be that their product will produce that happiness in the lives of those who use it.

The Impacts of Performance-Based Praise

Given how immersed our culture is in performance-based praise, it is hard to measure the negative impacts of it. And there are clearly very positive impacts from performance-based praise. High levels of academic and human achievement correlate to such praise, affirmation, and encouragement. A good friend of mine jokes that his Jewish mother was relentless in her desire for her son to achieve and excel. He admits he would have set his sights far lower without his mother's constant praise, expectations, and demands. Recent research has documented high levels of achievement in Asian American homes based on cultural expectations around hard work, performance, achievement, and success.[2] Numerous writers have documented a performance-based standard in immigrant families and the desire of immigrant parents to see their children do better financially and academically than their parents.[3] But a number of writers and researchers have looked at the issue from the negative impacts side. Mental health professionals too have experience in addressing the impacts of performance-based praise and have documented their work. I will focus on the three most obvious.

First, children growing up in a performance-based praise environment don't know who they really are or what they really believe about themselves. This correlates to both general mental health issues and to spiritual beliefs and values. My father raised me with very high expectations about academic achievement and athletic accomplishment. He was a strong, powerful man, and no one doubted who was in charge in our home. After my father died of a heart attack in 2009, I went to counseling for the first time in my life to process the trauma of his death. I was in a counseling session one day and was talking about some events in my life and the chronology of them. At one point, I said, "And then after God died ..." I did not even notice it at first. But my therapist had a funny look on her face.

Finally, she said, "Do you know what you just said?"

I did on some level. I responded, "Did I just say 'after God died'?"

"Yes, you did. Let's unpack that." Dang it. I hate it when a therapist says that to me. It means hard work ahead.

As she and I processed it, I had an epiphany. In my faith, God is always referred to as "Father." It is only natural. If you come out of a Christian tradition, it makes sense that you would relate your own notion of a father with your notion of God. If your father was abusive and controlling, you might view God in the same way. If your father had major rage issues, God likely seems angry with you most of the time. If your dad had a short fuse and did not understand forgiveness and grace, those concepts would be on short supply when you think about the God of the universe. If you were by raised by a father with no belief in God, you are far more likely to grow up an agnostic or an atheist. But if you do believe in God, the only human parallel to understanding who God is would be a human father.

Similarly, if their human father puts a high premium on performance and actions, children will naturally associate this with what life is about and who they are. They are likely to find their significance in what they do more than who they are. What they do will tend, in fact, to define who they are. It makes sense.

The research in a variety of settings has found a similar reality.[4] Performance-based parenting leads children toward authoritarianism, reduces empathy, and often gives rise to extreme political and social policy views.[5]

Second, children in performance-based praise environments rarely feel they have accomplished enough or done enough to earn what their parent is offering them—acceptance and love based on successful performance and achievement. They will feel more value when they achieve. They will find self-esteem in what they do more than who they are. It is so foundational to life for most of us, we don't even notice. We define people by what they do, rather than who they are. When you meet someone, early in the conversation you ask them "What do you do for a living?" It is a definition. It is a box to put them in, and it frames them for us. When we meet someone, we don't ask, "So, who are you inside? What are your top three character traits?" Imagine how different conversations might be if that was the big question when meeting someone new! I will often be at social events and ask someone I have met, "So, what do you do?" People always answer with their profession or job. I have never met anyone who says, "I try to love others every day, speak encouragement into their lives, and be open and vulnerable in sharing my emotions and letting others share theirs with me." I might stroke out and die on the spot if anybody ever answered that way, but it makes the point: we identify what we do with who we are.

Again, performance, achievement, and accomplishment are not bad. All cultures, economies, countries, and communities want people to strive, to achieve, and to accomplish. But understanding how insidious this can be in shaping what we value and who we value in the culture is important to understanding what happens when performance wanes, achievement declines, and accomplishments turn into failures in the context of violence, abuse, and trauma.

The depth of hopelessness in an abused child or teen who has grown up in a performance-based home, culture, and school environment is pronounced and far greater than it is in a child without trauma or abuse. Consequences, discipline, and condemnation are the natural results when children cannot perform in school, fall behind in grade-level reading, and are not able to compete with other children receiving strong support, affirmation, and encouragement in their home environment. The research on the impacts on abused and neglected children who receive inadequate affirmation and support shows deep deficits in most school-performance categories.[6]

Third, children who grow up with praise primarily focused on their appearance or achievement tend to pass it on, as adults, to their children and their grandchildren. We tend to raise children as we were raised. We tend to learn our parenting skills from our parents. In the absence of counseling, education, training, and strong mentoring from functional, healthy adults, we do what comes naturally and what we have seen and know. After Beth and I got married and started having children, I brought my performance-based standards to my parenting. It was not all bad, as we have discussed. I pushed my children to give it their all in sports, in school, in every hobby and endeavor they set their mind to accomplish. And often, they rose to the occasion. I coached my girls in fast-pitch softball, coached my son in basketball and baseball, and introduced them all to a host of sports and outdoor activities. The kids have many fond memories of those years and those adventures together.

But underneath all the positive reinforcement they got was a not-so-subtle message that value comes from what you do, not who you are. I talked much with my children about faith and beliefs but seldom focused on character traits, how they treated others, and how they built relationships with friends. None of those things were emphasized in my own home growing up. There was much more focus on outward appearances and outward achievement. As a result, my internal struggles and rage from childhood verbal, emotional, and physical abuse were suppressed—never discussed or processed—and I was left to internalize most struggles without ever sharing them. By personality type, I am an introvert. I really don't thrive in relationships with others, have never had many close friends, and enjoy time alone far more than engaging with large groups of people.

Perhaps you are an extrovert, perhaps your struggles are similar to mine, but I share all of this to help frame the challenges that can compound themselves based on personality type and life experience in a performance-based culture, family structure, or organizational culture. In the family context, this means we should be hypervigilant about asking a number of questions regularly:

- Am I praising my children regularly for who they are and who they are becoming, or do I focus more on achievement and accomplishment?
- Do I define happiness in relationships by whether others meet my expectations, or do I define it by our joint ability to share struggles from our lives and openly communicate without demanding they meet my expectations in order to "stay on the list"?

As we will talk about later, this is a complicated balance. The research is very clear that when at-risk and trauma-exposed children find they are competent in a sport or skill area, this *does* mitigate the impacts of trauma and gives them the ability to better deal with the bad things that have happened to them. But this also can easily mask the underlying issues they still struggle with from childhood trauma and abuse. Focusing on character and not achievement is far deeper and more meaningful in helping trauma-exposed children find healing and hope than simply challenging them to achieve and succeed.

The host of NFL players in the news in recent months and years highlights this issue in living color on national television. Ray Rice, Adrian Peterson, Jonathan Dwyer, Greg Hardy, Ray McDonald, Jovan Belcher, and many others found profound success playing football in high school, college, and the NFL. They enjoyed status, prestige, and financial success because of their competency as football players. They could channel their rage toward being highly successful in a sport that rewards aggression, dominance of others, and physical power. The competence they developed helped keep them out of jail and gangs and off other negative paths they could have traveled in their growing-up years.

But in a performance-based culture, they never dealt with the internal issues from childhood. I don't know any of these men personally, but I would bet money that they all grew up impacted by some form of child abuse, neglect, father abandonment, or domestic violence. They likely suffered and witnessed abuse and may even have perpetrated abuse on others as teens or young adults before their family-violence allegations made national and international news. Adrian Peterson was quoted early in his journey as saying, "I am the man I am today because of my father."[7] Adrian was saying it to defend his character, but what he was really telling us was his dad beat him, just as he beat his four-year-old son. The abuse is generational. Football was Adrian's competency. Football coaches, fellow players, and even the fans became his "cheerleaders." Adrian found significance, fame, and success through his amazing physical skills and abilities. He did not need an educational class on domestic violence while playing for the Minnesota Vikings. He needed help when he was five, six, and seven. He needed to be challenged about his view of women and girls when he was twelve, fourteen, and seventeen. His story is not really about using one switch on one of his children in Texas. He has fathered children with numerous women, and there have been abuse and abandonment issues with multiple children, including one who was killed by the mother's new boyfriend; Adrian was not even involved in the child's life.[8]

Competency—being good at something—is a protective measure for trauma-exposed children and is a great and powerful tool to help children grow up to be functional adults. But the underlying beliefs and values—who they really are and what they really believe—still must be addressed. If we don't help trauma-exposed children alter how they see themselves and who they are on the inside, they are going to repeat their violence and abuse with their children and grandchildren. Adrian Peterson needed coaches paying as much attention to his values and beliefs about women and girls as they paid to his skills on the football field.

Reflections

We should all do the tough soul-searching about how much we focus on achievement, performance, and accomplishment versus how much time we focus on character—who we are when no one is looking. Are we focusing on how children treat others in personal relationships, and what we do to help them focus on developing their own character, even while helping them become successful, productive adults? I know I need to spend far more time praising my children and grandchildren for who they are, rather than what they do. I need to see people as human beings of inherent value and worth, as eternal beings with value unrelated to their jobs, their accomplishments, or their achievements. And I need to focus on my self-talk about character and integrity so that I can more articulately praise observed character in the children in my life. How about you? How is the balance in your interactions with children? Is who they are as important to you as what they do? Do you communicate that clearly to every child in your life?

Nine

Learning How to Be a Child's Cheerleader

One of the first cases I ever dealt with where the man was executed was a surreal case. They shave the hair off the person's body before they put them in the electric chair, and we're standing there, [having a] very emotional conversation, holding hands, praying, talking. I remember him saying to me, "Bryan, this has been such a strange day. When I woke up this morning, the guards came to me and said, 'What do you want for breakfast?' And at midday, 'What do you want for lunch?' In the evening they said, 'What do you want for dinner?' All day long, he said, they kept saying, "'What can we do to help you? Can we get you stamps to mail your last letters? Can we get you water? Can we get you a phone to call your friends and family?'" I'll never forget that man saying ... "More people have said, 'What can I do to help you?' in the last fourteen hours of my life than they ever did in the first nineteen years of my life." I remember standing there, holding his hands, thinking, "Where were they when you were three years old being abused? Where were they when you were seven and being sexually assaulted? Where were they when you were a teenager and you were homeless and struggling with drug addiction? Where were they when you came back from war struggling with post-traumatic stress disorder?" And with those kinds of questions resonating in my mind, he was executed.[1]

—Bryan Stevenson,
Civil Rights Attorney

EVERY ONE OF us can be a child's cheerleader. We can learn to cheer for our own children or grandchildren. We can learn to cheer for at-risk, abused, and neglected children. We can learn to cheer for other children we might come in contact with in our neighbor-hoods, our churches, our schools, our sports programs, and any other setting. Being a cheerleader, affirmer, and encourager of children comes naturally to some. But for most of us, it is a learned skill. We must practice it over and over. We must figure out which approaches work best for us. We must figure out the most effective "language" for that child we want to affirm and encourage. And then we must do it again and again and again. Actions must become habits. I remember a Sunday school teacher, Norma Gintert, saying it to me when I was very young: "Sow a habit, reap a destiny." Bad habits can produce sad and tragic destinies and do for many. Good habits can produce great destinies—not only for us, but for others as well.

Our starting point in learning how to be a child's cheerleader here begins with my personal journey and experiences in learning how to be a cheerleader for children—my own and others. I made a host of mistakes with my children growing up. But I also did many things well, and I have learned from some of my mistakes over the years.

Early in my parenting life, I was influenced by a number of writers on the topic of parenting. Some wrote on it and then did not live it out so faithfully. Others wrote on it and lived it in spades. Both groups influenced me. And though I have shared some of the mistakes of my dad, he also did some things very well, and I am forever grateful for the ways in which he became my cheerleader, my affirmer, and the man who believed in me the most. He figured out how to "bless me," even amidst his own struggles.

Many years ago, Gary Smalley and John Trent wrote a book called *The Blessing*. They used a host of passages from the Jewish Bible and passages from the Christian Old Testament to make a case for the importance of parents passing on "the blessing" to their children in order to then see them grow up to be healthy, productive adults. The book played a role in my thinking early on, and I am thankful for their investment in my life as a father.

The Blessing

Gary Smalley and John Trent identified five major components from their study of ancient Jewish culture as they looked at how Jewish parents conveyed and passed on approval and blessing to their children. I would like to focus on three of them: *expressing high value, picturing a special future, and meaningful touch.* Their ideas no doubt have quite a bit of modern Western influence, but I believe in the truth of their ideas, the discussion of which is a great way to start a chapter on how to become an effective cheerleader for children.

First, looking at the Bible, the Old Testament, and even the teachings of Jesus, Gary Smalley and John Trent identified *expressing high value* to children as foundational to "the blessing" parents should bestow on their children.[2] They identify a host of examples where parents talked about how much they loved their children, how smart their children were, how valuable they were in the eyes of God, and how unique and special they were. One of the things I love about Jesus, which they point out, is that children were so special to him. He often rebuked his disciples and followers when they got annoyed with the children and tried to keep them from bothering Jesus. Jesus also spoke of profound condemnation and consequences for those who would harm a child or "cause a little one to stumble."

How are you doing? Do your children, grandchildren, or other children in your life regularly get that message from you of how much they are worth? Is it high on your list to make sure they realize how precious, unique, and gifted they are?

Second, Smalley and Trent focused on *picturing a special future.*[3] Successful parents down through the ages have helped their children think about a special future. Children who don't look past Saturday night often make destructive choices and end up wasting their long-term potential. Helping children early on think about what they might want to be when they grow up, how they might be able to impact the world or serve others, and how special that future can be frames the future for these kids.

During my tenure as the elected city attorney of San Diego, I would often speak in public schools in San Diego. I particularly liked middle schools. Kids are at such an awkward stage in middle school, and I remember my own embarrassing journey at that age. I had braces, my face was covered in acne, and I was growing at a pace too fast for my body. I liked older girls, but they saw me as an annoyance. I got bullied quite a bit, and I did not really have a good sense of where I was going in life. So when I would go into middle schools as city attorney, I always liked asking a whole class of students if they knew what they wanted to be when they grew up. It was always about the same: half the class thought they knew what they wanted to be, and half had no idea. Those who did have ideas were not always coming up with highly likely professions. Lots of boys would say "play in the NBA" or "play in the NFL." Professional skateboarders, video game testers, and television or movie stars were always plentiful. But I still enjoyed dialoguing with those who offered those pretty unlikely jobs along with those who said "teacher," "doctor," "firefighter," "scientist," or "police officer."

I was never hard on the kids who did not raise their hand. I would follow up with them and ask what subjects they liked in school the best or what hobbies or extracurricular activities they enjoyed the most. They all had answers to those questions, and then I would have the whole class discuss what kinds of jobs might someday connect to things that various kids liked to do.

It was a corporate version of picturing a special future! It was helping children think about future chapters of their lives. Often at Camp HOPE, we do the same thing. Once children share their dream of what they want to do when they grow up, we talk with everyone about how they can get there and what steps and choices and hard work might be needed on the pathway to their dream. It is helping them picture a special future.

How are you helping children in your life picture a special future? Are you helping them look down the road to that special future? If they don't know what they might be interested in doing, are you asking them about what they enjoy in life and talking about how it might connect to jobs or professions later in life? It is part of the "blessing" we convey upon children. But for children to receive the blessing, we actually have to help them engage in the dreaming and envisioning process for themselves.

Third, the writers of *The Blessing* said parents in ancient times focused on *meaningful touch*.[4] All the research cited in this book should only reinforce this reality. All human beings need meaningful touch. Babies need it enormously—the kind, caressing, loving touch of a mother, father, or care provider. Children need the hug, the soft hand on the shoulder, and the soothing hand through their hair. For abused children, inappropriate touch becomes abusive, sexual, and violative. Yet, they still need healthy, appropriate touch. One year at Camp HOPE, we had a child-welfare professional who announced to the whole camp on day one that there would be no physical touching during camp. She was not part of our staff and had never been to Camp HOPE, but she announced the rule! She said, "We all have a bubble around us, and no one should go inside anyone else's bubble. We need to keep our hands and our feet to ourselves. This will apply to campers and to counselors." I was stunned, angry, and then … amused. What a silly thing to say to children so desperately in need of meaningful, kind, loving, appropriate touch! While I understand her motivation (I think) and her desire to protect children from abuse (I think), she really missed the importance of meaningful touch in the lives of trauma-exposed children.

The touching of campers at Camp HOPE is always with boundaries, never in situations where an adult or counselor is alone with a camper, and always with permission of the camper. But meaningful touch is important, promotes healing, and conveys blessing to children, especially those who have been physically and sexually abused.

I worked hard in my children's lives to often and consistently touch them affectionately, hold hands with them, and hug them. I kissed my daughters and my son until they were into adolescence.

In fact, I remember the day my eleven-year-old son, Chris, decided that he did not want me to kiss and hug him when I dropped him off at middle school. He was starting to become self-conscious, and he decided it would be best if we only hugged at home! As a side note, he kept wanting to be hugged and still does to this very day! My daughters never went through a stage of not wanting to be hugged and it paid dividends throughout their teenage years. The ongoing respectful, physical affection from their dad was sexual assault prevention, domestic violence prevention, and self-esteem building. They grew up knowing they were loved. They grew up feeling secure in physical contact with a man who loved them. And it would later help them to recognize boys and men who treated them like their dad treated them—with respect, honor, and affection.

How are you doing with regard to passing on a blessing to children in your life through appropriate, meaningful touch? Are you conscious of it? Are you intentional in making sure that children in your life feel loved and valued through both words and gentle, kind, loving touch? If you grew up in a family with little or no physical affection, you might need to work harder at it. But it should be a high priority with both boys and girls. We all—children and adults—thrive with positive, meaningful touch.

Learning Every Child's Love Language

Another critical piece of my own journey is one I just spent time learning about with my adult children. I wish I had done it with them long ago. Gary Chapman has written about the importance of "love languages."[5] I have found his research and writing to be compelling. Chapman's research and writings identify five major emotional love languages:

- Words of affirmation
- Quality time
- Receiving gifts
- Acts of service

- Physical touch

During the writing of this book, I took Chapman's online quiz and challenged my wife and children to all take the quiz. You can take the quiz at http://www.5lovelanguages.com. At the end, it identifies and ranks the way you experience love and emotional connection using these five love languages. I recommend that you, your spouse or intimate partner (if you have one), and the children in your life all take the online quiz. It is an eye-opener. I was surprised to find that my wife, Beth, our children, and I all had different primary and secondary languages! For me, words of affirmation were number one. When people speak affirmation into my life, my emotional tank is filling, and I feel loved and appreciated. Physical touch was a close number two. For Beth, words of affirmation were number one, but her close second was quality time.

You can see the obvious disconnect that exists when we try to express love and appreciation to children or others in our life and their love language is different from our own and we fail to fully connect with them at the deepest level of communication they feel and hear. It quickly explained major disconnects for me with my children and, at times, my wife. For example, acts of service was number three for me but number five for Beth. I have regularly washed her car for thirty years. For me, it was my way of saying "I love you and appreciate you." To Beth, it meant virtually nothing! It did not make her angry and did not alienate her. But let's just say I could have saved a lot of water and soap and just written her notes more often and come out way ahead.

I will give you another example with my daughter Karianne. Karianne's number one love language is quality time. I would often speak words of affirmation, send her gifts, and give her money as my way of saying "I love you." Karianne, during her interview with me, said that she would have preferred that I just spent more time with her doing things she enjoyed doing. I would have saved a lot of money and spent far less time shopping for her if I had realized that time alone with me was far more important to her than the rest of it. Not that words didn't matter—Karianne astutely told me that she knew words of affirmation was high on my list of love languages, so when I wrote her notes and cards, she "translated" them into her love language to reassure herself how much I loved her. But it would have helped me be much more effective if I had known what love language was at the top of her list.

If you are investing your life in children and teens, ask them to take the love languages test and see how they best experience love and support. Gary Chapman developed it for marriages and intimate relationships. But it applies, in my opinion, to all relationships. It will help you better communicate with children and adults in your life.

Ben Hedberg's Words of Encouragement

I was probably in my late forties when a nine-year-old boy reminded me of the power of word pictures and encouragement. Ben Hedberg was a childhood friend of my son. Our families were friends. Later, we would vacation together. And even later in our relationship, we would support his parents as Ben was diagnosed with, and died of, a brain tumor at the age of nineteen.

At the time Ben encouraged me, our families were attending a church together in east San Diego County. We had just met the Hedbergs, and I had barely had one or two brief conversations with Ben. He was nine. But one Sunday morning, his mom, Debbie, walked up to me with Ben and said, "Ben needs to tell you about his dream." I was intrigued. Ben was quiet and somewhat shy and hesitated. I got down on his level always a good strategy whenever trying to connect to a child—and told him I would love to hear about his dream. He said he dreamed I was a mailman. I smiled. I wasn't sure this was going to be all that profound. I asked what I was doing as a mailman. He said, "You deliver the mail to people." It made no sense to me! Then he paused and said, "And the mail is notes with words that have sunshine, and the envelopes are bright, and when you deliver them to people, it makes them smile and be happy. It is your job. It is what you are supposed to do." I was spellbound.

Since my earliest days in life, I have always enjoyed writing. Sometimes it is hard for me to express my feelings or words verbally to be people in personal conversations. Writing is my way, as an introvert, to get my words out to people I care about. Quite frankly, when I am healthiest in life, I write a lot, and I write notes to others—my wife, my children, my friends, my coworkers, and those I care about in life. Ben Hedberg had a dream about me, and his dream challenged me to use my inclination to express things to those I care about. Ben passed away ten years later, but I will never forget how he reminded me about the power of my words in the lives of others. And it is not just my gift.

We all have the power to use our words to build up or to tear down. We have the ability to use our words to affirm and encourage or to be critical and negative. Many years ago a domestic violence survivor named Sarah Buel reminded me that it takes eleven positive things to overcome one negative thing said to a child. How are you doing? How am I doing? Cheerleading is hard work. But we need to work really hard to make sure our positive and affirming words far outweigh our negative and critical words. During the course of interviewing my children, I discovered how much my notes, cards, and letters had meant to them as they were growing up. They had saved them and still have them to this very day. Kelly said that the birthday cards were great, but the cards that were not connected to a birthday meant more to her. She said those times when I wrote to her while away on trips meant much more to her, as she knew that I was thinking of her and writing about her without any occasion in mind. Karianne said that she liked the letters that really focused on things I knew about her and understood about her from time I had spent with her. Chris said he often would go back and read my letters to him when he was having a tough time or struggling at a particular moment in his life.

We can all be mailmen and mailwomen. We can all deliver mail to our children and other children in our lives. We have to take the time to do it, though. We have to spend enough time with them to know them and be able to write something personal instead of empty platitudes. Most children and teens don't write on paper much. It is all about Instagram, Pinterest, Facebook, and text messaging. But children still long to feel special and receive words of blessing, encouragement, and affirmation. And we all have the power to deliver such words—in person or in writing.

How are you doing at writing notes to the children in your life? Not for birthdays or formal occasions only, but regularly at other times. More so today, than ever, children and teens will read handwritten notes and cards with personalized words of encouragement and affirmation. They will save them and read them again and again.

Ethical Wills

There are many ways to share our positive values and beliefs with our children. When my children were in their early teens, I read about ethical wills for the first time. The notion behind these wills was this: what do you want your children to inherit from you? It was not about cars or houses or bank accounts. It was about values and beliefs and things that matter in the context of eternity. The idea involved writing your "will" to your children while you are still alive and sharing it with them. Telling them what they mean to you, telling them what you want them to take from your mistakes, and expressing to them all the great character traits and values you see in them while you are still alive to say it!

I took it to heart. I spent many hours constructing and crafting ethical wills to my children. And then I gave them to my children in written form. I read some of it to them and then gave them copies to save and read later to themselves. When I asked the kids about it years later, they each said the words were priceless to them and they had saved the "wills" so they could read them while I was alive and still have them after I was gone.

I want to share what I wrote to our oldest daughter, Kelly, to help you think through how you might do the same for your children or grandchildren or other children you are mentoring. I would not suggest doing it for a child you don't know well, but it is a great tool for practicing how to become a cheerleader and how to pass on your values, both in words and actions, to the children you hope to impact. My faith, values, and beliefs come through in this letter, but whether you share my faith or not, I will tell you that letters have impacts. Kelly received this letter thirteen years ago and still has it and reads it regularly to this day.

Writing to Kelly (Age 15)

Dear Kelly,

The moment you were born, I saw determination on your face. Your drive and focus in life are two of the many gifts God has given you. God has big plans for you if you stay faithful to Him. He is going to use you in powerful and profound ways to touch the lives of many. I love seeing you develop into a woman of God. You can be moody (like me). You can get really uptight (like me). You can be impatient and unkind with those around you (like me). But beneath all of that, I see a focused, loving, deep, thoughtful, godly young woman. You have already begun to make your mark on your friends, your family, your church, your school, and on hurting kids across the world (Costa Rica). But the best is yet to come. God will slowly unfold His plan, step by step.

I am 42 years old, and today I can see so much more clearly His plan than I could at 15, or 20, or 25. I regret that I, at times, lost my eternal perspective and settled for a human perspective about my failures and struggles. But God's grace has always been sufficient. He restores me, forgives me, and pulls me closer and closer to Himself.

Kelly, long after I have gone to be with Jesus, I hope and pray that you will carry with you the values and priorities you learned in our home. Mom and I have not been perfect parents (but you already knew that, didn't you?). I certainly have made mistakes as a father and a husband. But the core values of our family will be a sure foundation for you to build your life on.

Follow Jesus. You will never regret staying close to Jesus Christ and living your life for Him. You can try to find happiness in money, or stuff, or achievements, or even romance—but none of it will fully satisfy. Only an intimate, dynamic, growing relationship with the God that made you will give you a sense of significance and ultimate satisfaction in life. The older I get, the more important my faith in Jesus becomes. None of us will live in this life or on this planet forever. So the focus and priority of your life should be crystal clear.

Guard Your Heart. Kelly, you are a loving, passionate, romantic girl. God has given you the drives and passion you have. And God will fulfill it in His time. Whatever you do, don't settle for second best. Don't settle for a consolation prize when you deserve the gold medal. So many guys will be more than happy to take your heart and satisfy their own needs. Don't let them! Pray for godly young men to spend time with. Pray (even now) for the godly man the Lord will have for you someday. Make wise choices. By the way, it just gets better the longer you are married. So many young people treat sex as a quick, entertaining, recreational activity. And they miss out on God's plan for intimacy—boundless fun and passion in a lifelong marriage.

Aim high! I know there will be lots of times in life when you don't feel like aiming high and giving it your all. Whether it is working hard in school now or pursuing the career of your dreams in the future—be the best. Set your sights high. Whatever you are doing, give it all you have. You will never regret it. You may not achieve all your dreams. God may redirect you from time to time, as He has redirected me. But God will reward your determination to do your best. It will bring honor and glory to God, and you will gain great satisfaction from it.

Pursue significance, not success. Whatever God calls you to in life, and wherever He takes you, don't buy the lie of the world that human success and achievement are the measure of your worth. You are of infinite value simply because you are a child of God. Nothing you ever do will earn God's love. He loves you completely right now.

There will be tough times though in life when you have difficult choices to make. The "world" might point you in one direction, while God may point you in another direction. Listen to your heart and God's leading. I said no to UC Berkeley Boalt School of Law (a higher ranked school) because I felt called to UCLA. I have passed up multiple career opportunities (even recently) because God has called me to be faithful to my work here in San Diego. And I have no regrets. Because I have learned that God's best is better than anything the "world" might define as success.

God may give you human successes along the way, but He does not call you to success. He calls you to faithfulness. And the rewards when you are faithful are so much better! God has special plans for you, Kelly.

Don't Take Yourself Too Seriously. Whatever happens in life, Kelly, keep your sense of humor and don't take yourself too seriously. You and I can both get pretty focused and pretty intense. That can be a very good thing. But it can also make you proud and self-absorbed and too focused on your own needs and your own problems. Our focus in life should stay on the needs of others as much as possible. Always look for opportunities to encourage other people and be a friend to those who need someone to care about them and cheer for them. Keep looking outward—it will keep you humble, and it will keep you sensitive to the needs of others. It will keep you from focusing too much on your own feelings and emotions. Whenever I have taken myself too seriously or become too self-absorbed, God humbles me and reminds me that only He is indispensable. My job is to live for Him, stand for Him, and love others.

Whether I am here to watch you serve Him with your life or I am cheering from the portals of heaven, I will always believe in you, always love you, and always expect the best of you. You will make many mistakes in life, but God's grace will always be available to you. I pray for you every day, Kelly, and I will keep praying for you until we are together forever in His presence. I love you more than words can describe.

—Your Loving Dad

I challenge you to give it a try. Even if you are not ready to give it to a child quite yet, write it and see how your goals and values lay out on paper. It will help you articulate the advice, goals, and values you want to pass on to children in your life.

Overcoming Our Own Trauma and Bad Habits

One of the biggest obstacles to becoming a cheerleader for children is often our own experience growing up. I grew up with physical abuse and varying levels of verbal and emotional abuse. My own trauma and bad habits have been a struggle to overcome. If you grew up in a home without a strong cheerleading parent, you are at a disadvantage with your own children or with the children of others. Parents who grew up with negative parents may tend more toward the negative. Parents who grew up with biting sarcasm tend to use more biting sarcasm with their own children. Children growing up with abuse or witnessing violence between their parents tend toward violence and abuse as adults, either as victims or perpetrators.

Being aware of our tendencies that stem from the way we were raised or from trauma or abuse we may have experienced is the first step toward beginning to unlearn bad habits or, more importantly, to learn good habits in how we talk to and treat our children.

If you don't have a good example in your life, I strongly recommend attending parenting classes, getting some good books on positive parenting (and reading them!), and trying to spend time with other parents who are engaging in positive, affirming parenting with their children. The best antidote to bad habits is learning good habits. The best way to change the way you affirm and support children is to start working at it, practicing positive affirming words, and staying at it. Chuck Swindoll, a great parenting expert and a mentor to me, calls it "a long obedience in the same direction." Chuck says the longer you keep doing good things with children, the more these things will become second nature. Let's spend a little time talking about some of the basics you can learn in a parenting class or from a parenting coach. If you have never attended a class or had a coach, you at least need to know the set of skills that need to be learned.

Parenting classes are primarily used by the child-welfare system when parents or children are facing issues in the juvenile court system. Most of the programs have been designed for parents who are considered high-risk candidates for child neglect or abuse. Often, domestic violence may have occurred or a substance-abuse problem has been identified. Research on the effectiveness of such classes is minimal, but the principles they teach are important for all adults interacting with children. Classes often focus on anger- and stress-management techniques, non-abusive disciplinary techniques, the importance of logical consequences with children, the importance of affirmation, useful tools for communicating with your children, and other topics connected to building on the strengths of your children. Personally, I would love to see parenting programs implemented, even required, before anyone becomes a parent.

If a parenting coach or parenting classes don't get you to a healthier place as a parent, I strongly recommend you pursue individual counseling to deal with the effects of childhood trauma in your own life. I just went to counseling for the first time three years ago. I wish I had done it when my children were very small. It was an eye-opening journey into transparency, vulnerability, and, ultimately, healing. Don't be ashamed if you need professional counseling to work through your own trauma and bad habits.

Learning to Build Character in the Lives of Children

We have talked about focusing on character instead of performance. To do this, we need to become very familiar with what character traits actually are, and then we need to start looking for evidence of them in the lives of children we are raising, working with, or trying to encourage. There are sixty-six identified character traits in most writings and research on character. Here is a list of those character traits:

Adaptability	Appreciation	Attentiveness
Availability	Commitment	Compassion
Concern	Confidence	Consideration
Consistency	Contentment	Cooperation
Courage	Creativity	Decisiveness
Deference	Dependability	Determination
Diligence	Discernment	Discretion
Efficiency	Equitableness	Fairness
Faithfulness	Fearlessness	Flexibility
Forgiveness	Friendliness	Generosity
Gentleness	Gratitude	Honesty
Humility	Integrity	Joyfulness
Kindness	Love	Loyalty
Meekness	Mercifulness	Observance
Optimism	Patience	Peacefulness
Perseverance	Persistence	Persuasiveness

Prudence	Punctuality	Purpose
Resourcefulness	Respect	Responsibility
Security	Self-control	Sincerity
Submissiveness	Tactfulness	Temperance
Thoroughness	Thriftiness	Tolerance
Trustfulness	Truthfulness	Virtue

I have to confess that I don't even know what some of these character traits are! But I do know that it helps to know what they are before we can actually see them emerging in the lives of children. Once you start becoming familiar with the core character traits in caring, loving, compassionate, and affirming people, you can determine what kind of character you want to build in children.

Personally, I think the top ten that we should encourage and focus on building should include:

1. Kindness
2. Courage
3. Perseverance
4. Compassion
5. Forgiveness
6. Friendliness
7. Affirmation
8. Patience
9. Gratitude
10. Respect

After thirty years of working with children who have witnessed domestic violence, I've realized that the top ten above all seem to be topics that children are able to understand, dialogue about, and emulate. They also connect to key needs in a child's life with regard to resilience, competency, and empathy. How could you identify and affirm the top ten above? Here are some ideas:

1. **Kindness**—Look for ways a child is kind during the day. Ask the school teacher to keep an eye out for acts of kindness at school. Talk regularly about what kindness looks like in acts and words. Learn to praise acts of kindness but not simply the act—learn to praise the child for being kind to others.

2. **Courage**—The prerequisite to courage is fear. Praising a child for being courageous first involves acknowledging fear. There can be no courage without fear. Look for opportunities to talk about fear of situations or fear of trying new things. Then praise decisions to overcome fear with acts of courage. Small fears and small acts of courage are usually the best place to start.

3. **Perseverance**—This is all about sticking to something and not giving up. Praise the child for times when he or she sticks to something that is difficult. Children at a very young age can start to understand the concept of staying at it and doing their best. Frame it as "finish well," even if they don't win or accomplish exactly what they hoped to accomplish. Perseverance is the antidote to "learned helplessness." Children who learn to give up easily will struggle their entire lives. Teaching them to do their best helps to increase the chance of competency and a sense of self-efficacy.

4. **Compassion**—Compassion is feeling sympathy for others in need and usually involves doing something kind for them. Children have an easier time with compassion than empathy, but both are important. Empathy really tries to engage a person in the feelings of another person to understand how he or she sees and experiences a situation. Empathy helps a child begin to the see the world from another person's perspective. Compassion may not go as deep as empathy, but it focuses more on action to help and encourage others. When you see a child actually reaching out to help someone in a tough situation,

you can praise the child for showing compassion. My personal feeling is that learning to show compassion is transformative for those struggling with their own trauma. It is feeling the sob of another's soul. It is learning to give away what most people cling to ferociously. It is a willingness to do whatever is necessary to demonstrate true concern.

5. **Forgiveness**—This makes my top ten list because resentment and anger toward others is such a poison in the life of a traumatized child. Helping children see how bitterness can eat them alive and how unproductive resentment is can really help them overcome their anger and rage. Don't ever confuse forgiveness, though, with tolerance for abuse and violence. Forgiving is not condoning or ignoring; forgiving is letting a wrong go without obsessing over it. But it does not mean the child should keep allowing abuse to happen.

6. **Friendliness**—Praising children for making friends, being a friend, and supporting friends is so powerful. Talk with a child about what makes a good friend. Draw pictures with a child of a good friendship. Focus on what it means to be a friend and let someone else be his or her friend.

7. **Affirmation**—Affirmation is building up another person. It is closely connected to encouragement. Encouragement is putting courage into someone else to help him or her overcome fear. Helping children see how they can encourage another should be a high priority for every adult. Life is always more fulfilling when we learn how to encourage and affirm others. Children can be cheerleaders for other children. Praise them for having the character trait of affirmation or encouragement when you see it. They will find such tremendous fulfillment in being an encouragement and support to others.

8. **Patience**—Patience and perseverance are closely related. Look for ways a child can be praised for waiting patiently for something—dinner, a special television show, or even when being picked up after school. Patience is not easily learned, and trauma-exposed children often have a very difficult time waiting for things in their lives. Talking about what patience is and then practicing it with them will pay dividends for the rest of their lives.

9. **Gratitude**—Learning to be thankful for what we have is a gift in life. Praising children for saying "please" and "thank you" is a great start. Helping children to appreciate what others do for them and praising them when they begin to understand the generosity of others will teach them about gratitude.

10. **Respect**—Children so often receive no respect from adults or other children in their lives, so we should not be surprised when they don't know how to give respect. Teaching them to treat others with respect (such as police officers, teachers, people in authority), even if that respect is not always earned, is an important discipline. Children can learn to respect others. Boys must learn to respect girls and women, and children must learn to respect themselves.

Our research over the last two years at Camp HOPE has consistently demonstrated the power of building up these key character traits in children. If we build these ten character traits into our work with children, we can transform their view of themselves and their futures.

Reflections

Bryan Stevenson's story at the beginning of the chapter haunts me. Once a man is on death row and facing the last day of life, we are kind, loving, and responsive to his needs. We have all the resources we need to hold him accountable for the consequences of childhood trauma and the poor choices he made through the darkness of his pain. But are we willing to invest the time and resources to help him before he ends up in jail, prison, or on death row?

Ten

Practical Steps to Success (Work the Plan)

If you fail to plan, you are planning to fail.
—Benjamin Franklin

MORE THAN TEN years ago, I fulfilled a lifelong dream of designing and building a house. We have always dreamed of building a home, but it did not become possible until after I left office as San Diego city attorney. Once we could live outside the city limits of San Diego, we got to design and build a home on two acres in East San Diego County. It was a challenging and difficult experience that involved working with a contractor friend and an architect. I was stunned by all the details that had to be decided, the complexity of the plans that had to be approved by the planning department of San Diego County, and the many, many issues that came up in the process. Having a plan was critical to our success. Without a plan, we would have failed—the house would never have been built successfully. We needed a plan, needed to regularly adjust the plan based on current realities, and needed to *follow* the plan. I am particularly thankful that our contractor, Greg Abell, knew the plan and followed it. We would have had a disaster on our hands if Greg had looked at the plan and then thrown it away and done his best based on instinct and intuition! We constantly looked at the plans. All the subcontractors looked at the plans before they bid on their part or actually did the work.

So, when you decide to love a child, build up a child, and become a child's cheerleader—*do you have a plan*? Have you thought it through? Have you received any professional advice and consultation? Have you leaned on the experts? Have you read books? If you have a plan, are you following it? Do you even remember what the key elements of the plan are?

If the children you are focused on supporting are your children, you might pay more attention with them. But even if they are your own biological children, I bet you don't have a plan. Most parents never form a plan, never follow clear intentional steps, and never regularly reevaluate their approach! With your own children, you do have the advantage of learning about them from birth forward. You see their tendencies, their "bents," and their particular personality traits come out early. This helps you better understand what works and what does not work with each child.

On the other hand, what if the child is not yours? What if you are trying to support and build up neighborhood children, your grandchildren, a mentor child, or perhaps the children of a friend or coworker? You need to spend time with these children in order to figure out who they are and what makes them tick. If they have suffered abuse, you need to learn more about trauma and the impact of trauma. What works with non-traumatized children generally will not work with children who have experienced severe abuse. Their experiences before you come in contact with them affect how they see the world, how they see themselves, and how they see their future.

Either way, in becoming a cheerleader for children, you need to have a plan, and then you need to work the plan. Cheering for the children is not a one-time, once-a-week, or once-a-month kind of event. It is a continual effort and may involve multiple strategies. Let's look at the basics of developing a plan first and then look at the practical challenges of working the plan.

Developing a Plan

Most child-development experts will tell you that connecting with a child takes time. It cannot be rushed and will rarely happen quickly. The older the child, generally the longer it takes to establish a connection. I am an introvert by nature, so early on I made the effort with my own children and with other children to try to establish a connection quickly! I did not have a lot of time. I was a busy guy. I would want to rush in, have some quality time, and move on to other priorities. It was a double whammy. I was an introvert, and I am not particularly a "kid person." It was not a good starting point for successfully impacting children in my life! I did not have a plan in those early years with my own children. Thankfully I realized early on the importance of being intentional in raising healthy, affirmed, and confident children and learned about key pieces that were necessary for success.

Start with Quantity Time

So, the first point is foundational: It is about quantity time and not just about quality time. Rarely can you have quality time without a lot of quantity time, during which nothing significant happens and no deep connection is evident. Early on I learned that I needed to be around my children for the special moments to happen. I could not simply come and go and expect to have a strong connection with any of my children. This principle applies whether we are talking about your own children or other children you want to develop a relationship with in order to become a cheerleader. The interviews with my children during the writing of this book yielded some consistent themes. One of them was that the children loved family vacations that involved us being together for many hours at a time without the interruption of television, work, or school. They really liked the quantity time just in and of itself! It was clear in each of their interviews, however, that quantity time was the prerequisite to quality time.

Turn Off the Electronics

The quantity time usually necessary for a connection is not time spent sitting in front of a television set or time together with every child plugged into headphones. Dr. Dre has become rich with his headphones, but I guarantee you that raising healthy children is not part of his business plan. Children spend hours in front of a television or plugged into music blaring in both ears every day. There are many benefits to getting children outside and getting their electronic devices away from them. It gives them and you a chance to have a personal connection and allows them to start using more of their senses than simply sight and sound. It also allows them to start using their bodies. I strongly support the NFL Play 60 program and other efforts that try to get children to do physical activity for at least sixty minutes a day. First Lady Michelle Obama has pushed this focus strongly, and she deserves praise for her work. At Camp HOPE, we are often amazed at how out of shape children are when they arrive at camp. They are children of the electronics era—Xbox, Game Boy, Nintendo, video games of all kinds, television, Internet surfing, cell phones, iPads, tablets, and so many more distractions—an era in which children don't need to even get out of a chair to entertain themselves for hours and hours. And in a world where parents are working full-time, dealing with their own issues, or distracted with their own priorities, it is easy today for children to find ways to entertain themselves.

Creating opportunities to spend time with a child without electronics or electronic stimulation should be a high priority. Children will groan and complain at first—particularly those addicted to electronics—but they will eventually engage with you, especially if less electronic options are available around them! This is why getting into nature and getting away from cell signals and Wi-Fi networks should be part of any starting point. Even if you cannot get away from cell signals, working out agreements with children for periods of time when you all agree that no one will use electronics can get you to that starting line for quality, uninterrupted time together.

Look for Those "Bents"

I love the old proverb that says, "Train up a child in the way he should go, and when he is old he will not depart from it."[1] We tend to think the formula for training up a child is the same for every child, but we are making a mistake if we think that is the point of the proverb. A closer look at the proverb discloses a more fundamental notion: Every child is unique. The proverb, properly understood in context, means "Train up a child in the way *that child should go.*" The original Hebrew text focuses on the "bents" of a child. No two children have exactly the same "bents," and no two children should be treated exactly the same.

This means we have to become students of our children and those children we want to be cheerleaders for in our lives. We need to figure out what makes them tick. One of the early failures of some parents who are strong, driven, type-A personalities is missing the sensitive, soft-spoken nature of a child who is not in any way like the parent. An aggressive approach with a sensitive, soft-spoken child can badly damage the child's self-esteem. Another child with a stronger personality or personal drive may not experience the same impact to self-esteem. There are a host of variables, of course, but different children will react to different approaches. Our oldest daughter, Kelly, was much more strong-willed than her younger sister, Karianne. I struggled harder with the decision not to spank Kelly because she was often defiant. On the other hand, I simply had to look at Karianne with a face of disappointment, and she would burst into tears. Had I been as verbally aggressive with Karianne as I was with Kelly, I have little doubt it would have been very traumatizing for her. Interviews with Kelly and Karianne during the writing of this book confirmed what I saw when they were much younger. Karianne internalized emotions much more than Kelly did. Karianne felt things more deeply than

Kelly did, and when I would not want to deal with her emotions, it often left her frustrated, lonely, and angry, even as a very young child.

Understanding how children differ and what strategy will work best with each child should be the highest priority of a parent, a mentor, and a cheerleader. I wish I had applied this truth much earlier with my children, and I wish I had been much more intentional in customizing my approach with each of our children. I have been able to do much more of this customizing with Camp HOPE children over the years because of my failures with my own children.

Prioritize Quality Time

Once we commit to quantity time with children, we should focus on quality time. I have found that quality time is most often one-on-one time with a child. With my own children, I decided to take one child on a trip with me at a time. I traveled a great deal during my children's growing-up years and decided that even though I could not always have as much time with my children as Beth had, I would try to have more time alone with each child. In my interviews with the children, each child said that special trips alone with me were significant in their lives. They did not call it "quality time," but that is exactly what they enjoyed. They also liked times when they knew I was totally focused on them and fully present (not one of my fortes). My son Chris remembered every trip we took by name, the places we went, and what we did. My daughter Karianne particularly liked time with just me alone—totally engaged with her alone.

You don't have to travel a lot for work to create these quality times with children. Beth used to have "dates" with each of our kids and still has telephone dates with them. Depending on the age of the children, a special date might be a trip to the playground, a dinner, or something else. Try to avoid activities that eliminate all interaction, such as movies, though movies may serve a purpose if you spend time afterward talking about the movie and processing it together. The purpose of special date times is to celebrate that child and focus on that child. It is why mentoring relationships have such power.

You are far more likely to have quality time with a child, whether your own or in a mentoring relationship, if you plan for time with the child and place him or her squarely in your schedule on a daily or weekly basis.

Many years ago, Dr. Stephen Covey told a story about an expert speaking to a group of business students that illustrates my point:

> As this man stood in front of the group of high-powered overachievers, he said, "OK, time for a quiz." Then he pulled out a one-gallon wide-mouthed mason jar and set it on a table in front of him. Then he produced about a dozen fist-sized rocks and carefully placed them, one at a time, into the jar.
>
> When the jar was filled to the top and no more rocks would fit inside, he asked, "Is this jar full?" Everyone in the class said, "Yes." Then he said, "Really?" He reached under the table and pulled out a bucket of gravel. Then he dumped some gravel in and shook the jar, causing pieces of gravel to work themselves down into the spaces between the big rocks.
>
> Then he smiled and asked the group once more, "Is the jar full?" By this time the class was onto him. "Probably not," one of them answered. "Good!" he replied. And he reached under the table and brought out a bucket of sand. He started dumping the sand in, and it went into all the spaces left between the rocks and the gravel. Once more he asked the question, "Is the jar full?"
>
> "No!" the class shouted. Once again he said, "Good!" Then he grabbed a pitcher of water and began to pour it in until the jar was filled to the brim. Then he looked up at the class and asked, "What is the point of this illustration?"

One eager beaver raised his hand and said, "The point is, no matter how full your schedule is, if you try really hard, you can always fit some more things into it!"

"No," the speaker replied, "that's not the point. The truth this illustration teaches us is: If you don't put the big rocks in first, you'll never get them in at all."[2]

Children need to be the big rocks in our lives if we truly want to change the world. Every parent reading this book needs to make sure his or her children go on the schedule first. And everyone who wants to change the endings for at-risk and abused children needs to make sure the time is committed to mentor a child, invest in a program, or volunteer with an organization helping children. Quality time will never happen if the children are not even in your jar.

Quality time clearly involves three key elements:

1. **What your children think is quality time!** Ask them what they would like to do with you. Let them help set the agenda, and you are likely to get far closer to quality time than you would on your own. Even in a mentoring relationship, it helps to ask children what they would like to do or what they would like to spend time talking about. Children, particularly teens, will appreciate being asked. If they don't have any ideas, you can suggest ideas and see which ones interest them. But the attempt at dialogue is worth the effort.

2. **Time together without distraction.** Make sure that spending time together is the main goal and not just a side benefit of doing a task or accomplishing some other responsibility. There are many times it can involve other activities, but such activities should not distract you from the goal of truly being with the child. While time with one child at a time is important in the quality-time discussion, don't forget that eating meals together as a family ranks very high in all research on positive impacts

on children. Now, if the time together is filled with tension and verbal and emotional abuse, this is of course not true. But positive time spent talking about everyone's day during a meal can be valuable quality time. My children each identified meals together in their growing-up years as significant times for them. And when you are with them, *be fully present!* Karianne and I talked in her interview about the importance of not answering your phone or text messaging when alone with your child. If you want a child to feel valued and special, be fully present when you are with him or her. It sends a message that the child is important to you.

3. **Time that helps your children discover more about themselves**. Activities and experiences that you are able to facilitate that help children know more about their gifts, strengths, and capabilities should always fall in the category of quality time. If you are there to affirm them and help them process those learning times, the impact will be even more positive in the long run. The things that children end up enjoying just by trying them have amazed me. We have had kids at camp that ended up loving archery or fishing, though they had no interest at first. You never know what children might enjoy, but helping expose them to many different activities and experiences will help them figure out what they enjoy.

Build Self-Esteem as the Foundation

The first, foundational step in every plan, however, should include building self-esteem. Most of the research around early childhood development identifies a child's self-esteem as one of the greatest predictors of future success in life.

Self-esteem is closely connected to the idea of self-worth. A child's sense of self-esteem starts very early in life and tends to ebb and flow throughout childhood and on into adulthood. I always liked the idea that self-esteem involves feeling loved and feeling capable. It takes both concepts. During my interview of my daughter Karianne, she articulated how her self-esteem had suffered when she struck out over and over in softball one season. I was the coach, and her performing well seemed to matter so much to me. She knew she was loved, but she did not feel capable in that sporting endeavor. When I asked what we could have done differently, she said she would have liked to have been encouraged to try other things, like music and creative arts. She has developed into a very gifted artist as an adult, but it is clear to me that I missed that when she was young because I don't have an artistic bone in my body. The balance of being loved and being capable was off for Karianne because of my obsession with girls' fast-pitch softball.

The older we get, the harder it is to change our level of self-esteem, so we know we must focus on developing it early in children. The process starts early of trying something (effort), persisting (perseverance), and succeeding or failing. Children will fail at some things but then succeed at others. They need adults, preferably parents, in their lives to help them navigate this journey. If it cannot be a parent (because of violence, abuse, or absence), then it needs to be another adult. This is where mentors and other role models come into play for at-risk and abused children. Self-esteem is not about convincing children they are great at everything. It is first about convincing children of their inherent value as human beings, as children of God, and as uniquely gifted people of character. But self-esteem is not just about inherent value and being loved for who they are (versus what they do). Self-esteem is also about an accurate self-perception that helps them identify strengths and weaknesses.

I have found that if children are encouraged to figure out what they enjoy and what they are good at, they will become more introspective in evaluating their strengths and weaknesses. Encouraging them in the journey of self-discovery and letting them know that no one is good at everything will give them the freedom to search for those things they enjoy and do well.

When my three children were very little, Kelly and I had a conversation one day. I think she was four years old at the time. We were playing on the floor (quantity time) and doing nothing in particular. I told Kelly I liked the way she played with me. She was being kind and sharing. She then said, "What else?" I was not sure what she meant at first. Then I realized she wanted me to say other things she did well. I decided it was a good teachable moment! So I said, "Kelly, how about if I think of one thing you do well, and then you can think of one?" She smiled at the thought of that game! And so we played! We sat there on the floor for twenty minutes while I listed something ("You do a great job of picking up your toys) and then she listed something ("I share my toys with Karianne"). It was a lesson in "bents." Kelly liked to talk about herself, and hearing things she did well inspired her to think of other things. Because of our strong family faith, over the course of the twenty minutes, I tried to weave in my view of Kelly as a uniquely gifted and talented child of God. She absorbed it, processed each statement, and then tried to come up with another thing she did well.

I realized as we sat on the floor that self-esteem does not always need to be tied to faith but it is a powerful foundation for a healthy self-image. *Merriam-Webster's Collegiate Dictionary* defines self-esteem as "a feeling of having respect for yourself and your abilities."[3] On the other hand, my definition of self-esteem comes from my faith: self-esteem is "a high regard for myself as a uniquely gifted and talented child of the Creator God." But whether it is connected to faith beliefs or not, regard for yourself is the core of self-esteem. And self-esteem is at the core of resiliency when children become teens and then adults. Resiliency, as we have discussed, is the ability to overcome trauma, stress, and catastrophe in life.

Actress Halle Berry was interviewed in 2012 about her multiple unhealthy relationships.[4] Her response was that her "picker" for picking good guys was broken. Berry was briefly married to baseball player David Justice and tried to kill herself after that marriage failed. She suffered through a marriage to Eric Benet filled with infidelity. And she ended up in an ugly custody battle with Gabriel Aubrey over their daughter. But as the interview went on, Halle Berry actually identified view of herself as the biggest issue in her failed relationships: low self-esteem. She said she never really had a father figure in her life, and her white mother was unable to help her understand the nature of being biracial or fully coming to grips with her African American heritage. Neglect (an ACE score marker) and abandonment (an ACE score marker) played a powerful role in Halle Berry's relationship struggles as an adult, and it all connected to her view of herself.

In my thirty years spent working in the domestic violence field, I have seen hundreds of young girls with low self-esteem who end up making poor choices in relationships because of their own low self-esteem and little sense within themselves of their own uniqueness, value, and giftedness.

Self-esteem is not about being arrogant. It is about having a healthy view of your abilities and what you can offer others. It is possible to think too much of yourself. Some parents often lean away from building self-esteem because they don't want their child to be self-absorbed, arrogant, or narcissistic. This decision is often a mistake. There are other ways to guard against arrogance or narcissistic tendencies. But with few exceptions, I don't think you can build too much self-esteem in a child.

The biggest problem today is children who lack self-esteem, particularly children experiencing trauma and abuse. Without self-esteem, it is tough to overcome the bad things that happen to you. It is also my strong view that bullies struggle with low self-esteem. They compensate for how bad they feel about themselves by making others feel bad about themselves. Tearing other people down becomes a powerful way for bullies to build themselves up. Often, bullies who use violence have learned violence as a power and control tactic from a parent or adult care provider in the home. Bullies are made, not born.

The research is very clear that high self-esteem can safeguard children against becoming a bully, succumbing to a bully, or dealing with teenage depression, eating disorders, early sexual activity, and a host of other unhealthy behaviors. Let's look at some of the behaviors that have been documented in children with low self-esteem:

- Angry outbursts and willful misconduct
- Internalizing emotions instead of processing them
- Difficult developing close friendships
- Self-deprecating language
- Unwillingness to take risks or risk failure

If self-esteem is the foundation of any successful "cheerleading plan," there is strong evidence that it will reap immediate benefits in the lives of children. Increased self-esteem will:

- Provide opportunities for a child to discover capabilities and competencies
- Enhance his/her ability to make decisions, particularly in stressful situations
- Give feedback on how to accept weaknesses
- Teach a child the importance of positive self-talk and self-praise
- Produce a wider social network in the child's life

Practical Ways to Build Your Own Self-Esteem

During the writing of this book, a great deal of self-reflection produced a number of significant personal revelations. As I talked to Beth, she shared how she felt that in recent years I had become less affirming with her in our marriage. It was a tough message to hear as I was writing a book on becoming a cheerleader for children. I tried to throw some empty praise at her from time to time, but she called me on it and said how much she wanted genuine encouragement and affirmation for real things, not made-up things! But it led to some personal reflection. Soon it became clear that my own self-esteem and sense of self-worth had taken some pretty major shots in recent years. The end of my political career, my failure in some important friendships in my life, and some personal heartbreaks had certainly impacted my view of myself. I had to begin studying ways to build my own self-esteem in order to be more effective at building esteem in others! But it was a powerful exercise, and virtually any of these personal recommendations can be applied to building self-esteem in others, particularly children. I am particularly grateful to psychologist Neel Burton for the excellent list of recommendations he provided.[5]

1. Make three lists: one of your strengths, one of your achievements, and one of the things that you admire about yourself. Try to get a friend or relative to help you with these lists. Keep the lists in a safe place and read through them regularly.

2. Think positively about yourself, and talk to yourself positively. Remind yourself that despite your problems, you are a unique, special, and valuable person and that you deserve to feel good about yourself. Identify and challenge any negative thoughts that you may have about yourself, such as "I am a loser," "I never do anything right," or "No one really likes me."

3. Exercise regularly. Go out for a brisk walk every day, get a good smartphone work-out application, and do more vigorous exercise (exercise that makes you break into a sweat) three times a week.

4. Ensure that you are getting enough sleep.

5. Manage your stress levels. If possible, agree with a spouse, close friend, or relative that you will take turns massaging each other on a regular basis.

6. Make your living space clean, comfortable, and attractive. Display items that remind you of your achievements or of the special times and people in your life.

7. Do more of the things that you enjoy doing. Do at least one thing that you enjoy every day, and remind yourself that you deserve it.

8. Get involved in activities such as painting, music, poetry, and dance. Such artistic activities enable you to express yourself, acquire a sense of mastery, and interact positively with others. Find a class through your local adult-education service or community center.

9. Set a challenge for yourself that you can realistically achieve, and then go for it! For example, take up yoga, learn to sing, or cook for a small dinner party at your apartment or house.

10. Do some of the things that you have been putting off, such as clearing out the garden, washing the windows, or filing the paperwork.

11. Do something nice for others. For example, strike up a conversation with the person at a checkout counter, visit a friend who is sick, or get involved with a local nonprofit organization.

12. Get others involved. Tell your friends and relatives what you are going through, and enlist their advice and support. Perhaps they have similar problems, in which case you might be able to band together and form a support group.

13. Try to spend more time with those you care for in your life. At the same time, try to enlarge your social circle by making an effort to meet people.

14. On the other hand, avoid people, places, and institutions that treat you badly or make you feel bad about yourself. This could

mean being more assertive. If assertiveness is a problem for you, ask a health care professional about assertiveness training or seek out a therapist to help you learn to say no.

I ended up actually using about ten of his recommendations during the writing of this book! And I am learning how to say no. "No" is a complete sentence. Use it when necessary.

Whether you create a list like this and follow it or develop other approaches, you need to do some soul-searching on this journey about your own self-esteem. It is very difficult to truly love others if you don't love yourself, and hard to build self-esteem in others if you don't possess high levels of it yourself.

Forgive Yourself

During a conference on Sexual Assault Response Best Practices in New Orleans, I shared with the audience some of my personal struggles because of trauma in my past and some bad decisions I felt I had made. A wonderful therapist named Jill came up to me and said, "Casey, I give you permission to forgive yourself. You need to forgive yourself, let it go, and claim freedom from it." I don't know if it was her body language, the way she took both my hands in hers, or just the caring look on her face, but I immediately realized just how much self-blame and self-shame I was carrying with me about a variety of things. I had been replaying mistakes in my head over and over. I promised her I would spend time alone and with my God and work on her challenge. It might be a message many of us need. Sometimes our biggest issue is not someone else forgiving us, it is our own willingness to forgive ourselves. Do you need to forgive yourself for anything? Do you need to let something go so you can start better positive self-talk? I did!

Soon after really focusing on recommitting to my own self-worth and value, I found it much easier to affirm Beth for her amazing gifts and abilities. She noticed it almost immediately. My affirmation and words of encouragement were focused on her character traits, things she actually did well, and not focused on pretending she did things well that she did not. And they are coming easier to me as I deal with my own self-loathing, negative self-talk, and shame.

Shame will eat at you like a cancer. Brené Brown, in *Daring Greatly*, calls shame the "master emotion." Shame is our fear that we don't measure up, that we can never measure up because of what we have done or what has been done to us. But we can deal with it. We can find people who will come alongside us and offer us grace, encouragement, and affirmation. We can tell the truth to those who love us. We can find honest people who will view our vulnerability as courage. And the loving acceptance of others will help us let go of our shame and open the door to self-esteem. Brown says it so well: "Empathy is the antidote to shame." We need to offer empathy and find those who will offer it to us. It will help us become people who realize we are gifted, talented, creative, and capable.

I have put a small saying on my bathroom mirror during the writing of this book: "I am important, deserving, loving, intelligent, worthy, compassionate, beautiful, creative, inspiring, brave, true, strong, competent, and able. I will keep acknowledging it until I finally realize it for myself."

And I posted it on my wife's mirror too. She needs it. I need it. We all need it.

The Goal: High Self-Esteem in Every Child

Healthy self-esteem is the armor of resiliency in a child. Children who fully understand their strengths and weaknesses feel better about themselves and tend to handle conflict better and resist negative peer pressure more effectively. Children with higher self-esteem hold their heads higher, smile more, and enjoy life more. They are realistic but are more optimistic than children with lower self-esteem.

In contrast, children with low self-esteem appear to have much higher anxiety levels and frustration levels when dealing with a challenging situation. All of my work over the years has consistently found that children with low self-esteem have a harder time finding solutions to problems. These children tend to have far more self-critical thoughts ("I am stupid," "I can't do anything well") and tend to become passive or withdrawn more easily than high self-esteem children. At Camp HOPE we see it all the time. They are the children who give up the fastest when trying to do something new or when challenged to do something they find difficult. Their immediate response is "I can't" or "I don't want to do this anymore."

Psychologists and parenting experts disagree on the basics of building self-esteem in children. Some agree with me that focusing on existing and developing character traits does build self-esteem. Others don't think that praise and affirmation alone build self-esteem. But what most experts agree on is that building self-esteem is about accomplishing something difficult or developing a competency or skill in something that takes effort.

Therapist Janet Lehman says it this way: "Kids cannot feel their way to better self-esteem, but they can behave their way to better feelings eventually."[6] This has certainly been my experience with Camp HOPE. Pushing children to accomplish difficult things they have never done before does, in fact, produce increased self-esteem. Conversely, the team athletic concept of "everybody gets a trophy" does not seem to build self-esteem. I remember when our kids were growing up and participating in sports, every child got a trophy and the coaches worked so hard to say something nice about every player. Sometimes it was totally empty praise! Empty praise, dishonest praise, or praise for something that is really easy and takes no effort does not seem to build self-esteem. When my kids were small and I praised them for learning to ride a bike, they beamed, and I could see their sense of accomplishment! But if I were to praise my children today for riding a bike, they would look at me like I was an idiot. It would not increase their self-esteem. Bike riding is no longer challenging, and they have been riding bikes for decades.

We need to look at self-esteem through the framework of achievement and problem solving. Increasing a child's self-esteem cannot be done externally. It has to occur internally, within the child. The child must do the work and accomplish the task or the challenge in order to produce increased self-esteem.

While most child therapists will say it is good for children to talk about their feelings, talking about it will likely only produce a fleetingly good feeling. The more effective approach to self-esteem focuses on problem-solving skill development and mastery of challenging tasks. It is like the old adage about fishing versus teaching someone to fish. If you get children talking, they may feel good about themselves for a while, but if you help them develop the skills for problem solving or help them master a craft, sport, or difficult task and see the benefits of that to their self-esteem, they will be able to build up their self-esteem themselves for the rest of their life.

But What If the Child Already Has Low Self-Esteem and Corresponding Bad Behavior?

To address or simply confront bad behavior in low self-esteem children is to miss the core of the problem. Focusing on the behavior is not a "trauma-informed" approach. The bad behavior is not the problem. The problem, as my dad used to say, is "stinking thinking." Therefore, we have to confront the thinking that a child might use to justify inappropriate behavior. Let's say that a child steals something from another child. You find out about it and confront the child who stole the item. You could march the child straight to the victim and demand a confession and return of the item. What would the child learn from this intervention? That getting caught has consequences. But will he or she learn not to steal again? That's doubtful. The child thinks that stealing something is morally OK and that he or she deserves the item more than the person it was taken from. Sitting down and talking to the child about his or her decision, helping the child articulate his or her thinking, and letting the child come to a different conclusion about his or her actions will, in the long run, produce better outcomes. If you then praise the child for returning the stolen item, he or she will associate a positive view of himself or herself with the decision to do what was right. Being forced to do it without processing the "why" of stealing will not get you to the core character issues that motivated the theft. At the child's core, he or she thought stealing the coveted item would make him or her feel better.

What about another example? What if you asked children to do something and they said they did it when you asked. But later you realized they did not do what they were asked to do and committed to do. As a parent or adult role model, you want children to respect authority and follow through with their commitments. You also want to let them know that lying about it is not going to help; you want to *challenge* that kind of stinking thinking. You could rage at the children and condemn their poor behavior. In fact, in a child with high self-esteem, this type of condemnation might produce a change in behavior. But in a child with very low self-esteem, you will likely only create shame and further self-condemnation. The goal should be to help children process and change the thinking that produced the failure to fulfill the commitment and then the choice to lie about it. Talking it through and helping children brainstorm how to make it right will always produce better results than shaming and scolding them.

Promoting Positive Self-Esteem by Setting Expectations

As we talk about self-esteem, I do want to spend some time on expectations. Expectations are powerful and generally positive in the lives of children. Children who don't know the rules, the boundaries, or the expectations of adults in their lives feel uncertain and often unstable. Children and teens need parents and other adults in their lives to be consistent and clear about expectations. You will see far more negative behavior from children, whether trauma-exposed children or not, if they don't know what you expect as an adult in their lives. And while we don't want to focus only on the behavior versus the issues and thinking behind the behavior, it is important to praise good behavior and make clear when a child's behavior does not meet your expectations.

One of the most important strategies connected to expectations is making sure you have explained your expectations, dialogued with the children about them, and hopefully grounded them in wisdom and logic. "Because I said so" is not an explanation of your expectations. Too many parents and adult role models don't want to spend the time reasoning with a child, when in fact reasoning out loud when you set expectations is exactly what children need. Don't make the mistake of thinking children are too young to be reasoned with or too old to be reasoned with about expectations. Dialogue is always going to produce better results than edicts.

Most parenting experts agree that children feel safer when parents or adults in their lives are clear and matter of fact. This objective lens can help you put a child's negative emotions into perspective. When emotions get in the way of following through on responsibilities or expectations, it's up to us as parents to focus on the behavior at hand. Then when your child does what he needs to do, you can be encouraging, reinforcing the positive behavior rather than the negative feelings and excuses that might have gotten in the way.

We all love positive reinforcement—we like to hear that we're doing a great job, and children do as well. Parents and other adults influencing the lives of children often get pulled into the emotional issues of children, especially when the child's self-esteem is shaky. But if you have a child who doesn't feel good about himself when you are working with him or her, focusing on positive behavior—and making sure he or she is held accountable for misbehaving—is even more important.

A number of years ago, I was running a domestic violence shelter in San Diego and began spending time with a teenage boy in the shelter who needed a positive male role model. I will call him Travis. One night, I went to one of Travis's high school basketball games. He had told me he did not play much, but it was much worse than that! His team got way ahead in a game, and the coach put him in during the fourth quarter. But he was only in for thirty seconds and never touched the ball, and then the coach took him out! Travis was angry and kicked the bench really hard when he came off the court. I felt his frustration and pain but could not condone his outburst at the coach. After the game, he was so upset that he kept kicking the bleachers and doing other inappropriate things. I felt terrible for him, but I also knew his poor behavior was not going to make him feel better about himself. I offered to take him out to eat but told him that I wanted to see him talk about his frustration instead of acting out violently in front of his coach and team. Once we sat down to eat, I was able to praise him for deciding to stop his behavior and talk it through with me. He shared his emotions even more openly as I praised him for verbalizing his discouragement and frustration. I could not condone his behavior. I needed to let him know the behavior was inappropriate but affirm the emotions he was dealing with in the process.

Let's be frank. The coach was a jerk. Putting a boy in for thirty seconds, and then taking him out without even letting him touch the ball? It is almost sadistic. But there are jerks in life, and Travis needed to be bigger than his coach. By the time dinner ended that night, I had praised him over and over for processing his emotions with me and spent no time condemning the inappropriate behavior. His unhappy experience with his coach was not the ultimate message of the night. The ultimate message of the night was how proud I was of him for being vulnerable, sharing his hurt and pain, and being honest in processing how he could deal with the situation differently in the future.

Let's look at another example. Your teen comes home from her sporting event and has just been cut from the "A" team and relegated to the "B" team. She's so upset that she says she can't clean her room and do her laundry. You feel terrible for her but know that having a messy room full of dirty clothes isn't going to help her feel any better about the situation. Instead, you gently remind her of your expectations, offer a little help getting started on cleaning her room, leave her to the task, and then let her know what a great job she's done when the room is clean and the laundry is done. It's not going to help her get back on the team, but it's going to give her some positive accomplishment in an otherwise unhappy day. While you cannot make the bad sports team result go away, you have been able to praise her for a different competency (cleaning her room), and she will finish the day with a feeling of accomplishment in a totally separate area of her life.

Have a Plan and Work It

Every parent's plan and every adult mentor's plan might be different, but I do want to suggest a few common strategies that should be included in most plans to cheer for children.

Use Your Words Wisely

Words matter. You can build up children or tear them down with your words. Sarcasm can destroy a child. Jokes made at a child's expense can easily cause damage that lasts a lifetime. We have done an exercise at Camp HOPE many times during which we have children squeeze all the toothpaste out of a tube and then have a race to see who can get the most toothpaste back into the tube. No one can ever get it all back in the tube. It is an object lesson. It is easy to shoot words out. It is very hard to take them back. Guard your words and always ask: Are my words giving grace to this child? Are my words building up this child or tearing them down?

The most effective communication is usually empathetic. You connect their struggle with your own weaknesses. A child who tries to sing and does not do well will always want me around. I cannot carry a tune in a bucket. I would tell the child what a great job he or she did compared to what I would have done. If I was good at something, I would still pick something I was not good at or a mistake I made in life and try to help the child see that making a mistake or not doing something well is just part of life for all of us.

Be a Role Model

Never forget that you are a role model for children. They record everything you do and say into their own developing brain. If you are hard on yourself or negative about yourself, they will likely be negative about themselves. If you are critical of others, your children will tend to be critical of others. I was raised by parents who were very critical of others—for appearance, weight, public displays of affection, and a host of other things that annoyed my parents. I am sorry to say that I picked it up and ... passed it on to my children. During our interview, my daughter Karianne identified that as a major struggle for her because of how critical I was about others in her presence growing up. We are role models for children all around us—the only question is what are we modeling for them?

Deconstruct and Reconstruct Negative Thinking

Children, just like adults, can end up with major negative thinking about themselves at very young ages. Parents and other adults in their lives need to be looking for it and ready to deconstruct it and then reconstruct a more positive approach. Our oldest daughter, Kelly, learned early on that she was not as gifted a singer as her sister. At a fairly early age, Kelly wanted to shy away from music and singing. But Beth helped her see that she could sing if she had someone near her who sang the melody with her. She went on to sing in her high school choir and enjoy music greatly, even though she was not going to be a professional musician. We worked hard to guard against her negative self-talk that could have become much more destructive.

Realism is not the enemy. If a child is not good at something, it is OK for the child to realize that, but try to reframe it as, "You probably need to work harder at that than you do at things you are naturally better at." If they are slow readers, don't let them say, "I can't read." Challenge them to realize they are good at math or at athletics but reading will likely take a little more work than things they are good at. If negative thinking takes root, it can become a cancer in a child. Letting children know you can help them work on whatever they struggle with will also help them to feel supported and not alone in their struggle.

Pour out Healthy Affection like Water

Never forget the importance of human touch and healthy affection for children. Affection is as important to human survival as water is. We will die without it. Loving touch will help boost self-esteem, self-image, and self-confidence. Hugs and gentle touch on a shoulder, arm, or head convey powerful support without a word being spoken. Beth would always put notes of love and encouragement in the children's lunches during their growing-up years. I always thought that was genius. Words of affection and love and physical gestures of affection and love all put gas in the emotional tanks of children!

Speak Positively and Honestly

Positive statements to a child will always produce better results than negative or condemning statements. Acknowledging frustration, anger, or other feelings is always good, but turning it toward a good choice that child made or tried to make in dealing with those feelings will reinforce healthy responses to such feelings. Nothing good will come from "You always get out of control so fast." The better approach, particularly with trauma-exposed children, is to acknowledge their anger but point them toward a healthy response: "I know you were angry with your sister, but I loved how hard you tried to use your words to talk it out instead of yelling at her or hitting her. Great job."

Create Safe, Loving Environments

Ideally, every child should have a safe, loving home environment. The reality is that millions of children do not. Children's self-esteem will drop if they live in fear and uncertainty at home. Children who are exposed to parents who fight feel no control over their environment and are more likely to feel helpless or become depressed. Whether you are parenting your own child after violence or abuse or mentoring a child who has experienced such trauma, you should make every effort to create safe and loving environments. This may mean less stimulation instead of more. This will generally always mean using a softer voice, even when you are frustrated with the child. And encouraging children to talk about their fears and frustrations and emphasizing your openness to helping them figure out issues and situations they are dealing with will help them know where they can go for help.

Don't Use Corporal Punishment

This is a hot topic. Corporal punishment is still legal in all fifty states. In most polling, 70 to 80 percent of parents say spanking is appropriate. If you want to juice up any book or public meeting, bring up the topic of corporal punishment and say, "Don't do it." Some cheer, some go from red faced to purple in seconds. I don't support spanking or other forms of corporal punishment. This is a very personal topic for me, and I know many disagree with me. Corporal punishment by my father became abuse. I had times when I could barely walk after my father's whippings with a belt.

As Beth and I began having children, I was running a child abuse/domestic violence unit as a prosecutor. I had to do some soul-searching and made the decision I would never hit my children, and I did not. It was too dangerous for me to use corporal punishment given the abuse I had suffered as a child. Beth did use a wooden spoon a few times with two of the children for misbehavior when they were very young, but I chose to never go down that road. I know many parents use it minimally (spanking with a hand or wooden spoon, for example) and feel strongly that it is appropriate in limited and specific circumstances. Many cite the adage—"spare the rod, spoil the child" to justify violence against children. The Bible is often the cited source for this statement though it does not appear in the Bible at all. My personal view is that "the rod" can be a variety of forms of discipline and logical consequences that don't need to involve physical violence. If you do use any form of spanking with your children, I firmly advise that you never do it in anger. But my best advice, supported by the American Academy of Pediatricians, is don't do it at all.[7]

As a parent, I strongly recommend that you consider this issue very carefully before simply doing to your children what was done to you. My primary issue with corporal punishment is that it is ineffective.[8] There is no research that says moderate or even severe spanking changes behavior positively.[9] It may stop it in the moment, but it does not change the rate of inappropriate behavior over days, months, or years. The ACE Study and other research cited earlier in the book show that physical violence actually increases negative side effects. These side effects can include the risk of mental health issues, short-term and chronic physical health problems, and altered immune systems. The better route is to focus on building up the behaviors that you want in a child instead of punishing the actions you don't want. Praising children for the good things they do produces better outcomes, in my opinion, than hitting them for the bad things they do. It is always easier to hit children than to reason with them and talk about the negative consequences of bad choices. Our children grew up to be healthy adults without years of corporal punishment for mistakes they made in their growing-up years. Our healthy, functional adult children are living proof that you don't need to physically assault children to have them grow into responsible, kind, loving human beings.

Consciously Engage Children in Constructive Experiences

Children and teens will always benefit from activities that encourage teamwork and cooperation with others. Much of life involves competition, and children have a hard time avoiding it, but self-esteem is usually better developed by working with others on a project or learning how to be part of a team. It is why mentoring programs are so beneficial and why cabin groups at a camp usually have a bond with each other by the end of the week. A good camp counselor is always pulling the whole cabin together in a way that builds cooperation and mutual support. Most trauma-exposed children don't have a good example of a family in which every member supports each other; so finding ways to build this sense of community support has a powerful impact on children.

Volunteering for community-service projects will always pay dividends in self-esteem. When our children were growing up, we worked hard to get them involved in building houses for the homeless in Mexico, bringing gifts and playing with children in orphanages, feeding the homeless, and letting them interact with victims of domestic violence and their children in shelters and other settings where they could show love and support for others. Teaching our children to serve others has paid immeasurable dividends.

Be Willing to Seek Professional Help if Needed

While the focus of this book is what we can all do to cheer for trauma-exposed and at-risk children, there are times when professional help is necessary. Children with very low self-esteem may have profound trauma issues. Sometimes professional help is necessary. I wish I had gone to counseling long ago to deal with some of my issues from childhood. If I had been able to get to counseling as a child, I would have processed them even sooner. Therapists and counselors can help children work through some of those issues. They can also help children and teens be able to sort out when they can deal with a problem and when they need to ask for help. The ability to discern between those two situations is part of developing self-esteem.

Reflections

For each child we are investing our lives in, we need a plan. Every plan may be different. Every child is unique. I have always said this, but interviewing my three children for this book brought it home so clearly. They each have different strengths. They each have different innate qualities and characteristics. They each process things that happen to them differently. Use this chapter to think through some of the key components you should include in your plan. Talk to the children in your life about what they need and what they would like to do with you and learn from you. Become a good question asker! Ask open-ended questions, and then listen to the answers from the children. Their wisdom and insight will help you develop a plan. Then, work the plan!

Eleven

Dealing with Trauma in Children of Faith

When trying to remember my share in the glow of the eternal present, in the smile of God, I return to my childhood ... for that is where the most significant discoveries turn up.

—Herman Hesse

THIS CHAPTER IS written for people of faith and those interested in matters of faith. I have many friends who do not share my faith, have deeply held beliefs that differ from my own, or who describe themselves strongly as being atheists or agnostics. With a deep respect for others who do not share my Christian faith, I have included this chapter because so many children do believe in God. In most studies, it is well in excess of 90 percent of children that believe in God or some type of higher power. Many abused children have grown up in homes where faith has been used as a tool of abuse, and even those who may share their faith don't know how to address it. *If you don't have an interest in things of faith, this chapter may be tough to read. But if you want to better understand those around you, particularly children, who do have strong beliefs, it will help you be more effective in working with them when they have been exposed to trauma and abuse.*

Most research on trauma has found that after a trauma victim's immediate physical and medical needs are met, the next profound set of needs include spiritual care.[1] And it does not matter what they believe. This has been well documented with victims of hurricanes, fires, tornadoes, violence, abuse, the death of a loved one, terrorist attacks, and other forms of trauma.[2] A good friend, Mickey Stonier, a pastor at the Rock Church in San Diego, spent nearly sixty days at Ground Zero after 9/11 in 2001. He was there as part of a national disaster-relief team to provide chaplaincy support for victims and their family members. After he returned, we had coffee at a Starbucks in San Diego, as we were planning the opening of the San Diego Family Justice Center. Mickey asked me what type of spiritual support services the center would be providing for victims and their children. I stammered and said that because of the presence of so many government agencies, we would likely be referring people elsewhere for spiritual support. Mickey lovingly reproved me! He said, "If you open a center for victims of violence and abuse and their children and don't offer spiritual support and care, the center will fail to meet the foundational needs of victims of trauma!"

Mickey went on to point out the obvious that I had missed. He noted there are reasons why every law-enforcement agency in America has chaplains, every one of the branches of the armed services has chaplains, and every hospital in America has chaplains. People experiencing trauma and people helping others through trauma, and therefore experiencing vicarious trauma, need access to spiritual-care services. He described experience after experience at 9/11 in which he prayed with atheists and agnostics at Ground Zero. It did not matter what they believed. They wanted his loving support and care, and he responded to their requests and provided the deep emotional/spiritual support they needed in the throes of the worst terror attack on American soil in the history of the country.

We listened to Mickey Stonier and developed spiritual-care support in the San Diego Family Justice Center. We later called for spiritual support to be provided in family justice centers and other community-based agencies serving victims and their children across America. This chapter is inspired by the powerful impact we have seen on victims of trauma and abuse by providing nondenominational spiritual support to all those who have asked for such help in family justice centers.

America has many faiths and belief systems. We need to be very sensitive to those faith systems and beliefs in the lives of all trauma victims, particularly children. This chapter is written help people of faith understand how to use their beliefs to support victims of trauma, and it may help those who do not have faith beliefs to support victims of trauma and abuse. This is an important piece. The feminist battered women's movement has failed to provide adequate spiritual-care services for victims and their children who do have spiritual beliefs. The church and organized religion have often failed to understand and address child abuse and domestic violence. And each side often blames the other for the very existence of violence and abuse. We must move beyond this and find ways to offer support to victims and their children that lets them believe in God if they choose to and lets them reject faith and religious belief systems if they choose to while still seeking to meet their emotional and physical needs.

God Has Abandoned Me

I should have figured out the importance of spiritual care for trauma victims long before we started Camp HOPE or opened the first family justice center in America. Early in my career as a prosecutor, I was handling a domestic violence case in which the victim was being abused by her Christian husband. I will call her Mara. Her husband was an elder in their church. He professed a strong Christian faith. And he used (well, misused) his faith beliefs and the victim's faith beliefs to justify his violence and keep her in the abusive relationship. Mara had separated from her husband because of the chronic violence and taken her young daughter with her. But the husband and others in the church were telling her that "divorce is not an option" and that she needed to come home and work through the issues and "heal" their marriage.

Mara was racked with guilt. She had briefly gone to a domestic violence shelter, where none of the advocates or case managers shared her faith or could relate to her faith. She left the shelter and ended up staying with a friend from work. But when she came to my office to talk about the criminal charges I had filed against her husband, she sobbed as she said, "God has abandoned me." I asked questions to help me understand her deep pain. Her religious beliefs did tell her that divorce was not an option. Her friends and family shared that view. Even her pastor felt she should forgive her husband and come home. He, without any specialized training in dealing with domestic violence or abuse, offered to provide couple's counseling for them. She felt that would do no good until her husband took full responsibility for his violence and abuse. Mara was right, of course. Her husband had committed multiple criminal acts against her, and he did need to take responsibility for his violence and abuse.

Mara's sense of abandonment by God should not have been ignored or minimized. And all the "professionals" working with her should have attempted to assure her that if she believed in a God of justice and fairness and compassion, she should realize that that God was not abandoning her. She needed to hear that deciding about divorce was a long way down the road and her first priority should be to keep herself and her daughter safe from the violence and rage of her husband. A "trauma-informed" approach to this issue would mean reflecting back to her all that she believed about God, Jesus Christ, and faith while continuing to affirm her value and worth in the eyes of her God. Well-trained advocates and other professionals could have and should have been doing this, even if they did not share her beliefs.

Soon after I met with Mara and explained the status of the criminal case, she called me to say she wanted to drop charges because her Christian friends and family members were encouraging her to forgive her husband and offer him "grace" and "mercy" by not pressing charges against him. As a person of faith and a domestic violence prosecutor, I had to tell Mara that offering forgiveness was her choice but committing a crime still required punishment, consequences would help create accountability, and grace did not mean we pretended like all the abuse had never happened. But I remember thinking how distorted faith beliefs can get in the midst of violence and abuse. She then shared with me how a leader in the church had reminded her that "love covers a multitude of sins." I asked her what that meant, and she said it meant if she really loved him, she needed to look past his sins and let his past violence go. She said she had a great deal of bitterness and resentment toward her husband and realized that she needed to learn to love him more deeply so she would be able to get over his violence and abuse (which also included forced sexual assault on her multiple times).

I was so thankful to be able to tell her that her journey of forgiveness and her personal choices/decisions about "loving" him were not my responsibility. Her husband committed a crime and needed to answer for his crime. I also reminded her that loving someone often requires "tough love," and tough love means you don't continue to let someone get away with violence without consequence. I required him to plead guilty to domestic violence charges. He never, by the way, truly took responsibility for his choices to be violent and abusive, and Mara divorced him two years later. Today, she is in a healthy, functional relationship with a Christian man who treats her with respect and dignity. But that case early in my career as a prosecutor reminded me how important and central faith may be for victims and perpetrators of domestic violence.

Working with Children of Faith Exposed to Trauma

Professionals and lay people working with trauma-exposed children may not be addressing the whole person if they are unwilling to talk about how a child's religious beliefs are being affected by trauma. For many young people and adults, neglecting the spiritual dimension of their lives is ignoring a core part of who they are and how they view the world.[3] Children or teens may end up in despair after trauma and abuse because their view of God or their view of good and evil has been undermined. When bad things happen to good people or when children experience the injustice of violence and abuse, their trust in their belief system may be deeply shaken.

Certain faith communities may immediately challenge an abused or traumatized child to forgive the wrongdoer because this is what "God expects you to do." In the midst of trauma and violation, children cannot accept that expectation and often face cognitive dissonance between their beliefs and their trauma reality. We must ensure that faith communities learn about trauma, and we must challenge them not to underestimate or over-spiritualize natural human physiological symptoms and reactions to traumatic events in a child's life. Too often the misuse of religious teachings is part of the abuse, and reinforcing those teachings in the midst of the child's struggle can exacerbate the trauma.

We also must be very sensitive to the diversity of religious and spiritual beliefs, and those in the faith community should be sensitive to people who do not believe in God or have decided they do not know if there is a God. In my experience working in the field of violence and abuse, I have concluded that being sensitive to spiritual matters and beliefs with victims is as important as being sensitive to head injuries, post-traumatic stress, and cultural diversity. I will not simply refer children or teens away to their particular faith community to seek spiritual guidance after trauma unless I know I am referring them to faith leaders who interpret their sacred texts and exercise their religious practices in ways that help trauma victims to heal and recover. Too much manipulation and abuse has happened in the name of faith for me to ignore the importance of the support that children and teens suffering from high ACE scores need to address spiritual issues.

I have found it is also important to know that every trauma victim reacts differently. Some victims of violence and abuse might go from believer to atheist and back to believer during their journey. Beliefs might change over time. A child's faith might be significantly affected by a traumatic experience or might not be changed at all. I recently found an overview of definitions that I think are helpful for all those working with children experiencing trauma:

- Spirituality refers to one's search for meaning beyond the ordinary human realm and centers on reality beyond the five senses. A person can be spiritual without being engaged in organized religious practice.

- Religion is an organized behavioral manifestation of values and beliefs within a certain form of spirituality. A person can be religious without being spiritual, perhaps valuing the tradition, symbolism, academic aspects, or social interaction of religious practice more than spiritual aspects.

- Faith is one's trust in or allegiance to his or her spirituality and/or religion.

- Soul/Spirit/Consciousness refers to the part of humanity that transcends the body, or what a spiritual person may consider the person's true essence.[4]

All of us working with children can find it challenging to set aside our own beliefs and values, particularly those of us with a strong religious faith, in order to validate those who hold different beliefs. In working with children and teens, we must all learn to genuinely understand and respect their beliefs. Facial expressions and body language can communicate judgment or ridicule. Tone of voice often can be interpreted as criticism or condemnation. Native American, Hindu, Buddhist, Muslim, and other children may avoid eye contact or try to avoid sharing their beliefs or values in order to show respect for an adult. I have found I tend to think they are lying to me or being dishonest when this happens. In fact, it is often their way of showing me respect.

I have also found that when I use my own faith language with someone who does not share my faith, I can put up walls between us very quickly. Learning to reflect the beliefs of a child (meeting them where they are and honoring what they believe) and listening for how he or she expresses any views of God or faith are an important part of later being able to reflect the child's beliefs back to him or her. In my work through Camp HOPE and in other settings, I tend not to bring up spiritual matters unless the child brings them up. I try not to share my beliefs unless the child asks about them. Generally, if a child trauma victim wants to talk about spiritual things, he or she will bring them up. I might ask a question such as, "How are you feeling about yourself right now?" I also might ask, "Where do you find the strength to deal with what you are going through?" If children want to talk about spiritual things, their answer will usually disclose that. If there are mixed messages, I might just ask if they want to talk about faith or their spiritual beliefs. If the answer is no, I do not explore it further.

I recently was referred to *The Complete Idiot's Guide to World Religions*. I loved a number of the ideas in the book about talking to people when you don't know what they believe.[5] I liked the idea that we should not assume that just because a child says he or she is "Muslim" or "Hindu" or "Christian," we immediately know what the child believes or how the child wants to talk about his or her beliefs. As a Christian, I have found I have to work particularly hard not to view other belief systems in the context of my views. I need to make sure that I let the children process their issues around spirituality without injecting my own faith-based views and interpretations. We should all be sensitive to not spiritually manipulating or re-victimizing trauma-exposed children through inappropriate responses to their struggles and journey toward hope and healing.

Spiritual needs in child and teen trauma survivors are often significant. Spirituality can be a strengthening factor in healing from trauma and abuse. On the other hand, some children find that the use or misuse of religious beliefs and practices has caused their abuse.

Other children have no spiritual perspectives in their lives and should not have spiritual expectations placed on them as they are trying to find hope and healing.

Personal Reflections for People of the Christian Faith

If you are not interested in my views as a follower of Jesus, move on to the next chapter. If you want to understand how to deal with trauma in children with some version of Christian faith, read on. I do want to help those who work with children who have a predominantly Christian belief system to help them understand some of the dynamics that come up for trauma-exposed children. I am not competent to share any perspective on other faith communities or belief systems.

If we are truly going to help adults and particularly victimized children with Christian beliefs and notions of God and good and evil, we need to know how to help them understand the abuse they have experienced and then help them talk about it and process it. In spiritual terms, for children with Christian beliefs, we need to let children call abuse what it is—a sin. Then we can help them understand it and deal with it without blaming themselves or thinking it is their fault. I have found two categories of sin are helpful when talking to children of faith about abuse.

The Splash Zone

The first kind of sin is when someone does something to or causes consequences for someone else, and the person experiencing the pain, loss, and heartbreak did not do anything wrong. It is the worst kind of injustice. A friend of mine describes the innocent person in this scenario as being in the "Splash Zone." Anyone who has ever been in the first ten rows at SeaWorld when Shamu splashes the crowd knows exactly what that phrase means. SeaWorld has lost some of its luster in the wake of the *Blackfish* documentary, but the image is still a helpful one to understand the concept of the Splash Zone.

The Splash Zone can hit the victims of a sniper, the family wiped out by a drunk driver, the badly burned survivors of a fire set by a pyromaniac (so common now in San Diego), a woman stalked and raped by a serial rapist, the child molested by her mother's boyfriend, and a thousand other situations like this which occur every day around the world. One person makes a choice that causes pain, trauma, or even death for another. The victim is in the Splash Zone of someone else's sin—in spiritual terms! The victims are innocent. They did not do anything to deserve it. They were just in the wrong place at the wrong time in a fallen world where evil and injustice exist.

We see this in so many Native American communities, where historic oppression—yes, the sins of others from centuries ago—still impacts those who lost their land, lost their culture, and lost their way of life because of European settlers. Many don't like to talk about it or like to write it off as "old news" or historical facts that are irrelevant to current-day realities. This is a mistake. The profound oppression and inhumanity of that chapter of American history, just like the oppression and sin of slavery, continue to play out in the lives of many Native Americans and communities of color. The recent death of a young African American man in Ferguson, Missouri, is connected to the Splash Zone of slavery going back hundreds of years. It is not simply about what a white cop did to an unarmed young black person.

When I was in high school, my brother and I were driving home one night from a party at the roller-skating rink, and a drunk driver came around a corner and sideswiped us—destroying the left side of our family station wagon. My dad was angry when we got home, but my brother and I had done nothing wrong. We were in the Splash Zone of a drunk driver, and his sin caused us pain, trauma, and consequences. I can still relive that moment to this day, over forty years later. I can place myself there emotionally and mentally. I can feel the car slamming into us. I can see the indifferent face of the drunk driver. I can hear the screeching and metal on metal. I can smell the burning oil from the engine in his car as it spilled out onto the road when his car came to a stop. It was not as traumatic as a child witnessing her parents fighting or feeling the dirty unwanted hands of an uncle or even a stranger on the intimate and private parts of her body. But it is still vivid to me all these years later.

The children of domestic violence and abuse are in the Splash Zone of the sins of others. If you grew up in a healthy family with supportive parents, you are blessed. If you never experienced the terror, the pain, or the trauma of violence in your home, you should be extremely grateful. You will have other challenges in your life, but dealing with the brain-development issues, the devastating memories, and the long-term consequences of witnessing violence between your parents will not be one of your challenges. But if you did grow up experiencing domestic violence, abuse, or the other types of trauma identified in the Adverse Childhood Experience Study discussed in chapter 1, you are dealing with the fallout. You may have had to struggle with how to parent your own children. You may have needed counseling to work through the trauma of those experiences. Or you may never have fully addressed these issues in your life.

In talking to children of the Christian faith about abuse against them, I have found that explaining the Splash Zone of someone else's sin is a good way to help them understand that they did not do anything wrong—they are victims of someone else's choices, and these choices have created complex issues and consequences in their lives.

Many in the faith community don't want to work through these terms and don't want to help children process them and understand the consequences they now have to deal with, whether emotionally, physically, or spiritually. But children do need to process all of it and their healing often depends on it.

We try to ignore the impacts in the Christian community, as in many other faith communities. The great lie of the twentieth century is that children are resilient. In churches, synagogues, and parishes, we love this notion. In fact, we all love to use the line whenever bad things happen to children—children are resilient. They will be OK. But the research does not support that statement unless resiliency is innate and unharmed in some children or is developed in other children. Children are resilient if they get the counseling they need and if they have someone who passionately loves them, cheers for them, and helps them find what they are good at. Children are resilient if the trauma has a beginning and an end, instead of chronically trapping them in violence and abuse for years and years. Children are resilient if they have mitigating factors in their lives that help their brains develop more fully after the trauma has slowed or stunted development of the hippocampus or the frontal cortex of their brain. But children are not simply resilient in the abstract.

Sin has consequences. The choices of others cause consequences for the innocent. Children end up in the Splash Zone. We all end up in the Splash Zone at times. It is not our fault, and it does not mean God does not love us or want us to heal and overcome the bad things that have happened to us.

Self-Inflicted Wounds

The second type of bad choices (sin) in a Christian worldview that create consequences in our lives involves our own bad choices. When I do things that harm myself and create guilt and shame, I have no one to blame but myself. I am at times extremely self-centered, and I make choices that hurt others and indirectly hurt me as well. I make a decision to have too many adult beverages, and the next day, the consequences are all mine. Sometimes my choices are just plain stupid, and I end up with a dislocated shoulder from diving in a whiffle-ball game. It was a self-inflicted wound when I was twenty-eight years old!

An enormous amount of research has documented the poor choices that victims of trauma and abuse may make after experiencing the Splash Zone of other people's choices. Victims of childhood trauma may turn to alcohol or drugs to dull the pain or mask the trauma. If this does not happen in childhood, it is still more likely to happen in adulthood. As we saw in chapter 1, the ACE Study has found dramatically higher rates of drug and alcohol abuse if an adult has an ACE score of four or greater. Child sexual-molestation victims may become sexually active and often promiscuous in search of love and acting out of a sense of hopelessness. Victims of childhood sexual and physical abuse make up the largest segment of the human trafficking population in the United States today.[6] As noted earlier, many trauma victims make poor health choices and fail to address chronic health issues, thereby lowering their life expectancy. As we saw earlier, if an adult has an ACE score of six, his or her life expectancy goes down by nineteen years compared to an adult with an ACE score of zero.

Adults should take responsibility for their adult choices. We cannot live our lives blaming all our bad choices on our parents, grandparents, or some adult from our past. Bad choices do often become self-inflicted wounds. But it is ignoring reality and ignoring the Splash Zone effect to not realize what is happening to us and to others we love.

Very often children don't know why they are filled with rage, and we don't help them figure it out. We just try to deal with the anger, the poor conduct in school, or the foul mouth, instead of dealing with the underlying trauma that is causing the behaviors that concern or offend us. It is more effective to help children open up about what has really happened, get it all out, and then understand why their decisions may be compromised or unhealthy at times because of the trauma they have suffered due to someone else's sin.

Messages of Value and Hope

Children of faith who have experienced violence and abuse need you to say the following:

- You did not deserve to be treated like this.
- Feeling angry about what happened is OK.
- You can talk about your feelings with me anytime.
- What happened to you was wrong.

- You are of infinite value.
- I am sorry this happened to you.
- It was not your fault.
- You can overcome this.
- You are a survivor.
- You can be stronger and more powerful in life because of it.
- I am so proud of the way you are working through what happened.
- You are loved by so many people.
- We all want to help you move forward.
- Thank you for sharing your story with me.
- I am here for you anytime you need me.
- You have an incredible future ahead of you.
- Nothing that has happened can stop you from pursuing your dreams.
- This does not have to define you; you can decide who you want to be and what you want to do in life.
- God has a special plan for your life.
- God loves you so much—that is why I am here to help you.

Statements like this will rarely be delivered at one time. Relationships with children take an investment of time and energy. Statements of affirmation and support may be delivered in the course of letting children tell you what happened to them. They may be woven into conversations as children talk about their feelings. They may be delivered in small bites over time. But the statements above need to be delivered with love and acceptance. The list is not exclusive, but it gives you a sense of how to speak truth and life into children who have been violated or hurt by someone they trusted.

Love Your Neighbor as Yourself

The last spiritual-impact piece I want to touch on in this chapter is the principle of self-love. We touched on it earlier in the book, but it is worth visiting more deeply here. There is a spiritual teaching that was spoken by Jesus two thousand years ago: "Love your neighbor as yourself."[7] Jesus at the time was challenging the people of his day to truly care for the downtrodden, the outcasts, and the marginalized. One of the powerful themes of much of his teaching as an itinerant Jewish rabbi was focused on caring for those who were sick, isolated, lonely, and hurting. It is that theme of helping those in need that has helped launch many of the world's largest relief organizations, including the American Red Cross, the Salvation Army, the Rescue Mission movement, World Vision, and Samaritan's Purse. Jesus's words have also inspired Mother Teresa's work and the work of so many others.

But the value that Jesus gives to your "neighbor" is supposed to be equal to the value that you assign to yourself! "Love your neighbor *as* yourself." It assumes you love yourself. It assumes you assign high value to who you are in your own eyes. This creates profound challenges for those who despise themselves, live in shame, and fail to see their value or worth in their own eyes, in the eyes of others, or in the eyes of God!

It is why focusing on how trauma victims view themselves, the guilt and shame they carry, and the self-loathing they hold inside is crucial. Many with deep self-hatred, shame, and loathing may need a counselor or therapist to help them work through these feelings. They blame themselves for bad things others did to them or bad choices they made in their own lives after someone did bad things to them. It is very hard to truly learn to love others when you hate yourself!

I am convinced that the spiritual truth of needing to love yourself before you can love others is like gravity; whether you believe it or not, it is true. Many angry and abusive boys and many violent and aggressive bullies actually despise themselves. And because of their own self-loathing and ugly self-talk, they don't know how to "love their neighbor."

Though Camp HOPE is a values-based and not a faith-based camping model, I do talk about this principle with kids at Camp

HOPE. Because whether you have spiritual beliefs or not, it is still true that it is very hard to truly learn to love others unconditionally and treat others well if you despise yourself and treat yourself badly!

We all need greater self-awareness around this issue of loving yourself. I have made many mistakes in my life—some large and some small. My mistakes produce shame and very negative self-talk. "I am stupid." "I am a liar." "I don't care about others." I hear my voice in my head all the time. I have to catch myself and change the dialogue. "I did something stupid [versus "I am stupid"] but I can make a different choice tomorrow." "I lied to my wife about that [versus "I am a liar"], but I can tell her the truth and ask for her forgiveness." Distinguishing between what I do and who I am helps me work through my challenges in life and maintain a healthier self-image.

Children need the same thing that I need. They need to hear positive words of affirmation in their head. In her book *Daring Greatly*, Brené Brown tells the story of her six-year-old daughter, Ellen, correcting her teacher one day in class. Ellen had made quite a mess during an art project. The teacher came over and exclaimed, "Ellen, you're a mess!"

Ellen immediately corrected her. "I made a mess, but I am not a mess!" Truth from a six-year-old! We need all children to define themselves around their significance, irrespective of things that are done to them or things they might do to themselves.

Brené Brown notes that in her research the spiritual dimension of these challenges: "Spirituality emerged as a fundamental guidepost in Wholeheartedness. Not religiosity but the deeply held belief that we are inextricably connected to one another by a force greater than ourselves—a force grounded in love and compassion. For some of us that's God, for others it's nature, art, or even human soulfulness. I believe that owning our worthiness is the act of acknowledging that we are sacred. Perhaps embracing vulnerability and overcoming numbing is ultimately about the care and feeding of our spirits."[8]

Most children I have worked with in the world of violence and abuse do have a spiritual sense within them. I believe it is their soul. I believe we all have a soul that is the deepest part of who we are. But whether you believe in a soul or not, you need to understand the truth of this reality in most children who have been abused. And we must acknowledge it and help them embrace their sense of worthiness, irrespective of what they have done or what has been done to them. We cannot truly love others until we learn to love ourselves. Children of trauma and violence also must learn to love themselves and see themselves as valuable and even sacred.

Loving Others

Once we are able to love ourselves, we are far more effective in being able to love others. We can then begin to help trauma-exposed children experience unconditional love. Such love is not something that comes naturally to me. I have had to practice it. I have had to work hard to see children from God's perspective—looking past their messes to the essence of who they are on the inside and who they are in a sacred view of life. When I get to that point, I begin to stop noticing their problems, their deficits, and their shortcomings and start to notice their potential to love, to help others, and to pursue their dreams. My love for them starts to cover their "sins," which I don't notice as quickly. I also find it easier not to judge them or be critical of them. It is the "covering" that Paul talks about in the Bible—"Love covers a multitude of sins."[9] If you truly love someone, you notice their shortcomings and failures less than if you don't love them because your love for them "covers" up their mistakes, weaknesses, and problems.

If you are a person of faith, are you applying those principles to see children in your life as sacred beings that need to find their way to self-love and self-acceptance? If you are not a person of faith, are you engaging with children in a way that respects their religious beliefs and meets them where they are in their journey of healing and hope? Do you ignore their spiritual beliefs, or do you support them even if you don't share them? Are you attempting to impose your beliefs on others, or are you allowing children to navigate with your encouragement, affirmation, and support?

Reflections

I hope this chapter has helped you think through some of the spiritual dynamics of abuse (sin) and some of the ways you need to frame it and talk about it with children who feel that God has abandoned them or that God must be angry, rage filled, and violent, just like the father figure in their lives. Whether you share my Christian faith or have a different religious or spiritual belief system, you cannot ignore the spiritual dimension of children exposed to trauma. Hopefully, this chapter will also give you strategies and tools to help children realize that being caught in the Splash Zone of someone else's sin is not their fault and not their responsibility. Sharing this truth may help them forgive themselves, reject the shame and self-loathing they might feel, and realize that the God they believe in longs to see them be healthy and happy.

Twelve

What Works in Dealing with Childhood Trauma

Gabriel Davis and Casey Gwinn

The wound is the place where the Light enters you.
—Rumi

My name is Gabriel Davis. I am the youngest of four in my family. My brother Kyle was a year and a half older, my sister, Raelynn, is three and a half years older, and my brother Jeromiah was nine years older. I share this because my family is my main source of my trauma and my inspiration.

I remember my brother Kyle and me taping baseball cards into the spokes of our bicycles, giggling and imitating the sounds of motorcycles as young children. My happy memories with Kyle were cut short. My brother Kyle was hit by a truck and killed in front of Bostonia Elementary in El Cajon, California, on April 17, 1990. The crosswalk guards gave the OK to cross too soon, and as my brother Kyle was running to greet my father, he was hit. Rushed to Children's Hospital by Life Flight, Kyle died from internal bleeding. In memory of my brother, I switched to be left-handed to wear his baseball glove. To this day, I am still left-handed.

My parents divorced when I was nine, four and a half years after the death of Kyle. Unfortunately, I was caught in the middle. One day, after baseball practice at El Cajon National Little League, my mother and father came to pick me up, both claiming it was their day to have me. My father snatched my baseball bag out of my left hand, putting it over his right arm. My mother responded by attempting to grab my bag from my father, tugging his arm. I stood between my parents, confused, hurt, and embarrassed. It was my mother's day to pick me up. I knew the schedule better than either of them.

A day passed. My father had a bruise on his right bicep from my mom attempting to acquire my baseball bag. My father took pictures and called Child Protective Services against my mother. CPS came to our house. I remember the woman; she was kind, had short hair, and wore a badge. The woman from CPS helped me find clothes to pack and told me I was going to go to my grandmother's. I did not understand why she was taking me from my mother. I felt disoriented, confused, upset, and extremely violated.

In the days and months afterward, I would bounce back and forth between my parents as they fought over custody. My father bragged about how he represented himself and how he was making my mother pay for lawyer's fees. Many more incidents occurred at other sporting events. At a basketball game, my father showed up drunk, shouting at my mother and verbally attacking my mother's boyfriend. In response to my father's actions, my mother wanted me to write a statement to the judge. I felt torn. I loved both my parents. My mother had me stay with my Uncle Mark for an extended period of time, not informing my father of my whereabouts. It felt like weeks. Both parents wanted me to testify against the other in court. Fortunately, I refused. The feeling that everything was my fault did not go away. I wanted to die.

My biological father teased me and called me names. I became a victim of bullying. I remember all through my baseball experiences, especially Pony League when I was twelve, my baseball coaches treated me differently and failed to protect me from bullying from my peers. I was already an isolated child who had no confidence to stand up for himself. I was an unwanted athlete, because my biological father would show up to games drunk and start conflict. Literally, I would be up to bat, the umpire could call a strike, and my father would argue. In Little League, an umpire who was my friend's dad actually threw my father out of the stands, because he was so verbose and drunk. I was stigmatized because of my father's drunkenness and further socially isolated. I felt unworthy when people would try to be kind to me because of my father's alcoholism. It made me feel like a charity project.

Most of my childhood and youth were consumed with me crying myself to sleep out of emotional exhaustion. I grew up hating my life and myself. I inflicted self-harm. I burned myself, often using matches on the backs of my hands. I punched wooden boards with my knuckles until my hands were raw and bloody. Only one person ever noticed my suffering. His name was Jeromiah. He was my half brother. My mother was raped at the age of sixteen and became pregnant. She kept the child and named him Jeromiah.

My brother Jeromiah and I grew closer as I grew up. He introduced me to martial arts through Bruce Lee and Chuck Norris films. Jeromiah taught me about exercise, nutrition, and philosophy. He also taught me to be mentally adaptive in order to absorb knowledge physically, as well as spiritually. My brother grew up socially awkward, not quite being black, not quite Mexican—my mother never shared the race or identity of the man who had raped her. Jeromiah grew up unaware of his biological father and suffered from identity issues. My biological father was an alcoholic who never accepted Jeromiah as his son and beat him when inebriated. Jeromiah attempted to escape his suffering through drug use.

Throughout high school and into college, I worked hard to encourage Jeromiah. He was the Hulk, and I was Captain America. During my undergraduate program in one my classes, we hosted a dinner and speaking engagement for the Syrian Ambassador; there I was being recruited by the State Department at the age of nineteen and volunteering to work for Homeland Security to fight "The War on Terrorism." My brother got clean for a time; I inspired him, and he signed up with the Coast Guard. As fate would have it, my brother was sent to Guantanamo Bay. There my brother witnessed firsthand the treatment of our prisoners, our inhumanity.

I was in the Middle East working for the State Department in Amman, Jordan, while Jeromiah was in Guantanamo. I learned of a new world. I saw refugees, the displaced, the war-torn, the persecuted, the forgotten. I saw suffering, and I saw a dying culture. From Jordan I moved to London to acquire my master's degree in Middle Eastern Studies and then back to San Diego.

When I returned to San Diego, my brother Jeromiah's life was spiraling out of control. He fell into major depressive episodes. He was tired of seeing suffering, tired of seeing the world tear itself apart. Compounded by life without a father, an abusive stepfather, and not feeling his place in the world, working at Guantanamo sent him to a darker place. One day, Jeromiah used crystal meth and ran around until the police were called. He was shot and killed by the police. He got what he wanted—a police-assisted suicide. In their ignorance, the police officers even received medals for killing my mentally ill brother—a child of trauma and abuse.

I too have struggled with thoughts of suicide in my life. Many times I have prayed to not exist. I am the product of a man who had no empathy for his son, which allowed me to be continuously traumatized and an easy target for bullies. Yet, I have survived multiple attempts to kill myself through overdose, asking God to allow me to die. I never used a gun. Once my brother Jeromiah died, I determined to never again attempt to end my life, even though the thoughts and feelings persisted. I did not want my mother to have to endure another death of a son. But sometimes I wished my mother would die, that way it would be easier to kill myself.

My heart has always gone out to those who are mistreated, misunderstood, and marginalized. I tried to express this to my father. One time when he was drunk, he told me I was going to hell for my beliefs and that I was the Antichrist and God did not love me because I wanted peace and love on Earth for all beings. The verbal and emotional abuse from my biological father and its connections to the belief of so many others in society is still raw in my life.

In recent years, I have followed my passion to help those facing social stigma and discrimination. I have worked with Save the Children, the International Rescue Committee, the San Diego Gang Commission, the San Diego Police Department (Mid-City), the LGBT community, and the San Diego Center for Children. I have volunteered to do nonviolent communication trainings with murderers, rapists, drug dealers, gang members, and youth. Two years ago, I decided to pursue a joint degree in law and social work.

During my second year of law school, one of my professors told me all of my accomplishments in life were because I was good-looking and charming. She had no idea how I would be triggered. That semester I failed law school and lost my scholarship, because I fell into a major depressive episode. I relapsed and once again contemplated how to kill myself but make my death look like a mystery disappearance, so my mother would know nothing about it. I was ready to use a gun to end my life, drive to Mexico, and shoot myself in a remote area. It has been a challenging journey to navigate forward from the setback of dropping out of law school. Understanding my own trauma, back into childhood, has been part of that journey.

I met a kind, loving man named Casey Gwinn right before I left law school. He asked me to help with Cheering for the Children, helped me find hope, and offered me opportunities to help children in different ways than being a lawyer. Mentors matter in the lives of children and adults. Casey Gwinn mattered in my life.

I am not an expert. I am a survivor.

I am not my stigma, and I will not continue to be stigmatized. I will not be defined by my trauma. I am not my biological father. I will not be defined by an addiction. I am not the ignorance of my species. I will not allow myself to exist in the depths of darkness, the hell inside myself, the waste dump of emotional chaos from childhood, the black hole devouring love in self-hatred and self-loathing.

I am the last son of my family. I have to remind myself to live so that my brothers did not die in vain, to live for my mother and decide that my life can allow other children and families to not suffer or persecute each other as I have been persecuted. In telling the truth, there is love, there is forgiveness, healing, growth, and understanding. The journey is real, and there is a path to discovery that gives us the ability to love. I am learning to have even greater empathy. It is my hope that we will all learn to have greater empathy for those around us still help captive by the pain of childhood trauma.

Initial Observations about What Works

We now know the facts. Large percentages of children and adults are experiencing or have experienced significant childhood trauma.

Research in California has found that two-thirds of Californians have experienced at least one major childhood trauma.[1] Twenty-five percent have experienced three or more major traumas. As research is continuing across the country, the national numbers do not appear to be any different. Childhood trauma is one of the top predictors of misbehavior in teenagers, major health issues, poor academic performance, substance abuse, risky sexual behaviors, criminality, and juvenile and adult incarceration in the county, state, or federal jail and prison system.

The good news is that programs are beginning to develop and emerge across the United States that are showing promise in reducing and ameliorating the impacts of childhood trauma on children and adult survivors. It needs to be the calling of our generation and our children's generation to figure out how to change the endings for those living with the impacts of high ACE scores and significant childhood trauma. I have little doubt that in twenty years, writers on these topics will read of our programs today and chuckle at how much more they have learned in developing successful prevention and intervention models. But we must celebrate the progress we are making and continue to aspire, dream bigger, and strain to see into the future.

There is a burgeoning movement across the country in many different arenas around "trauma-informed care" and "trauma-informed practices." Being "trauma-informed" means recognizing that people have many different types of trauma in their lives. My focus in this book is on children who have been traumatized and need support and understanding. Children exposed to trauma are often re-traumatized and re-victimized by well-meaning adults, care providers, and even professionals who don't understand the impact of the trauma and therefore are not compassionate and supportive when these children act out in unhealthy or destructive ways. Trauma-informed care is both an organizational construct and a treatment framework that involves fully understanding, recognizing, and responding appropriately to the effects of trauma. Trauma-informed approaches emphasize physical, psychological, and emotional safety for survivors of trauma and the professionals, family members, and friends trying to help them. It often focuses on helping survivors regain or rebuild a sense of control and power over their lives, bodies, and choices. We cannot go deeply into them here but there are excellent resources available for those interested in going deeper into the work around trauma-informed care.[2]

There are many complex ideas related to trauma-informed care and practices, but so many of these concepts can be boiled down to letting trauma survivors tell their story, being kind and supportive in the process, and helping them navigate the natural and normal human reactions to often terrible and unnatural events in their lives.

A deficit-based (or non-trauma-informed) approach says to a trauma survivor, "What is wrong with you?" A trauma-informed approach says, "What happened to you?" Powerful healing and validation come with simply being able to tell your story and being believed, accepted, and supported. It was apparent even in the ACE Study. Follow-up doctor visits were 37 percent lower for those who completed the original ACE questionnaire than for those who did not. Dr. Felitti rightly notes that the process of Confession in the Catholic Church has survived for nearly eighteen hundred years because of the cathartic power of telling the truth and being forgiven and blessed by a priest.

Virtually all of the successful trauma-informed interventions are strengths-based. Strengths-based approaches are not just working with trauma survivors. The Gallup organization has developed a powerful movement in the business and educational community around focusing on what works, instead of focusing on what is wrong. Gallup has popularized its work in Strength Finders 2.0. The nonprofit organization I lead, Alliance for HOPE International (www.allianceforhope.com) has used it with our own staff and with family justice center and community-based domestic violence and child abuse agency directors across the country.[3] Strengths-based approaches don't ignore what is wrong; they put emphasis on repeating success. This approach works with businesses, in personal improvement, and with at-risk, trauma-impacted children and adults. In the trauma world, we need to decipher and decode bad behavior and poor choices and figure out where they are coming from. Then, we need to reframe the bad into a positive so that every day there are many chances for success and progress for childhood-trauma survivors. It has worked with some of the highest trauma-exposed children I have met.

The Pain Behind F--- You

Last summer at Camp HOPE, we had a boy who I will call Gordy. Gordy had an ACE score of eight. He was fourteen years old. Gordy had been kicked out of a group home at age twelve and spent nearly two years on the streets, running with a street gang. The abuse, neglect, and abandonment issues for Gordy went all the way back to infancy. I don't actually know all the violence he witnessed or the abuse he experienced, but he was a rage-filled young man when he arrived at camp. He had medicated his trauma with drugs and alcohol. When he arrived at camp, he was a three-pack-a-day cigarette smoker. We don't allow smoking at Camp HOPE, so he needed to use a nicotine patch through the course of the week. It helped only marginally. Gordy spent the week angry, cranky, and enraged. For most of the week, he wore a baseball cap and sunglasses. It was a protective mechanism to hide him physically and emotionally from others.

I had a hard time loving Gordy. His favorite phrase was "fuck you." He used it whenever he got angry. With the goal of being trauma-informed, we tried not to focus on his profanity and swearing, but it impacted the other kids significantly. Every time I confronted him about his language or his actions, I got a "fuck you." One day he got very amped up and was chest bumping a female camper. My daughter Karianne intervened and told him that was not OK at Camp HOPE. Gordy said, "Step off, bitch" to my daughter.

I intervened, took him by the arm, spun him away from my daughter, and said, "Let's take a walk."

Gordy said, "Fuck you." In fact, he said it so much, I must confess I began referring to him (not to his face) as the "Fuck-You Boy." All week long this went on.

"Gordy, that is not OK!"

"Fuck You!"

"Gordy, please walk away from that situation."

"Fuck You!"

As the week went on, though, Gordy began to soften. It was clear he loved being at camp. He began to engage in activities. He even laughed at times. He started to relax for minutes here and there, and his rigid body and limbs seemed to release a small amount of the rage and pain he held within so powerfully. On the last day of camp, we played a slide show with pictures from the whole week. The slide show was set to music with songs the kids all enjoy (minus any songs with lots of profanity!). As they watched the show, I noticed Gordy down in the front without his baseball cap and sunglasses. He was laughing, smiling, and even singing along at times with the songs! About an hour later, the kids went to get on the buses to head home. As we passed out Camp HOPE bracelets to each child, Gordy came up to me and hugged me! Because we try to focus on affirmation and encouragement with every child, I wanted to build on Gordy's strengths as he left camp. But it was hard to be positive and affirm character traits I had seen during the week in Gordy. I struggled and even prayed a quick prayer for wisdom. And it came to me!

"Gordy, I am so proud of you. You didn't hit me all week. You wanted to hit me, didn't you?"

"I fuckin' did!"

"But you made a choice not to hit me, and I am proud of you for that. You are a leader, Gordy. Other kids will look up to you if you help them find their way in life. I love you, Gordy, and I am glad you came to Camp HOPE."

"Thanks!" And he hugged me again on the bus. I was finally able to see past his crap and his "fuck yous" and realize that Gordy needed to be loved. When I truly loved him, his "fuck yous" that so bothered me all week faded away, and I saw a teenager who has the potential to be a leader, a role model, and a protector of others. Focusing on his strengths and building on his successes was and is the only thing that will work with Gordy in relieving some of his pain and helping him find a way toward hope and healing.

Evidence-Based Programs in Addressing Childhood Trauma

There are many evidence-based approaches emerging that show promise in dealing with high-ACE-score children. I don't believe every childhood-trauma survivor needs professional help or intervention. Many need a mentor, need a caring adult in their lives, need someone to believe in them. But some do need professional programs. High-ACE-score kids have a tough time in school and in a host of other structured settings. Girls are even more profoundly impacted by high-ACE scores, as demonstrated by the research of the National Crittenton Foundation and its programs with girls and young women. When they end up in the juvenile justice system, we need better responses than the arcane system that exists today. When they end up in our health care or social service system, we need far more informed approaches. This chapter seeks to highlight a few of those approaches and tries to draw some lessons we can all learn from what is working in the mental health community, social service world, and education arena.

Child and Family Traumatic Stress Intervention (CFTSI)

The Child and Family Traumatic Stress Intervention was developed through the Childhood Violent Trauma Center at Yale University and later studied with nearly five hundred childhood-trauma victims and their care providers (usually a parent) through Safe Horizon in New York City. CFTSI focuses on working with children and their parents or adult care providers through four to six structured sessions with trained clinicians. The first session is with just the care provider. The second session is with just the child. Two sessions are then conducted with the care provider and the child together. Other follow-up sessions may then be used as needed. The goals include helping the parents or care providers know how to talk to and support the children experiencing the trauma, helping them understand what trauma does to the body and mind, and then helping them learn how to navigate the experience.

In the study at Safe Horizon, the program showed marked reductions in post-traumatic stress symptoms, such as sleep disturbances, intrusive thoughts, depression, anxiety, tantrums, or feelings of helplessness or hopelessness.

One of the key successes of CFTSI is clearly helping parents or care providers understand childhood trauma and the impact of traumatic events so they can better support the children and teens. There is no evidence to say that four sessions heals all trauma impacts in the children in the long term, but it is encouraging to see a short-term reduction in PTS signs and symptoms.

Eye Movement Desensitization and Reprocessing (EMDR)

Eye Movement Desensitization and Reprocessing (EMDR) is an evidence-based treatment for trauma recognized on a national and international level.[4] It is an integrated psychotherapy approach and includes psychodynamic, cognitive behavioral, interpersonal, experiential, and body-centered therapies. EMDR focuses first on the past trauma experiences (history) and then on the current symptoms, including emotions, beliefs, sensations, and positive experiences, in order to help children and adults develop or enhance adaptive behaviors to deal with the trauma.

There are eight phases to EMDR. The first phase is a history-taking session. This is the "What happened to you?" part of trauma-informed work. The history taking often includes the trauma, subsequent stress, and related emotional struggles. But the history session generally also includes beginning to identify the specific skills and behaviors that a trauma survivor needs for the future.

The second phase includes an assessment by a trained therapist to make sure the client is in a stable mental and emotional state. It also includes an evaluation of coping skills. Stress-reduction techniques to be used during the treatment process are usually taught during this phase.

In phases three to six, a survivor identifies the most vivid visual image related to a trauma memory or memories, a negative belief about himself or herself, and any related emotions and body sensations. The survivor also identifies a preferred positive belief. After the survivor is instructed to focus on the negative image or thought and related body sensations, the survivor is told to use his or her eyes to follow the therapist's fingers as they move across the field of vision. This may last for twenty to thirty seconds at a time. Eye movements are the most commonly used stimulus, but many therapists use auditory tones, tapping, or other types of tactile stimulation. This process is repeated numerous times in each treatment session. After the distress from the negative image or memory begins to recede, the therapist will encourage the survivor to replace it with the positive image and repeat the EMDR process multiple times. In EMDR, the process is often repeated again and again to address negative feelings and sensations and replace them with positive feelings and thoughts.

In phase seven of EMDR, the survivor will use journaling to document progress and use the self-calming activities from phase two. In the eighth phase of EMDR, the therapist will evaluate progress and help the survivor be able to practice these techniques on his or her own when needed. EMDR has been shown to reduce or eliminate emotional stress from childhood and adult trauma. Much of the research has shown that a well-trained therapist and fully engaged survivor can produce spontaneous behavioral and personal changes in relatively short periods of time.

Trauma-Focused Cognitive Behavioral Therapy (TFCBT)

Trauma-focused cognitive behavioral therapy (TFCBT) is a psychotherapy approach that addresses the unique needs of children with PTSD (or PTS, our preferred name for it when talking to children and naming it around children) symptoms, depression, behavior problems, and other difficulties related to traumatic life experiences.

The goal with TFCBT is to reduce or ameliorate PTS symptoms and related problems in as few as twelve sessions through specific components. The National Traumatic Stress Network has produced an excellent manual on TFCBT that describes the core components:

- Psychoeducation is provided to children and their caregivers about the impact of trauma and common childhood reactions.

- Parenting skills are provided to optimize children's emotional and behavioral adjustment.

- Relaxation and stress-management skills are individualized for each child and parent.

- Affective expression and modulation are taught to help children and parents identify and cope with a range of emotions.

- Cognitive coping and processing are enhanced by illustrating the relationships between thoughts, feelings, and behaviors. This helps children and parents modify inaccurate or unhelpful thoughts about the trauma.

- Trauma narration, in which children describe their personal traumatic experiences, is an important component of the treatment.

- In vivo mastery of trauma reminders is used to help children overcome their avoidance of situations that are no longer dangerous but remind them of the original trauma.

- Conjoint child-parent sessions help the child and parent talk to each other about the child's trauma.

- The final phase of the treatment, Enhancing Future Safety and Development, addresses safety, helps the child to regain developmental momentum, and covers any other skills the child needs to end treatment.[5]

Most of the outcome research on TFCBT has found that it reduces many of the significant symptoms of post-traumatic stress, including the following:

- Intrusive and upsetting memories, thoughts, or dreams about the trauma
- Avoidance of people, things, or situations that are trauma reminders
- Emotional numbing
- Physical reactions of hyperarousal, trouble concentrating, or irritability[6]

TFCBT is particularly helpful for children with major trauma symptoms and exposure, and the outcomes include additional benefits for both children and for parents. The children often show significant improvement with the following:

- Depression
- Anxiety
- Behavior problems
- Sexualized behaviors
- Trauma-related shame
- Interpersonal trust

- Social competence[7]

The TFCBT research has been found to benefit the parents and adult care providers who participate with the children in treatment. It helps them:

- Overcome general feelings of depression;
- Reduce PTS symptoms;
- Reduce emotional distress about the child's trauma;
- Improve parenting practices; and
- Enhance their ability to support their children.[8]

TFCBT has demonstrated the importance of many of the things I talked about earlier in the book, including the need of children to tell their story, be believed, learn about how trauma can impact their brains and bodies, and learn how to self-regulate and use activity and stress-management skills to overcome the stress created by the abnormal events they have experienced. The parenting-skills component is clearly important as well. We will see this even more in the next evidence-based practice.

Parent-Child Interaction Therapy (PCIT)

Parent-child interaction therapy (PCIT) is an innovative, evidence-based treatment that has been shown to help children whose behavior is disruptive and causing serious problems at home or school.[9] It has been identified as effective in addressing defiance, aggression, inability to follow directions, and other behaviors often related to prior trauma and abuse. PCIT focuses on restructuring interactions between a parent and a child in order to reduce disruptive behavior and symptoms of childhood trauma. PCIT helps parents focus on the behaviors they want to encourage. PCIT has also been very beneficial in helping parents, particularly moms, interact with their children after the children have witnessed domestic violence in the home. We began using PCIT, in conjunction with the Chadwick Center for

Children and Families at Rady Children's Hospital in San Diego, at the San Diego Family Justice Center nearly ten years ago.

PCIT involves two phases of treatment, each of which includes coaching sessions with the parent and the child and the introduction of a set of skills for the parent to master. The first phase aims to improve the parent-child relationship by concentrating on positive behaviors and trying to reduce the parents' focus on inappropriate behaviors by children in what is often called Child Directed Interaction (CDI). The second phase is called Parent Directed Interaction (PDI). In this phase, the focus is on helping parents give effective direction, set appropriate limits, understand better how to problem solve discipline situations, and decrease ongoing negative behaviors in their children. The general length of the PCIT program is twelve to fifteen sessions.

PCIT often involves placing a hearing device in a parent's ear so the parent can be monitored by a therapist during interactions with a child. The therapist can coach the parent in positive interaction with the child so the parent can build trust, create open dialogue, and focus on encouraging and affirming parenting approaches.

PCIT outcomes are very impressive, and we now have more than ten years of strong evidence of the positive impacts it has on children who have witnessed violence or abuse and their parents. PCIT has also been identified as a best practice for working with military families with high stress levels and trauma histories.[10]

There are similar lessons to be learned from PCIT's success in therapeutic settings. Children and adults can overcome trauma and abuse. Parents can learn new techniques for interacting with their children, even after violence and abuse. Children can learn to better process the impacts of childhood trauma with the help of better trained and educated parents, even if those parents have been the victims of violence themselves. Parents with significant trauma exposure can still become the cheerleaders their children need.

Trauma Smart (Kansas City, Missouri)

Trauma Smart is an innovative, evidence-based practice model provided in Head Start preschool programs in Kansas and Missouri.[11] The Crittenton Children's Center (CCC) developed Trauma Smart. Many school-based trauma-informed programs are developing across the country, but Trauma Smart was developed out of a long history of work affiliated with both the CCC and Head Start. It helps preschool children (ages three to five) and adults who care for them to navigate the impacts of childhood trauma and stress. The CCC is affiliated with St. Luke's Hospital in Kansas City, a leader in so many areas associated with sexual assault, child abuse, and trauma-informed care and practices. Trauma Smart works primarily with children exposed to the following:

- Family and/or community violence
- Family members' arrest and/or incarceration
- Caregivers' substance abuse or untreated mental illness
- Homelessness
- Separation from their parents

Trauma Smart focuses on helping school and program staff and parents understand the symptoms of trauma, identify its impact on children, teach specific skills for responding, and provide access to therapeutic intervention when appropriate. I love the "calm-down box" they have with specific toys and activities for children when they trigger or struggle to self-regulate!

Trauma Smart is one example of a program that offers high-ACE-score kids more than expulsion. We need to help these children navigate their issues and not ostracize and isolate them in the public school system.

The lessons learned from the Trauma Smart program and similar models will continue to become evident. I am particularly interested in the connections to attachment theory and the importance of attachment for young children, which we talked about in chapters 1 and 2. Attachment theory focuses on the importance of those relationships that children form, primarily with their mother and secondarily with their father or other adult care providers, early in life. The strength and health of those attachments clearly impact how children approach relationships throughout the rest of their lives. When children have warm, trusting, and predictable relationships, they learn to expect the same from future relationships. This allows them to form close friendships and trusting relationships later in life. As children spend more and more time in day-care and child-care programs, teachers are becoming more important early-life attachment figures, along with parents and family members.

As research has found in many early childhood development programs, so many issues later in life connect to the existence of healthy relationships and normal development in children from birth to five years old.[12] I don't want us to see teachers and school educators as the primary solution to trauma exposure and impacts, but they are important. For children with significant trauma, teachers may be even more critical. Traumatized children whose trust has been violated need to relearn trust in the world around them, and teachers, like other important adults in their lives, may provide a predictable, safe, nurturing environment for the rebuilding of trust.

Solution-Focused Brief Treatment (SFBT)

The solution-focused brief treatment model is a unique method of communication that invites children and adults to be their own authority on what they want in their life, rather than what others want for them. Instead of focusing on children's negative decisions or problems or telling children how to solve the situation, the practitioner empowers children to problem solve and develop their own goals and solutions.[13] SFBT uses what is called "The Miracle Question."

Miracle Question Test: Suppose you woke up one morning, and by some miracle, everything you ever wanted, everything good you could ever imagine for yourself, had actually happened—your life had turned out exactly the way you wanted it.

Think about it now.

What will you notice around you that let you know that the miracle had happened?

What will you see?

What will you hear?

What will you feel inside yourself?

How would you be different?[14]

Solution-focused brief therapy focuses on the solution, not the problem. It concentrates on what can be done, instead of focusing on what cannot be changed. Solution-focused brief therapy is about here and now, not what happened in the past.

Research has shown SFBT is highly effective with adolescents.[15] Youth who are engaged in "solutions focus" have an increase in hope and cognitive hardiness/resiliency and decreases in depression.[16] Solutions focus is an empowerment philosophy that works with adolescents who are at risk of or have experienced and witnessed domestic violence and related child abuse. Children and teens have shown remission in depressive and post-traumatic stress symptoms, improved academic achievement, and improved parent relations.[17] SFBT has also shown positive results in decreasing concentration difficulties.[18] SFBT has demonstrated an increase in the ability to solve problems and increase rates of learning [19/20]

The following is an excerpt of SFBT applied to an interaction with a homeless teen referred to as "SP":

Therapeutic Intervention: I (Gabriel Davis) inquired with SP about how he has been since the last session. I provided a familiar space for SP to communicate and express himself. Through unconditional positive regard, I provided positive feedback for SP about obtaining a sleeping bag to meet one of his basic needs. I utilized motivational interviewing techniques—open-ended questions and reflections to assist SP in exploring how his relationship with his girlfriend and cannabis use had affected his housing options. I normalized SP's challenges by recognizing his barriers. I instilled hope in SP in exploring personal goals and educated SP on goal-setting strategies, such as short-term, midterm, and long-term goals. On a scale of one to ten, I asked SP how important finding housing was. I empowered SP by asking for his thoughts on how he would accomplish his goal of finding a place to live with his girlfriend. I assisted SP in exploring barriers to his goals and housing options, such as shelters, sober living, and transitional housing. I asked SP when he thought the soonest he could find housing (to enhance his planning skills). I aimed to assist SP in exploring his goals, including access to basic needs, privacy, and a safe place to live. I asked SP what assistance he might need in meeting his goals.[21]

SFBT allows the practitioner to meet children where they are at emotionally and then help them focus on their goals through self-determination approaches—highlighting the children's hopes for the future and helping them find the pathway to seeing their hopes become a reality.

It Really Is About the "Talking Cure"

In the beginning of this book, I talked about Jean-Martin Charcot, Sigmund Freud, Joseph Breuer (Freud's collaborator in Vienna), and the story of Anna O. near the end of the 19th century. Anna O., a patient of Joseph Breuer, coined the phrase the "talking cure" for the process of doctor and patient working together to figure out what trauma and abuse had occurred to so many women being diagnosed with "hysteria." Anna O. realized more than one hundred years ago that telling the story is cathartic, being believed brings healing, and addressing the trauma puts you on a pathway to hope. Though virtually all the doctors investigating "hysteria" and its connection to childhood sexual abuse, including Freud, recanted their work and ignored the truth of their findings, Anna O., a survivor of child sexual abuse, found her way forward and became a pioneer in the early women's liberation movement.[22] Anna O., the woman who invented the "talking cure", recovered from her post traumatic stress and went on become a prominent feminist social worker. Her real name was Bertha Pappenheim. During her amazing life, she founded a feminist organization for Jewish women, ran an orphanage for girls, and campaigned against the sexual exploitation of women and children. I love a quote about her from philosopher Martin Buber, who wrote these words shortly after her death: "I not only admired her but loved her, and will love her until the day I die. There are people of spirit and there are people of passion, both less common than one might think. Rarer still are the people of spirit and passion. But rarest of all is a passionate spirit. Bertha Pappenheim was a woman with just such a spirit. Pass on her memory. Be witnesses that it still exists."[23]

In her will, Bertha Pappenheim made clear what she wanted if people visited her grave. She asked that each visitor leave a small stone "as a quiet promise...to serve the mission of women's duties and women's joy...unflinchingly and courageously." It just went on my bucket list—leaving a small stone at Bertha's grave.

Reflections

Many dedicated and caring professionals, investors, and government leaders are contributing enormous amounts of time and energy in learning about the impacts of childhood trauma, the importance of early childhood development, and successful intervention and prevention measures. We can all learn from the evidence-based work being done by professionals in the area of childhood trauma. Trauma narration and storytelling are cathartic and therapeutic in virtually all settings for survivors. We need to focus on the underlying adversity and not on the behaviors of survivors if we truly want to meet their needs and mitigate the potential long-term impacts of childhood trauma. The sooner we engage with children, the better. The longer we wait, the more complicated and expensive the solutions are. Many of us have exposure to trauma, and we can and must relate with love and care to those with even more profound impacts. Focusing on strengths and pointing children toward the future, instead of letting them stay stuck in the past, helps create a pathway to hope and healing. For me, Gabe, Bertha Pappenheim, and so many other childhood-trauma survivors, the wound was the place where the Light was able to enter and the journey to hope and healing began.

Thirteen

Leaving a Legacy

Time is too slow for those who wait, too swift for those who fear, too long for those who grieve, too short for those who rejoice, but for those who love, time is eternity.

—Henry van Dyke
Author, Educator, Clergyman

YOUR GREATEST CONTRIBUTION in life will be made in the lives of those you love. Whether you are a person of faith or not, what outlives you will be your investment in children and others, who will live their lives differently because of you. I worked with an attorney many years ago who did not believe in God or life after death, but I remember asking her what caused her to care so much about her children. She said, "My children are my life after death. After I am gone, I will live on through them because of the way I loved them, taught them, and cared for them." I do believe in life after death, and I do believe that decisions and actions in this life matter in the context of eternity, but she spoke truth from her own beliefs. In our quietest places, deep in our hearts, we all want to leave a legacy—some evidence that it mattered we were here on Earth. For some, mistakes and bad decisions have created a wake of pain and heartbreak, and it is hard to see how we can leave a legacy that is positive and affirming. But if you are still reading this book, you have made it through a lot of difficult concepts and ideas, and you have the opportunity to still leave a legacy of hope and healing. If you have breath, it is not too late.

A dear friend of mine, whom I will call Al, now in his late eighties, has an enormous amount of regret about how he raised his children. But he told me many years ago that he wanted to invest in Camp HOPE because it was his way of making a difference in the lives of other children. He also told me how he began investing in his grand-children in ways that he had never invested in his own children. Al is leaving a legacy that will outlive him—with his grandchildren and with many children he will never personally meet. *Cheering for the Children* is an opportunity to renew your commitment to children, no matter what mistakes you have made in the past. Reach out to your children or grandchildren if forgiveness and healing are necessary. If you have never been invested in children, engage for the first time in trying to make a difference in children in your community who need to be loved and cheered for by someone outside their own immediate family.

Legacy discussions are always difficult. We cannot decide person-ally what our legacy will be. Others will decide that for us after we are gone. Thinking about legacy means thinking about the finite nature of life. Nobody makes it out of this life alive. We all have a beginning and an end. My life began in 1960. Right now, I am in the "–"; my life is the dash. There will be another year put after the dash. It might be 2015. It might be 2025 or 2035. I don't know. We don't get to decide the first number or the last number. But we do get to decide what the dash means in between the two numbers. And the dash is always made up of good things and bad things. No one does all "good," and no one does all "bad." I have bad things in my dash that I cannot change. I can choose to live with the shame and guilt of those mistakes, or I can focus on the opportunities I have to do good things for those I love and those God brings into my life before the second number gets tagged onto my dash.

I choose to move forward—every day, one day at a time. It is why family justice centers and Camp HOPE are two of the great passions of my life. It is why I just interviewed each of my children for the writing of this book. I want to be a *hope* giver. I want to be someone who is honest and vulnerable enough to admit my mistakes and try to learn from them. Shame is never a platform for healing and hope. If *hope* brings healing, then I need to be a person of *hope*. I need to eliminate the ugly, negative self-talk that sometimes fills my head and replace it with the truth about who I am—a unique, gifted person who has gifts and abilities that can encourage others around me. We all need to do that. We need to surround ourselves with people who encourage and affirm us. Negative, critical people are like a cancer. But people who speak grace and forgiveness and share their own mistakes so we can know that we are not alone—those are the people we need to be around.

We all need to make sure we are getting the care, love, affirmation, encouragement, and support we need in order to be able to help others. No one with an empty emotional gas tank can do much to offer hope and encouragement to others around him or her. The impact of vicarious trauma (the trauma others are experiencing and discussing with you) is significant and cumulative. You end up needing the same kinds of care and support that those you are helping need. You need to be loved and encouraged. You need to maintain and build up your own resiliency. You need to maintain healthy self-esteem and regularly evaluate how you are personally doing in the face of all you are dealing with on a daily basis.

You need to make sure you love yourself in order to be able to love others. And if you don't find that you love yourself, you need to take steps to find your way back to that place of loving yourself, valuing who you are and who you are becoming. It might take some counseling and professional help. It did for me. It might take the courage to be really honest with those around you who can love and support you. Brené Brown in her book *Daring Greatly* says: "*Courage starts with showing up and letting ourselves be seen.*" She also writes: "*Vulnerability sounds like truth and feels like courage. Truth and courage aren't always comfortable, but they're never weakness.*" My journey in writing this book has been a difficult one. I am a very imperfect cheerleader for children. I have sometimes focused like a laser on being a cheerleader and other times have allowed my own issues and struggles to totally sidetrack me from truly caring about my own children or other children who have come into my life. But being honest about our mistakes always enables us to start looking forward.

If you really want to take stock of how you are doing or how you did as a parent, interview your children like I interviewed mine for this book. Here are the questions I asked my adult children:

How would you describe growing up in our home in general terms?

Do you feel we expressed our love for you enough?

Gary Chapman says there are five love languages:

- *Words of affirmation*
- *Acts of service*
- *Receiving gifts*
- *Quality time*
- *Physical touch*

How would you rank those five concepts in how you best experience love and support?

How did we do in meeting those needs based on the way you best experience feeling loved?

What are your best memories?

What are your most difficult memories?

What do you think I did best as a parent?

What do you think Mom did best as a parent?

What things did I do as a dad that caused you pain or difficulty in life?

Are there things you saw in Mom or me as a parent that you want to do differently when you become a parent?

Do you think we encouraged you enough? Were there times when you needed more encouragement or support and we did not provide it?

How could we have encouraged or affirmed you more?

Are there other things you wish we had done or things you wish we had not done with you or said to you?

Interviewing your children is not for the faint of heart. You have to come to it with an open heart and be willing to hear hard things if your children need to say them. But it will help you reflect on how you can better support your grandchildren or other children who may come into your life. It can also help begin the healing process for your children with their own struggles. Asking for forgiveness might be high on your list of priorities after you dialogue with your children about these questions. It was for me. But it was not all bad either. Many of the things we did with our children were very positive and played a role in their own resiliency in life.

Some powerful things jumped out from these interviews—things we did that I never realized the power of until my children shared it with me. My children said they valued the following:

- Individual trips and special activities with each child separately
- Family vacations where we were all together and there were few distractions (camping, house boating)
- Notes, cards, and letters written to them expressing love, affir-

mation, and personalized encouragement (especially when it was not for a birthday or formal occasion)

- Affection and physical touch throughout their growing-up years
- Regular, verbalized "I love yous" and clear statements of appreciation for who they were or about character traits we saw in them
- Us being there for their events, activities, sports teams, and significant moments
- Us asking questions about their days, lives, and relationships
- Us praying with them every night and debriefing them about their day (especially when they were younger)
- Having a home where all their friends wanted to come and hang out
- Our messages to our daughters about high standards for boys in their lives ("Don't settle")

Our son also noted that witnessing how I treated his mother taught him how to respect and honor girls. And our daughters said that seeing the way I treated their mother showed them what kind of man they wanted in their lives.

I wish I had been humble enough and open enough to interview my children while I was still raising them. Their insight was very accurate and helpful to me, but they are all adults now, and the lessons learned from the interviews won't allow me to make mid-course corrections like I could have if I had crafted some age-appropriate questions when they were in their teens or even younger.

As we wrap up this book, let me share a few of the lessons I have learned from the research for this book and some of my own reflections on leaving a legacy of hope in the lives of children. My perspective is framed by my experience as a man and as a father, so I cannot speak as well to the role of moms and women in the lives of children, but the lessons are still applicable to both men and women.

We all leave a legacy to our own children and other children in our lives. If your experience with your father and mother was healthy and positive, you have an advantage in leaving a healthy legacy to your children. If your experience had negative elements, as most of ours did, your goal should be to leave a different or better legacy for your children and the children who come into your life.

1. **You can never be too positive or affirming with children.** Find ways every day to encourage children and praise them for character you see in them, efforts made in various tasks and responsibilities, and ways they encourage or help others.

2. **Ask questions that expect narrative answers.** Too often as we dialogue with children, we ask them, "How was your day at school?" And the conversation ends with, "Fine." My wife and I always found that asking our children about their favorite part of the day and their toughest part of the day produced more discussion than one-word answers or yes-or-no questions.

3. **Empathy always opens doors.** It is generally always better to find a way to connect with children and let them know that their experience is similar to yours in some way. Therapist David Wexler calls it "twinship" experiences.[1] If children don't think you can relate and you don't help validate their feelings or experiences, it is tough to make a connection that can grow into a hope-giving relationship.

4. **Listen more than you talk.** As a man, I tend to want to be a fixer. Tell me your problem, and I will help you solve it. But children, especially trauma-exposed children, need to tell you what happened. They need you to ask good questions. They need you to validate and not judge them. They don't need you to try to fix it or push past their feelings quickly. Throughout

the book, from the ACE Study on, we have seen the power of listening and kind, thoughtful responsiveness.

5. **Try to be trauma-informed in your responses.** We have looked at how trauma impacts human beings. We have seen how children act out because of trauma and often engage in behaviors that we don't like and want to discourage. But if we get distracted by their behavior and focus on it, we will not help them process the underlying trauma that is causing the behavior. For all the complex work being done by professionals around "trauma-informed care" and "trauma-informed practices," I remain convinced that being trauma-informed means we are compassionate, kind, and loving in our response to what children (and adults) have gone through. We don't blame or shame if we are sensitive to the trauma people have experienced. We listen and let them share their pain and loss, instead of trying to steer them to only talk about the things in their story we are interested in. We try to help them see that they are not abnormal or suffering from a "disorder" because of the way they reacted to a very abnormal situation.

6. **Focus on strengths, not on weaknesses or deficits.** We should always look at the strengths that children exhibit amid the pain or the trauma they are experiencing. The strengths they have will allow them to move forward. Focusing on their failures or their weaknesses will not help them overcome them. Resiliency is all about finding ways to build children and teens up and increase their self-esteem and sense of self-efficacy—their ability to solve problems and work through issues in their lives.

7. **Engage in healthy physical affection.** Children, especially abused children, need to know what healthy, nonsexual affection feels like. They need to see and feel the universal language

of affection—soft touches, hugs, gentle touches of the head and hair, hand holding when appropriate, and even kisses on the forehead or cheek. This is always a controversial subject in the world of child maltreatment professionals, but children need it, and we all need to figure out how to express affection in a way that is appropriate, consensual, and nonthreatening. We all need affection in our lives, and children who have experienced trauma and abuse probably need it more than other children. Most children get it naturally, but when physical touch has been experienced as sexual or physical abuse, we must not then refrain from any touch or affection with those children. They need it more than ever.

8. **Use your power and influence to bless children.** Adults have enormous power and influence in the lives of children. Most of the children experiencing violence and abuse have suffered at the hands and words of adults who have misused their power and influence. Caring, loving adults must counteract that misuse of power with positive use of their position. Children long for approval and are shaped by the examples that adults set for them. Even teenagers, who often describe their parents as idiots and morons, still say that approval or disapproval of their parents is one of the most significant social forces in their lives. We need to use this power to build them up and help them feel blessed and favored.

9. **Say you are sorry when you need to.** It is healthy and good for parents to apologize. Sadly, it is way too rare. During the interviews of my children, they all said they wished I had apologized more when I did something wrong or reacted inappropriately. They were glad for the times I did apologize, but they each said those apologies were few and far between. My attempts to project an image of perfection did not fool my

children." All of us should apologize more, but not flippantly. Save it for when you really screw up and everyone knows it. You are not fooling anybody by pretending you were right when a child that your mistake impacted knows just how wrong you were. My son, Chris, told me it would have been helpful if I had been more honest about my mistakes in my life (of which there were many) so that he did not think he was the only one with struggles.

10. **Become an expert on each child you invest yourself in.** You need to become an expert in the uniqueness of each child, whether that child is your own or someone else's. Children, even in the same family, are so totally different. Learn to study children, see their personality traits, see how they deal with different situations, and understand their strengths and weaknesses. Don't try to fit them into a box or into the image of the child you think they are or want them to be. I made that mistake to some extent with our middle daughter, Karianne. She was so different from her brother and sister—far more in tune with her own feelings and the feelings of others. She tended toward transference (internalizing the feelings of others around her), and I did not see it and therefore could not help her figure out how to process those feelings and her reaction to them. She needed different encouragement and support, and I was not very effective at providing it to her. I wish I had known her language of love sooner, as well. I thought she felt love the same way I felt love—through words of affirmation and support. Those did play a positive role, but her primary language of love is quality time. Her close second is physical touch. Quality time barely made my personal top five, so I did not prioritize that personalized time alone with her as much as I should have.

We can all change the ending for ourselves, even if we have ACE scores greater than zero. We can change it for our children. Remember, my dad was a six on the ACE score index. I had three ACEs. My adult children, now two generations away from their extremely abusive great-grandfather, each have an ACE score of zero. We can get the help we need, make different choices with the children in our lives, and lean into the hard work of creating pathways to hope for others.

Come Home

I want to conclude this book with one final story a friend shared with me. A young girl, who I will call Carrie, grew up in a home with violence and abuse. Carrie ran away from home to get away from her abusive father and ended up in a human trafficking ring in a major city. She became drug and alcohol addicted. She was lost in shame and pain. But her mother, a survivor herself, never gave up on her daughter. She didn't know where she was but she kept searching for her; putting up posters in city after city. The posters included a picture of her mother and a phone number, and this compelling invitation: "Whatever you have done, whatever you have become, I still love you, come home." Years passed as the mother hoped and prayed for her teenage daughter's return. And finally, nearly three years after the first poster went up, the exhausted, broken, shame-filled teenager climbing up a stairway in a run down apartment building was stunned to see her mother's picture on a piece of paper on the wall. She read the words on the poster with tears streaming down her face and found her way home toward hope and healing.

May we all be that passionate and loving in our effort to save the children of America—children trapped in trauma and heart-break because of the actions of abusive adults and then their own poor choices in trying to cope with the unbearable pain. May those of us struggling with our own trauma be willing to accept the same message: "Whatever you have done, whatever you have become, you are still loved, come home."

Final Reflections

We know the negative impacts for so many children of growing up with violence, abuse, and neglect. We know the enormous costs of trying to deal with the consequences of unmitigated trauma in the lives of children and adults in the health care system. We know of the large percentage of inmates in local, state, and federal jails and prisons who have come out of homes with child abuse, domestic violence, and/or drug and alcohol abuse. We know who is most likely to kill law-enforcement officers in the line of duty. We know what ACEs mean for children and later for adults. We know the legacy of violence and abuse and the trauma it causes in the lives of children and later in their lives as adults. The questions are now before us: Are we willing to try to change the endings? Are we willing to invest the time and the resources to change the probabilities for those with ACEs? Are we willing to help children leave a different legacy for their children?

Each of us has the ability to do something. Some have the power and influence to change public policy in America. Others have the power to invest far more corporate and philanthropic dollars in at-risk and high-risk children and teens. Some have the power to change the priorities and strategies of their church youth programs. Others have the ability to raise awareness in a school, place of work, or community organization. We all have the ability to invest our own time and resources in mentoring a child. What will your legacy be? What will you do to help the children in your life have a different legacy than their parents or stepparents? We each have choices to make every day in how we can express love for the children of this generation and the next generation. Our choices today will impact eternity through the lives of those we love. It is my hope and prayer that we will all learn to leave a legacy of cheering for the children.

About the Author

CASEY GWINN, JD, is president of Alliance for HOPE International (formerly the National Family Justice Center Alliance), a frequent speaker in communities across America and the visionary behind the Family Justice Center movement. Previously, he served for eight years as the elected city attorney of San Diego. During a twenty-year career as a prosecutor, he focused on the prosecution of domestic violence, child abuse, and sexual assault offenders.

He served on the U.S. Attorney General's National Advisory Committee on Violence Against Women, the American Bar Association Commission on Domestic Violence, and the U.S. Department of Defense task force studying the handling of family violence throughout the department. He also chaired the California Attorney General's Task Force on Domestic Violence.

He has received many local and national awards, including the California Peace Prize from the California Wellness Foundation.

He is the author of numerous articles on domestic violence and has coauthored nine books, including *Hope for Hurting Families: Creating Family Justice Centers Across America*, *Hope for Hurting Families II: How to Start a Family Justice Center in Your Community*, and *Dream Big: A Simple, Complicated Idea to Stop Family Violence*.

Gwinn is the founder of Camp HOPE, the first specialized camp in America focused exclusively on children exposed to domestic violence. All of the proceeds from the sale of this book will benefit Camp HOPE.

Acknowledgements

IT IS ALMOST impossible to thank all those who have made this book possible. Hundreds of dedicated friends, supporters, colleagues, survivors, and others have shared the vision for this book and the work of changing the destinies of children both in San Diego and across the United States. Thank you to Lori Leavitt and Grael Norton at Wheatmark Press for believing in this project. A special thank-you to my amazing wife, Beth, and my uniquely gifted children, Kelly, Karianne, and Chris, for sharing their hearts and lives with me in the writing of *Cheering for the Children*. To our "dream team", our Board and staff members at Alliance for HOPE International—Gael Strack (our tireless and relentless cheerleader), Ashley Walker, Robert Martin, Clint Carney, Jerrilyn Malana, Mike Scogin, Michael Mason, Ted Bunch, Sarah Buel, Dean Hawley, Kim Wells, Oliver Williams, Denise Gamache, Jennifer Anderson, Michael Burke, Natalia Aguirre, Michela Farnsworth, Chris Burlaka, and Ruth Samson—for putting up with me during this journey and giving tremendous feedback and input to the ideas and concepts in the vision shared here.

I must give a special thank-you to the funders and supporters who have helped start and develop the family-justice-center movement and others now supporting the Camp HOPE movement. The California Endowment, the U.S. Department of Justice, Office on Violence Against Women (including Bea Hanson, Darla Sims, and Susan Williams), the Qualcomm Foundation, Mount Hermon Association, San Diego Gas & Electric, Price Charities, the Discount Tire Driven to Care Foundation, the Donner Foundation, the Walmart Foundation, In-N-Out Child Abuse Foundation, San Diego County District Attorney Bonnie Dumanis, the Verizon Foundation, Blue Shield of California Foundation, the Charles and Mildred Schnurmacher Foundation, the Walt and Mary Zable Foundation, and hundreds of individual donors who have contributed tirelessly to our vision for changing the destinies of trauma-exposed children. And to Barbara Bethel, who has joined her life with ours to develop Camp HOPE Bethel Ranch.

We have had some very strategic thinkers, in nearly ninety family justice centers, to ensure trauma-informed services, survivor-defined success, and integrated approaches to helping adult survivors and their children. Thank you to Lisa Olson (Director of Programs, Mount Hermon/Kidder Creek), Charles Wilson (Chadwick Center for Children and Families at Rady Children's Hospital), Rebecca Lovelace (Boise Family Justice Center), Suzann Stewart (Tulsa Family Safety Center), Mary Claire Landry (New Orleans Family Justice Center), Alameda County District Attorney Nancy O'Malley, Raeanne Passantino (Alameda County Family Justice Center), Melissa Erlbaum (A Safe Place Family Justice Center of Clackamas County), Dr. Chan Hellman (University of Oklahoma), and Lt. Misty Cedrun (San Diego Family Justice Center). A special thank-you to one of the most passionate advocates for children in the family-justice-center and Camp HOPE movements today—Michael Burke, the Director of Community Engagement at Alliance for HOPE International.

I want to single out and thank Gabriel Davis, a graduate student at San Diego State University, for his tremendous research support for this book. Gabe coauthored chapter 12 on evidence-based programs and shared his own childhood trauma journey in the book. He is an amazing young man who has already impacted thousands of children. Gabe, so many other survivors of childhood trauma, and the amazing children of Camp HOPE inspire me every day.

Endnotes

Chapter 1

1. S. Bowles, "Did Warfare among Ancestral Hunter-Gatherers Affect Evolution of Human Social Behavior?," *Science* 324, no. 5932 (2009): 1293–98.

2. Jon Bois, "Home Advantage in Sports: A Scientific Study of How Much it Affects Winning," SB Nation (blog), January 19, 2011, accessed October 11, 2014, http://www.sbnation.com/2011/1/19/1940438/home-field-advantage-sports-stats-data. A major longitudinal study of NBA, NFL, MLB, and NHL teams found home-field advantage existed at varying levels for all teams in all sports. There is little basis to find this has any other cause than the presence of hometown fans and, in many cases, the deafening cheers of the hometown crowd in support of their team and in opposition to the visiting team.

3. N. J. Balmer, A. M. Nevill, and A. M. Williams, "Home Advantage in the Winter Olympics (1908–1998)," *Journal of Sports Sciences* 19, no. 2 (2001): 129–139.

4. "Trauma-Informed Approach and Trauma-Specific Interventions," Substance Abuse and Mental Health Services Administration, accessed January 2, 2015, http://www.samhsa.gov/nctic/trauma-interventions. According to SAMHSA's concept of a trauma-informed approach, "A program, organization, or system that is trauma-informed: *Realizes* the widespread impact of trauma and understands potential paths for recovery; *Recognizes* the signs and symptoms of trauma in clients, families, staff, and others involved with the system; *Responds* by fully

integrating knowledge about trauma into policies, procedures, and practices; and Seeks to actively resist*re-traumatization.*"

5. R. Lanius, E. Vermetten, and C. Pain, eds., *The Impact of Early Life Trauma on Health and Disease: The Hidden Epidemic* (Cambridge University Press, 2010).

6. Center on the Developing Child, *Building the Brain's "Air Traffic Control" System: How Early Experiences Shape the Development of Executive Function* (working paper no. 11), 2011, accessed December 6, 2014, http://www.developingchild.harvard.edu.

7. R. Listenbee and J. Torre, *Report of the Attorney General's Task Force on Children Exposed to Violence*, National Task Force on Children Exposed to Violence, 2012, accessed June 5, 2014, http://www.justice.gov/defendingchildhood/cev-rpt-full.pdf.

8. V. J. Felitti, R. F. Anda, M. D. Nordenberg, M. S. Williamson, and S. James, "Relationship of Childhood Abuse and Household Dysfunction to Many of the Leading Causes of Death in Adults: The Adverse Childhood Experiences (ACE) Study," *American Journal of Preventive Medicine* 14 (1998): 245–258. For more information on the Adverse Childhood Experience Study, go to http://www.acestudy.org. Accessed December 13, 2014.

9. V. J. Felitti and R. F. Anda., "The Relationship of Adverse Childhood Experiences to Adult Medical Disease, Psychiatric Disorders and Sexual Behaviors: Implications for Healthcare. R. Lanius, E. Vermetten, and C. Pain, eds., *The Impact of Early Life Trauma on Health and Disease: The Hidden Epidemic* (Cambridge University Press, 2010), pp.77-87.

10. Ibid.

11. V. J. Felitti, "The Relationship of Adverse Childhood Experiences to Adult Health: Turning Gold into Lead," *Zeitschrift fur Psychosomatische Medizin und Psychotherapie* 48, no. 4 (2002): 359–369.

12. Ibid.

13. G. Griffin, Z. Martinovich, T. Gawron, and J. S. Lyons, "Strengths Moderate the Impact of Trauma on Risk Behaviors in Child Welfare," *Residential Treatment for Children and Youth* 26, no. 2 (2009): 105–118. The ACE Questionnaire is a powerful tool now being used with both adults and teenage children to evaluate the trauma exposure in their lives.

14. "About ACE," Centers for Disease Control and Prevention, accessed October 20, 2013, http://www.cdc.gov/ace/findings.htm.

15. "About ACE," Centers for Disease Control and Prevention, Accessed October 21, 2013, http://www.cdc.gov/ace/prevalence.htm#ACED.

16. Lanius et al., *Impact of Early Life Trauma*, 80.

17. Ibid.

18. Ibid, 82.

19. J. A. Reavis, J. Looman, K. A. Franco, and B. Rojas, "Adverse Childhood Experiences and Adult Criminality: How Long Must We Live Before We Possess Our Own Lives?," *The Permanente Journal* 17, no. 2 (2013): 44–48.

20. See http://acestudy.org/ace_score, accessed October 21, 2014.

21. Exodus 20:5 (New International Version).

22. Anonymous, "Dear Doctor," *The Permanente Journal* 6, no. 1 (2002). Printed with permission.

23. Herman, J. (1992), Trauma and Recovery: The aftermath of violence—from domestic abuse to political terror, (Basic Books, New York, NY), 7-13.

24. Ibid.

25. Ibid, 14.

26. Ibid.

Chapter 2

1. Center on the Developing Child at Harvard University (2011). *Building the Brain's "Air Traffic Control" System: How Early Experiences Shape the Development of Executive Function: Working Paper No. 11*, accessed January 15, 2015, www.developingchild.harvard.edu.

2. Interview with TKF mentors and former gang members, April 21, 1999.

3. K. A. Fox, K. A. Ruffino, and G. A. Kercher, "Crime Victimization and Gang Membership," Crime Victims' Institute, Sam Houston University, 2011, accessed October 20, 2013, http://dev.cjcenter.org/_files/cvi/Gang_Crime_Victimization_final.pdf.

4. M. De Santis, "The Youth Gang Connection," Women's Justice Center, 2014, accessed November 21, 2014, http://justicewomen.com/help_gang.html.

5. R. Karr-Morse and M. S. Wiley, *Scared Sick: The Role of Childhood Trauma in Adult Disease* (City of Publication: Atlantic Monthly Press, 2012).

6. S. Drury, E. Mabile, Z. H. Brett, K. Esteves, E. Jones, E. A. Shirtcliff, and K. P. Theall, "The Association of Telomere Length with Family Violence and Disruption," *Pediatrics* 134, no. 1 (2014): e128–e137, accessed December 12, 2014, http://pediatrics.aappublications.org/content/early/2014/06/10/peds.2013-3415.

7. A. L. Kirkengen, "Ghosts from the Nursery: Tracing the Roots of Violence by Robin Karr-Morse and Meredith S. Wiley," *The Permanente Journal* 18, no. 2 (2014).

8. A. L. Kirkengen, "Ghosts from the Nursery: Tracing the Roots of Violence by Robin Karr-Morse and Meredith S. Wiley," *The Permanente Journal* 18, no. 2 (2014).

9. J. A. Reavis, J. Looman, K. A. Franco, and B. Rojas, "Adverse Childhood Experiences and Adult Criminality: How Long Must We Live Before We Possess Our Own Lives?," *The Permanente Journal* 17, no. 2 (2013): 44–48.

10. Kirkengen, "Ghosts from the Nursery," e129.

11. R. Boynton-Jarrett, L. Rosenburg, J. R. Palmer, D. A. Boggs, and L. A. Wise, "Child and Adolescent Abuse in Relation to Obesity in Adulthood: The Black Women's Health Study," *Pediatrics* 130, no. 2 (2012): 245–53.

12. S. E. Hadland et al., "Suicide and History of Childhood Trauma among Street Youth," Journal of Affective Disorders 136, no. 3 (2012): 377–80; C. Jaite et al., "Etiological Role of Childhood Emotional Trauma and Neglect in Adolescent Anorexia Nervosa: A Cross-Sectional Questionnaire Analysis," *Psychopathology* 45, no. 1 (2012): 61–66; S. H. Shin and D. P. Miller, "Exposure to Childhood Neglect and Physical Abuse and Developmental Trajectories of Heavy Episodic Drinking from Early Adolescence into Young Adulthood," *Drug and Alcohol Dependence* (2012); and E. Y. Tenkorang and S. Obeng Gyimah, "Physical Abuse in Early Childhood and Transition to First Sexual Intercourse among Youth in Cape Town, South Africa," *Journal of Sex Research* 49, no. 5 (2012): 508–517.

13. C. E. Cavanaugh, J. T. Messing et al., "Patterns of Violence against Women: A Latent Class Analysis," *Psychological Trauma: Theory, Research, Practice and Policy* 4, no. 2 (2012): 169–176.

14. "Adrian Peterson Releases Statement," Minnesota Vikings (press release), September 15, 2014, accessed December 9, 2014, http://www.vikings.com/news/article-1/Statement-From-Adrian-Peterson/aabb41f8-1afe-4133-8b30-71390b6a3fbf.

15. Accessed December 21, 2014, http://ww.daddyfiles.com.

16. A. Gouveia, "Adrian Peterson, Child Abuse, and Why It Doesn't Matter If That's How You Were Raised," *Huffington Post* (blog), November 19, 2014, accessed December 12, 2014, http://www.huffingtonpost.com/aaron-gouveia/adrian-peterson-child-abuse-and-why-it-doesnt-matter-if-thats-how-you-were-raised_b_5842642.html.

17. Cavanaugh and Messing et al., "Patterns of Violence," 169–176.

18. S. DeGue and C. Spatz Widom, "Does Out of Home Placement Mediate the Relationship between Child Maltreatment and Adult Criminality?," *Child Maltreatment* 14, no. 4 (2009): 344–355.

19. Mark 9:42 (New International Version).

20. R. Maniglio, "The Impact of Child Sexual Abuse on Health: A Systematic Review of Reviews," *Clinical Psychology Review* 29, no. 7 (2009): 647–657.

21. B. Perry and M. *Szalavitz, Born For Love* (New York: Harper Collins Publishers, 2011).

22. T. L. Messman-Moore, K. L. Walsh, and D. Dilillo, "Emotion Disregulation and Risky Sexual Behavior in Revictimization," *Child Abuse & Neglect* 34, no. 2 (2010): 967–976.

23. Felitti et al., "Relationship of Childhood Abuse," 245–258.

24. S. Joseph, H. Mynard, and M. Mayall, "Life-Events and Post-Traumatic Stress in a Sample of English Adolescents," *Journal of Community & Applied Social Psychology* 10 (2000): 475–482.

25. K. Knight, S. Menard, S. Simmons, L. Bouffard, and R. Orsi, "Generational Cycles of Intimate Partner Violence in the US," Crime Victims' Institute (research brief), 2013, accessed December 9, 2014, http://dev.cjcenter.org/_files/cvi/Generation%20Cycles%20IPVforweb.pdf.

26. Ibid.

27. R. Karr-Morse and M. S. Wiley, Scared Sick: *The Role of Childhood Trauma in Adult Disease* (Atlantic Monthly Press, 2012).

28. C. Gwinn and G. Strack, *Hope for Hurting Families: Creating Family Justice Centers Across America* (Volcano Press, 2006).

29. A. Fortin, M. Doucet, and D. Damant, "Children's Appraisals as Mediators of the Relationship between Domestic Violence and Child Adjustment," *Violence and Victimology* 26, no. 3 (2011): 377–392.

30. J. C. Spilsbury, S. Kahana et al., "Profiles of Behavioral Problems in Children Who Witness Domestic Violence," *Violence and Victims* 23, no. 1 (2008): 3–17.

31. E. M. Cummings, M. El-Sheikh et al., "Children and Violence: The Role of Children's Regulation in the Marital Aggression-Child Adjustment Link," Clinical Child and Family Psychology Review 12, no. 1 (2009): 3–15.

32. H. J. Gotham and K. J. Sher, "Children of Alcoholics," in *Clinical Manual of Substance Abuse*, ed. J. Kinney (St. Louis: Mosby, 1996), 272–287. See also R. E. Drake and G. E. Vaillant, "Predicting Alcoholism and Personality Disorder in a 33-Year Longitudinal Study of Children of Alcoholics," *British Journal of Addiction* 83 (1988): 799–807.

33. Listenbee, *Report of the Attorney General's Task Force*, accessed June 5, 2014, http://www.justice.gov/defendingchildhood/cev-rpt-full.pdf.

34. C. B. Cunradi, R. Caetano et al., "Neighborhood Poverty as a Predictor of Intimate Partner Violence among White, Black, and Hispanic Couples in the United States: A Multilevel Analysis," *Annals of Epidemiology* 10, no. 5 (2000): 297–308.

35. D. Adams, *Why Do They Kill: Men Who Murder Their Intimate Partners* (Vanderbilt University Press, 2007).

36. Ibid.

37. D. Adams, *Why Do They Kill: Men Who Murder Their Intimate Partners* (Vanderbilt University Press, 2007), Kindle edition, 1652.

38. G. Fineman, "Strangulation and the Homicidal Link to Law Enforcement" (2013), Training Institute on Strangulation Prevention Online Library, accessed December 29, 2014, http://www.strangulation-traininginstitute.com/index.php/library/viewcategory/843-scholarly-works-and-reports.html.

39. Ibid.

Chapter 3

1. K. Hunt, "Pharrell Williams Talks Race, Black Women and Social Justice," *Ebony*, November 2014, accessed December 13, 2014, http://www.ebony.com/entertainment-culture/pharrell-williams-talks-race-black-women-and-social-justice-cover-story#axzz3LnUhjg3Y.

2. H. Hammer, D. Finkelhor, and A. J. Sedlak, "Runaway/Thrownaway Children: National Estimates and Characteristics," 2002.

3. S. M. Buel, "Why Juvenile Courts Should Address Family Violence: Promising Practices to Improve Intervention Outcomes," *Juvenile and Family Court Journal* 53 (2002):1–16.

4. M. Anne Powell, "Peer Tutoring and Mentoring Services for Disadvantaged Secondary School Students," *California Research Bureau California State Library* 4, no. 2 (1997).

5. Gwinn and Strack, *Hope for Hurting Families*, 79–84.

6. "About Criminal Justice," California Correction Peace Officers Association, accessed December 9, 2014, http://www.ccpoa.org/.

7. "About Prisons," International Center for Prison Studies, accessed December 9, 2014, http://www.prisonstudies.org/highest-to-lowest/prison-population-total?field_region_taxonomy_tid=All.

8. Ibid

9. P. Yost, "Eric Holder Proposes Drug Sentencing Reform," Huffington Post (blog), August 12, 2013, accessed December 10, 2014, http://www.huffingtonpost.com/2013/08/12/eric-holder-drug-sentences_n_3744717.html?utm_hp_ref=politics.

10. J. Petersilia, K. J. Hinds, C. Keel, M. Owens, and C. Vilkin, "Voices from the Field: How California Stakeholders View Public Safety Realignment," 2014, accessed December 26, 2014, http://papers.ssrn.com/sol3/results.cfm.

11. Ballotpedia, s.v. "Proposition 47," accessed December 26, 2014, http://ballotpedia.org/California_Proposition_47,_Reduced_Penalties_for_Some_Crimes_Initiative_(2014).

12. Ronald Goetz, "Do Prevention or Treatment Services Save Money? The Wrong Debate," *Health Affairs* 28, no. 1 (2009): 137–41.

13. Report of the Attorney General's National Task Force on Children Exposed to Violence (2012), accessed December 20, 2014 at http://www.justice.gov/defendingchildhood/cev-rpt-full.pdf.

14. Ibid.

15. Interview with Gael Strack, September 13, 2014.

16. C. Gwinn and G. Strack, *Dream Big: A Simple, Complicated Idea to Stop Family Violence* (Wheatmark Press, 2010).

17. M. L. Sturgle-Apple et al., "The Role of Mothers' and Fathers' Adrenocortical Reactivity in Spillover between Interparental Conflict and Parenting Practices," *Journal of Family Psychology*, 23, no. 2 (2009), 215–25.

18. Former San Diego County Sheriff Bill Kolender ran for office in 1994 using this line in his standard political stump speeches. He was, at the time, the director of the California Youth Authority dealing with a burgeoning population of juvenile criminals.

19. J. Washburn et al., "Psychiatric Disorders among Detained Youths: A Comparison of Youths Processed in Juvenile Court and Adult Criminal Court," *Psychiatric Services* 59 (2008): 965.

20. C. Wilson and C. Gwinn, "Rethinking How We Define Child Maltreatment and Family Violence Work" (Presentation, 29th annual San Diego International Conference on Child and Family Maltreatment, San Diego, CA, January 27, 2015), accessed December 28, 2014, http://www.sandiegoconference.org/index.html.

21. E. Van Voorhees, E. Dedert et al., "Childhood Trauma Exposure in Iraq and Afghanistan War Era Veterans: Implications for Posttraumatic Stress Disorder Symptoms and Adult Functional Social Support," *Child Abuse and Neglect* 36, no. 5 (2012): 423–432.

22. In 2012, the VA estimated that military-related suicides averaged twenty-two per day between all the services. No research however has been done looking at childhood-trauma histories for these suicides.

23. "Ending Domestic Violence," No More, accessed December 10, 2014, http://www.nomore.org.

24. "Engaging Communities to End Violence against Women and Girls," NFL Game Changer, accessed December 15, 2014, http://www.nflgamechanger.org/. NFL Game Changer was a related attempt to create such influence, but it too was unable to generate the political and social

influence necessary to compel the NFL to truly invest in a major social-change campaign.

25. "About Community," Seattle Department of Neighborhoods, accessed December 15, 2014, http://www.seattle.gov/neighborhoods/npi/documents/Cooperation-Coordination-CollaborationHandouts.pdf.

26. Ibid.

27. "Inspirational US Policy Wins Prestigious International Prize on Ending Violence against Women," United Nations Women (press release), October 14, 2014, accessed December 15, 2014, http://www.unwomen.org/en/news/stories/2014/10/future-policy-awards#sthash.nOEDgHbZ.dpuf.

28. E. Pence and M. McMahon, "A Coordinated Community Response to Domestic Violence," The National Training Project, Duluth, Minnesota, 1997, accessed December 14, 2014, http://files.praxisinternational.org/ccrdv.pdf.

29. J. C. Campbell, J. Dienemann, J. Kub, T. Wurmser, and E. Loy, "Collaboration as a Partnership," *Violence Against Women* 5, no. 10 (1999): 1140–1157.

30. Gwinn and Strack, *Dream Big*.

31. H. S. Boon, S. A. Mior, J. Barnsley, F. D. Ashbury, and R. Haig, "The Difference between Integration and Collaboration in Patient Care: Results from Key Informant Interviews Working in Multiprofessional Health-Care Teams," *Journal of Manipulative and Physiological Therapeutics* 32, no. 9 (2009): 715–722.

Chapter 4

1. R. Louv, Last *Child in the Woods: Saving Our Children from Nature-Deficit Disorder* (Algonquin Books of Chapel Hill, 2008).

2. Dr. Chan Hellman, "Title of Presentation" (presentation, 14th annual International Family Justice Conference, Name of Venue, San Diego, CA, April 2014).

3. H. Chancellor and C. Hellman, *The Impact of Camp HOPE on Children Exposed to Domestic Violence*, The University of Oklahoma, Schusterman Center (preliminary report), 2013, accessed December 30, 2014, http://www.familyjusticecenter.org/jdownloads/viewcategory/41-evaluation-a-outcomes.html.

4. Ibid.

5. Ibid.

6. Ibid.

7. Pursuant to our protocol with the University of Oklahoma, all ACE-score questionnaires were de-identified before being provided to the research team for evaluation.

8. Karianne Gwinn, "The Camp HOPE Goodnight Song," accessed January 2, 2015, https://www.youtube.com/watch?v=y0HWLDILD8Y.

Chapter 5

1. F. D. Harper, J. A. Harper, and A. B. Stills, "Counseling Children in Crisis Based on Maslow's Hierarchy of Basic Needs," *International Journal for the Advancement of Counselling* 25, no. 1 (2003): 11–25.

2. C. R. Snyder, "Hope Theory: Rainbows in the Mind," *Psychological Inquiry* 13, no. 4 (2002): 249–275.

3. Interview with C. Hellman about hope study, December 2014; and J. D. Salgado, F. P. Deane, T. P. Crowe, and L. G. Oades, "Hope and Improvements in Mental Health Service Providers' Recovery Attitudes Following Training," *Journal of Mental Health* 19, no. 3 (2010), 243–248.

4. "About Hope," National Association of Social Workers, Mental Health Section Connection, Fall 2012, accessed January 4, 2015, http://www.socialworkers.org/sections/areas/archives.asp?sVal=mentalhttp://www.socialworkers.org/sections/areas/archives.asp?sVal=mental.

5. C. R. Snyder, B. Hoza, W. E. Pelham, M. Rapoff, L. Ware, M. Danovsky, and K. J. Stahl, "The Development and Validation of the Children's Hope Scale," *Journal of Pediatric Psychology* 22 no. 3 (1997): 399–421. This measure is comprised of six self-report items with a six-point Likert-Type response format (1 = none of the time; 6 = all of the time). Scores can range from a low of six to a high of thirty-six. Thus, higher scores reflect higher hope.

6. A. D. Naik, C. D. White, S. M. Robertson, M. E. Armento, B. Lawrence, L. A. Stelljes, and J. A. Cully, "Behavioral Health Coaching for Rural-Living Older Adults with Diabetes and Depression: An Open Pilot of the HOPE Study," *BMC Geriatrics* 12, no. 1 (2012): 37; and W. Duggleby, A. Williams, L. Holstlander, D. Cooper, S. Ghosh, L. K. Hallstrom, and

M. Hampton, "Evaluation of the Living With Hope Program for Rural Women Caregivers of Persons with Advanced Cancer," *BMC Palliative Care* 12, no. 1 (2013): 1–11. Validity studies have been established both psychometrically and substantively. However, reliability is sample specific and must be established in each individual study.

7. Snyder et al., "The Development and Validation of the Children's Hope Scale," 399–421, accessed January 4, 2015, http://jpepsy.oxfordjournals.org/content/22/3/399.full.pdf.

8. Kara, not her real name, completed the ACE Index and the Hope Scale with authorization from her mother. Her scores were all de-identified after they were gathered and before they were turned over to the University of Oklahoma.

9. Snyder et al., "The Development and Validation of the Children's Hope Scale," 399–421, accessed January 4, 2015, http://jpepsy.oxfordjournals.org/content/22/3/399.full.pdf.

10. Ibid, 400.

Chapter 6

1. "President Obama Calls on Americans to Volunteer as Mentors," Harvard School of Public Health, accessed December 12, 2014, http://www.hsph.harvard.edu/news/hsph-in-the-news/president-obama-call-on-americans-to-volunteer-as-mentors/.

2. "About Mentoring," National Mentoring Project, accessed December 12, 2014, http://www.mentoring.org/news_and_research/news_releases/mentor_invites_corporations_to_take_the_corporate_mentoring_challenge.

3. "Harvard Mentoring Project," Harvard School of Public Health, accessed December 12, 2014, http://www.hsph.harvard.edu/chc/harvard-mentoring-project/.

4. "OJJDP Mentoring Programs," US Department of Justice, accessed December 12, 2014, http://www.ojjdp.gov/programs/mentoring.html.

5. "About Mentoring," National Mentoring Project.

6. "Mentor," Elements of Effective Practice for Mentoring, 3rd ed., accessed December 12, 2014, www.mentoring.org/downloads/mentoring_1222.pdf.

7. N. L. Deutsch and R. Spencer, "Capturing the Magic: Assessing the

Quality of Youth Mentoring Relationships," *New Directions for Youth Development* 2009, no. 121 (2009): 47–70.

8. Ibid.

9. T. Cavell, D. DuBois, M. Karcher, T. Keller, and J. Rhodes, *Strengthening Mentoring Opportunities for At-Risk Youth*, 2009, http://www.mentoring.org/downloads/mentoring_1233.pdf; S. Jekielek, K. A. Moore, and E. C. Hair, *Mentoring Programs and Youth Development: A Synthesis* (Washington, DC: Child Trends, 2002); D. L. DuBois, F. Doolittle, B. T. Yates, N. Silverthorn, and J. K. Tebes, "Research Methodology and Youth Mentoring," *Journal of Community Psychology* 34, no. 6 (2006): 657–676; and "Ensuring Brighter Futures for Youth through Federal Mentoring Programs," Federal Mentoring Council, accessed December 15, 2014, http://www.federalmentoringcouncil.gov/.

10. "About Mentoring," Mentoring Coalition of San Diego County, accessed December 12, 2014, http://www.sdmentorcoalition.org/.

11. "About Mentoring," Friends of the Children, accessed December 15, 2014, http://friendspdx.org/.

12. "Longitudinal Study," Friends of the Children, accessed December 5, 2014, http://friendspdx.org/it-works/research-results.

13. Ibid.

14. These numbers are all significant to anyone working with at-risk youth. Friends of the Children is not participating in a longitudinal study with a randomized sample and control group, but this early data is clearly promising and significant.

15. Telephone interview with T. Sorenson, May 16, 2013.

16. C. Herrera, J. B. Grossman, T. J. Kauh, A. F. Feldman, and J. McMaken, "Making a Difference in Schools: The Big Brothers Big Sisters School-Based Mentoring Impact Study," Public/Private Ventures, 2007.

17. J. P. Tierney, J. B. Grossman, and N. L. Resch, "Making a Difference: An Impact Study of Big Brothers/Big Sisters," 1995.

18. Ibid.

19. Ibid.

20. *Youth Outcomes Survey Report*, Big Brothers Big Sisters, accessed December 15, 2014, http://www.bbbsnew.org/news-detail.php?story=219.

21. "Childhood Development," 4-H, accessed December 5, 2014, http://www.4-H.org.

22. R. M. Lerner, A. von Eye, J. V. Lerner, and S. Lewin-Bizan, "Exploring the Foundations and Functions of Adolescent Thriving within the 4-H Study of Positive Youth Development: A View of the Issues," *Journal of Applied Developmental Psychology* 30, no. 5 (2009): 567–570.

23. R. Lerner, J. Lerner, et. al. (2011). The Positive Development of Youth: Comprehensive Findings from the 4-H Study of Positive Youth Development, accessed January 25, 2015 at http://www.4-h.org/about/youth-development-research/positive-youth-development-study/.

24. Ibid.

25. Ibid.

26. Ibid.

27. D. Anderson-Butcher, W. Newsome, and T. Ferrari, "Participation in Boys and Girls Clubs and Relationships to Youth Outcomes," *Journal of Community Psychology* 31, no. 1 (2003): 39–55.

28. "Recent News," National Youth Crime Prevention Program, accessed December 5, 2014, http://nationalpal.org/.

29. "Programs Offered," National PAL, accessed December 5, 2014, http://nationalpal.org/programs.

30. "Youth Mentoring Opportunities," Mentor Youth, accessed December 5, 2014, http://www.mentoryouth.com/.

31. "Creating a Community of Respect," Coaching Boys Into Men, accessed December 5, 2014, http://www.coachescorner.org/.

32. M. Carr and L. Lee, *Coaching Boys Into Men Playbook*, Family Violence Prevention Fund, 2008, accessed December 5, 2014, http://coachescorner.org/filelibrary/CBIM%20Playbook%202008.PDF.

33. "Child Advocates," Court Appointed Special Advocates for Children, accessed December 5, 2014, http://www.casaforchildren.org.

34. "About CASAs," Voices for Children, accessed December 5, 2014, http://www.speakupnow.org.

35. "Confronting Abuse," Royal Family Kids, accessed December 5, 2014, http://royalfamilykids.org/. Royal Family Kids Camp has also produced a movie simply called *Camp*. I was honored to attend one of the premiere showings of it in 2013 with the founder, Wayne Tesch.

36. Ibid.

37. Chancellor and Hellman, *The Impact of Camp Hope.*

38. Camp HOPE Texas documented increases in HOPE scores, but the increases were not statistically significant in the first year. Camp HOPE Idaho's HOPE scores have not been analyzed by the University of Oklahoma.

Chapter 7

1. S. Jaynes, *The Power of a Woman's Words* (Harvest House Publishers, 2007), 59.

2. Interview with Linda Chamberlain, December 2014. See also http://ww.fosteringresilience.org. Dr. Ken Ginsburg has done excellent work on the topic of fostering resilience in trauma-exposed children.

3. M. E. Seligman, Flourish: *A New Understanding of Happiness, Well-Being, and How to Achieve Them* (Nicholas Brealey Pub, 2011).

4. M. E. Seligman, *Learned Optimism: How to Change Your Mind and Your Life* (Random House LLC, 2011).

5. "Positive Thinking: Stop Negative Self-Talk to Reduce Stress," Mayo Clinic, March 4, 2014, accessed January 3, 2015, http://www.mayo-clinic.org/healthy-living/stress-management/in-depth/positive-think-ing/art-20043950.

6. M. E. Seligman, "Positive Psychology, Positive Prevention, and Positive Therapy," Positive Psychology Center, accessed January 3, 2015, http://www.ppc.sas.upenn.edu/ppsnyderchapter.htm.

7. "Spirit and Joy," Survivorship Now, accessed January 3, 2015, http://www.survivorshipnowvt.org/basics/spirit-joy/.

8. A. Miller, "A Critique of Positive Psychology or 'the New Science of Happiness,'" *Journal of Philosophy of Education* 42, no. 3-4 (2008): 591–608.

9. C. R. Snyder and S. Lopez, eds., *Handbook of Positive Psychology* (New York: Oxford University Press, 2002). The heart of the positive psychology movement (along with its roots in the power of positive thinking) is important to this book on a number of levels. It lays the foundation for Hope Theory, and it connects to current strengths-based approaches to helping victims of trauma and abuse.

10. C. Peterson, "What Is Positive Psychology and What Is It Not?" *The Good Life* (blog), *Psychology Today*, May 16, 2008, accessed January 3, 2015, http://www.psychologytoday.com/blog/the-good-life/200805/what-is-positive-psychology-and-what-is-it-not. In 2008, one of the early positive-psychology thinkers, the late Christopher Peterson, said, "Positive psychology is … a call for psychological science and practice to be as concerned with strength as with weakness; as interested in building the best things in life as in repairing the worst; and as concerned with making the lives of normal people fulfilling as with healing pathology."

11. Ibid.

12. N. Constantine, B. Benard, and M. Diaz, "Measuring Protective Factors and Resilience Traits in Youth: The Healthy Kids Resilience Assessment" (7th Annual Meeting of the Society for Prevention Research, New Orleans, LA, 1999).

13. E. E. Werner and R. S. Smith, *Overcoming the Odds: High Risk Children from Birth to Adulthood* (Cornell University Press, 1992); and R. J. Lifton, *The Protean Self: Human Resilience in an Age of Transformation* (New York: Basic Books, 1993).

14. Constantine, Benard, and Diaz, "Measuring Protective Factors."

15. R. Karr-Morse and Meredith S. Wiley, *Ghosts from the Nursery: Tracing the Roots of Violence* (New York: Atlantic Monthly Press, 1997), 159, 163, 201.

16. R. Karr-Morse and M. S. Wiley, *Scared Sick: The Role of Childhood Trauma in Adult Disease* (Atlantic Monthly Press, 2012), 201–202.

17. K. Weintraub, "Structural Brain Changes Found in Romanian Orphanage Children," *Common Health*, July 23, 2012, accessed January 3, 2015, http://commonhealth.wbur.org/2012/07/brain-changes-orphanage.

Chapter 8

1. The Character Education Partnership is helping schools focus on character across the United States. A mentor of mine, Michael Josephson, has helped lead this effort. For more information, go to http://www.josephsoninstitute.org and http://www.character.org.

2. M. Chang, "Cultural Differences in Parenting Styles and Their Effects on Teens' Self-Esteem, Perceived Parental Relationship Satis-

faction, and Self-Satisfaction," 2007, accessed December 28, 2014, http://repository.cmu.edu/hsshonors/85/?utm_source=repository.cmu.edu%2Fhsshonors%2F85&utm_medium=PDF&utm_campaign=PDFCoverPages.

3. A. Usher, "What Roles Do Parent Involvement, Family Background, and Culture Play in Student Motivation?," The George Washington University, 2012, accessed December 28, 2014, http://www.cep-dc.org/publications/index.cfm?selectedYear=2012; and R. G. Rumbaut, "Children of Immigrants and Their Achievement: The Role of Family, Acculturation, Social Class, Gender, Ethnicity, and School Contexts," Michigan State University (unpublished paper), 2000, accessed December 28, 2014, http://www.hks.harvard.edu/inequality/Seminar/Papers/Rumbaut1.pdf.

4. B. Duriez, B. Soenens, and M. Vansteenkiste, "In Search of the Antecedents of Adolescent Authoritarianism: The Relative Contribution of Parental Goal Promotion and Parenting Style Dimensions," *Eur. J. Pers.* 21 (2007):507–527; and B. Duriez, B. Soenens, and M. Vansteenkiste, "The Intergenerational Transmission of Authoritarianism: The Mediating Role of Parental Goal Promotion," Journal of Research in Personality 42, no. 3 (2008): 622–642.

5. Ibid.

6. E. L. Lyman and S. S. Luthar, "Further Evidence on the 'Costs of Privilege': Perfectionism in High-Achieving Youth at Socioeconomic Extremes," *Psychol. Schs.* 51 (2014)913–930.

7. J. Feinstein, "NFL's Ineptitude Overshadows the RealStories," John Feinstein Blog, November 20, 2014, accessed December 10, 2014, http://feinstein.radio.cbssports.com/2014/11/20/john-feinstein-blog-nfls-ineptitude-overshadows-the-real-stories/.

8. L. Boyle and J. Daniel, "Man 'Who Killed Adrian Peterson's Son' Beat His Ex-Girlfriend's Three-Year-Old Little Boy So Hard He Was Left With Welts Last Year—But Judge Spared Him Jail And Sent Him To Counseling Instead," *Daily Mail,* October 15, 2013, accessed December 10, 2014, http://www.dailymail.co.uk/news/article-2454622/Adrian-Petersons-son-killed-man-prior-abuse-charges.html.

Chapter 9

1. B. Stevenson, *Just Mercy: A Story of Justice and Redemption* (Scribe Publications, 2015).

2. J. Trent and G. Smalley, *The Blessing: Giving the Gift of Unconditional Love and Acceptance* (Thomas Nelson Inc., 2004).

3. Ibid.

4. Ibid.

5. G. Chapman, *The Five Love Languages: The Secret to Love That Lasts* (Zondervan Publishing, 2010).

Chapter 10

1. Proverbs 22:6 (New International Version)

2. S. Covey, R. Merrill, and R. Merrill, (1994), *First Things First: Coping With the Ever Increasing Demands of the Workplace*, (Simon & Schuster, New York, New York), pp.

3. *Merriam-Webster,* s.v. "Self-esteem," accessed December 1, 2014, http://www.merriam-webster.com/dictionary/self-esteem.

4. A. Bueno, "Halle Berry on Why She's Had Bad Choices in Men," Yahoo News, October 19, 2012, accessed December 1, 2014, https://tv.yahoo. com/news/halle-berry-why-shes-had-bad-choices-men-161400233. html;_ylt=AwrBT9bR2HxUOIAAGyhXNyoA;_ylu=X3oDMTEzdD JkMGM2BHNlYwNzcgRwb3MDNARjb2xvA2JmMQR2dGlkA1ZJ UDQ0Ml8x.

5. N. Burton, "Building Confidence and Self-Esteem," *Hide and Seek* (blog), *Psychology Today*, May 30, 2012, accessed December 1, 2014, http://www.psychologytoday.com/blog/hide-and-seek/201205/building-confidence-and-self-esteem.

6. J. Lehman, "How to Build Self-Esteem in Children and Teens," Empowering Parents, accessed December 1, 2014, http://www.empowering-parents.com/how-to-build-self-esteem-in-children-and-teens.php#.

7. "Where We Stand: Spanking," The American Academy of Pediatrics, October 10, 2014, accessed January 2, 2015, http://www.healthychildren.org/English/family-life/family-dynamics/communication-discipline/Pages/Where-We-Stand-Spanking.aspx. The American Academy

of Pediatrics strongly opposes striking a child for any reason. Spanking is never recommended; infants may be physically harmed by a parent who strikes the child. If a spanking is spontaneous, parents should later explain calmly why they did it, the specific behavior that provoked it, and how angry they felt. They also might apologize to their child for their loss of control. This usually helps the youngster to understand and accept the spanking, and it models for the child how to remediate a wrong.

8. C. A. Taylor, J. A. Manganello, S. J. Lee, and J. C. Rice, "Mothers' Spanking of 3-Year-Old Children and Subsequent Risk of Children's Aggressive Behavior," *Pediatrics* 125, no. 5 (2010): e1057–e1065, accessed January 2, 2015, http://pediatrics.aappublications.org/content/early/2010/04/12/peds.2009-2678.abstract.

9. Ibid.

Chapter 11

1. I. Ivtzan, C. P. Chan, H. E. Gardner, and K. Prashar, "Linking Religion and Spirituality with Psychological Well-Being: Examining Self-Actualisation, Meaning in Life, and Personal Growth Initiative," *Journal of Religion and Health* 52, no. 3 (2013): 915–929; J. L. McBride and G. Armstrong, "The Spiritual Dynamics of Chronic Post-Traumatic Stress Disorder," *Journal of Religion and Health* 34, no. 1 (1995): 5–16; D. N. McIntosh, M. J. Poulin, R. C. Silver, and E. A. Holman, "The Distinct Roles of Spirituality and Religiosity in Physical and Mental Health after Collective Trauma: A National Longitudinal Study of Responses to the 9/11 Attacks," *Journal of Behavioral Medicine* 34, no. 6 (2011): 497–507; S. Mihaljević, B. Vuksan-Cusa, D. Marcinko, E. Koic, Z. Kusevic, and M. Jakovljevic, "Spiritual Well-Being, Cortisol, and Suicidality in Croatian War Veterans Suffering from PTSD," *Journal of Religion and Health* 50, no. 2 (2011): 464–473; J. F. Peres, A. Moreira-Almeida, A. G. Nasello, and H. G. Koenig, "Spirituality and Resilience in Trauma Victims," *Journal of Religion and Health* 46, no. 3 (2007): 343–350; J. A. Sigmund, "Spirituality and Trauma: The Role of Clergy in the Treatment of Posttraumatic Stress Disorder," *Journal of Religion and Health* 42, no. 3 (2003): 221–229; and M. B. Werdel, G. S. Dy-Liacco, J. W. Ciarrocchi, R. J. Wicks, and G. M. Breslford, "The Unique Role of Spirituality in the Process of Growth Following Stress and Trauma," *Pastoral Psychology* 63, no. 1 (2014): 57–71.

2. McIntosh et al., "The Distinct Roles of Spirituality," 497-507; K. E.

Senter and K. Caldwell, "Spirituality and the Maintenance of Change: A Phenomenological Study of Women Who Leave Abusive Relationships," *Contemporary Family Therapy* 24, no. 4 (2002): 543–564; P. Stratta, C. Capanna, I. Riccardi, G. Perugi, C. Toni, L. Dell'Osso, and A. Rossi, "Spirituality and Religiosity in the Aftermath of a Natural Catastrophe in Italy," *Journal of Religion and Health* 52, no. 3 (2013): 1029–1037; and I. Ungureanu and J. G. Sandberg, "Broken Together: Spirituality and Religion as Coping Strategies for Couples Dealing with the Death of a Child: A Literature Review with Clinical Implications," *Contemporary Family Therapy* 32, no. 3 (2010): 302–319.

3. H. G. Koenig, M. McCullough, and D. B. Larson, *Handbook of Religion and Health* (New York: Oxford University Press, 2001).

4. J. H. Lord, "How to Provide Spiritually Sensitive Trauma Care," PTSD Support, 2015, accessed January 2, 2015, http://www.ptsdsupport.net/ptsd_and_spiritually.html.

5. B. Toropov and L. Buckles, *The Complete Idiot's Guide to World Religions* (New York: Alpha Books, 1997), 21–25.

6. K. Countryman-Roswurm and B. L. Bolin, "Domestic Minor Sex Trafficking: Assessing and Reducing Risk," *Child and Adolescent Social Work Journal* (2014): 1–18; H. Hammer, D. Finkelhor, and A. Sedlak, "National Incidence Studies of Missing, Abducted, Runaway, and Thrownaway Children," US Department of Justice, 2002; G. C. Hammond and M. McGlone, "Entry, Progression, Exit, and Service Provision for Survivors of Sex Trafficking: Implications for Effective Interventions," *Global Social Welfare* (2014): 1–12; and S. Hepburn and R. J. Simon, "Hidden in Plain Sight: Human Trafficking in the United States," *Gender Issues* 27, no. 1-2 (2010): 1–26.

7. Matthew 22:39 (New International Version).

8. B. Brown, *Daring Greatly: How the Courage to be Vulnerable Transforms the Way We Live, Love, Parent, and Lead* (Penguin, 2012).

9. I Peter 4:7 (New International Version)

Chapter 12

1. "Findings on Adverse Childhood Experiences in California," Center for Youth Wellness, accessed January 4, 2015, https://acestoohigh.files.wordpress.com/2014/11/hiddencrisis_report_10141.pdf.

2. J. Becker, R. Greenwald, and C. Mitchell, "Trauma-Informed Treat-

ment for Disenfranchised Urban Children and Youth: An Open Trial," *Child and Adolescent Social Work Journal* 28, no. 4 (2011): 257–272. See also http://www.nasmhpd.org/TA/nctic.aspx.

3. T. Ruth, *Strength Finder 2.0* (Flipkart, 2007).

4. "About EMDR," EMDR Institute, accessed January 4, 2015, http://www.emdr.com/general-information/what-is-emdr.html.

5. How to Implement Trauma-Focused Cognitive Behavioral Therapy (TF-CBT) (2004), accessed January 21, 2015 at http://www.nctsnet.org/nctsn_assets/pdfs/TF-CBT_Implementation_Manual.pdf.

6. C. Webb, A. M. Hayes, D. Grasso, J. P. Laurenceau, and E. Deblinger, "Trauma-Focused Cognitive Behavioral Therapy for Youth: Effectiveness in a Community Setting," *Psychological Trauma: Theory, Research, Practice, and Policy* 6, no. 5 (2014): 555.

7. Ibid.

8. Ibid.

9. M. Brinkmeyer and S. M. Eyberg, "Parent-Child Interaction Therapy for Oppositional Children," in *Evidence-Based Psychotherapies for Children and Adolescents,* eds. A. E. Kazdin and J. R. Weisz (New York: Guilford, 2003), 204–223.

10. E. M. Flake, B. E. Davis, P. L. Johnson, and L. S. Middleton, "The Psychosocial Effects of Deployment on Military Children," *Journal of Developmental & Behavioral Pediatrics* 30, no. 4 (2009): 271–278.

11. J. Becker et al., "Trauma-Informed Treatment." For more information, go to http://www.traumasmart.org.

12. "Child Development," First 5 California, accessed January 4, 2015, http://www.first5california.com/parents/learning-center.aspx?id=9. First 5 California has provided tremendous leadership and associated funding to major initiatives for children ages zero to five.

13. S. de Shazer, I. K. Berg, E. Lipchik, E. Nunnally, A. Molnar, W. Gingerich, and M. Weiner-Davis, "Brief Therapy: Focused Solution Development," *Family Process* 25 (1986): 207–221; I. K. Berg and Y. Dolan, *Tales of Solutions* (New York: Norton, 2001); and I. K. Berg and T. Steiner, *Children's Solution Work* (New York: Norton, 2003).

14. Cool Intervention #10: The Miracle Question, accessed January 22, 2015 at https://www.psychologytoday.com/blog/in-therapy/201001/cool-intervention-10-the-miracle-question.

15. S. Green, A. Grant, and J. Rynsaardt, "Evidence-Based Life Coaching for Senior High School Students: Building Hardiness and Hope," *International Coaching Psychology Review* 2 (2007): 24; K. M. Burns and H. M. Hulusi, "Bridging the Gap Between a Learning Support Centre and School: A Solution-Focused Group Approach," *Educational Psychology in Practice* 21, no. 2 (2005): 123–130.

16. Green et al., "Evidence-Based Life Coaching," 24.

17. S. D. Georgiades, "A Solution-Focused Intervention with a Youth in a Domestic Violence Situation: Longitudinal Evidence," *Contemporary Family Therapy* 30 (2008): 141–151.

18. C. Lam and M. Yuen, "Applying Solution-Focused Questions with Primary School Pupils: A Hong Kong Teacher's Reflections," *Pastoral Care in Education* 26 (2008): 103–110.

19. R. Thompson and J. M. Littrell, "Brief Counseling for Students with Learning Disabilities," *Professional School Counseling* (1998).

20. J. J. Murphy and M. W. Davis, "Video Exceptions: An Empirical Case Study Involving a Child with Developmental Disabilities," *Journal of Systemic Therapies* 24, no. 4 (2005): 66–79.

21. Ibid.

22. Herman, J. (1992), Trauma and Recovery: The aftermath of violence—from domestic abuse to political terror, (Basic Books, New York, NY), 7-13.

23. Ibid, 19–20.

Chapter 13

1. David Wexler, *When Good Men Behave Badly* (New Harbinger Publications, 2004), 63.